INTERNATIONAL MARITIME
TRANSPORT COSTS

T0330712

International Maritime Transport Costs
Market Structures and Network Configurations

GORDON WILMSMEIER
*United Nations Economic Commission for Latin America
and the Caribbean (UN-ECLAC)*
and the
University of Applied Sciences, Bremen, Germany

Routledge
Taylor & Francis Group

LONDON AND NEW YORK

First published 2014 by Ashgate Publishing

2 Park Square, Milton Park, Abingdon, Oxfordshire OX14 4RN
711 Third Avenue, New York, NY 10017

Routledge is an imprint of the Taylor & Francis Group, an informa business

First issued in paperback 2018

British Library Cataloguing in Publication Data
A catalogue record for this book is available from the British Library

The Library of Congress has cataloged the printed edition as follows:
Wilmsmeier, Gordon.
   International maritime transport costs : market structures and network configurations / by Gordon Wilmsmeier.
     pages cm – (Transport and society) ISBN 978-1-4094-2724-7 (hardback)
  1. Shipping– Economic aspects. 2. Shipping–Costs. 3. Shipping–International cooperation. 4. Shipping–Latin America–Costs. I. Title. II. Series: Transport and society.
   HE582.W55 2014
   387.5'1–dc23
                                                                                        2014006162

ISBN 978-1-4094-2724-7 (hbk)
ISBN 978-1-138-54719-3 (pbk)

Contents

List of Figures and Boxes

Figures

Boxes

List of Tables

Foreword

International trade grows two to three times faster than global GDP, and 80 per cent of this trade is transported by sea. Especially developing countries depend on maritime transport for most of their imports and exports. As trade is being liberalized through lower tariffs and quotas, it is the shipping costs that play an ever more important role within global supply chains. The understanding of the determinants of international maritime transport costs has thus become a cornerstone of any analysis of international trade and development.

Gordon Wilmsmeier is among the leading researchers in this domain, and his book presents a comprehensive and up-to-date picture of the advances made during the last decade. Traders and carriers, private operators and policy makers, just as practitioners and academics will find in this book a wealth of analysis of the key aspects that explain differences and trends in maritime freight costs. Why is it cheaper to ship a container from Miami to Buenos Aires than to St Johns in Antigua? What would be the potential impact of dredging my port to attract larger vessels? How important are trade imbalances for trade costs? These and many other questions are being answered in the book you are holding in your hands. While the empirical results are based on Latin American trade transactions and their transport costs, the conclusions can well be generalized and are in line with other recent research undertaken for example by UNECLAC and the OECD.

The book's empirical analysis draws on the International Transport Data Base ('BTI' for its Spanish acronym) of the United Nations Economic Commission for Latin America and the Caribbean UNECLAC. During his time working for UNECLAC, Gordon Wilmsmeier himself successfully expanded and developed this data base, enabling him now to make the most comprehensive use of the BTI's wealth of information. In particular, the book benefits from ten years of data, which allows for an analysis of the impact of different variables over time. This is important in view of changing demand (trade volumes), supply (vessel capacity) and cost components (e.g. the price of bunker).

Many of the results will not come as a surprise to industry insiders. Economies of scale, port characteristics and trade imbalances are generally seen as more important than the simple geographical distance. The contribution of this book is the inclusion of practically all relevant variables within one comprehensive empirical and theoretical framework. This allows the reader to understand the mutual relationships between many of the variables, while at the same time providing quantifiable estimates for their expected impact on transport costs.

Some of the determinants of maritime transport costs are beyond the influence of policy makers. National governments cannot do much about a country's geographical position or the overall trade volumes and imbalances. However, as Wilmsmeier shows, there is ample scope for reforms and improvements in the seaports, customs, and the legal and regulatory environment. Port reforms and investments in transport infrastructure can empirically reduce the operating costs for carriers, and with a regulatory framework that assures competition the reduced operating costs will translate into lower freight costs for the importers and exporters.

As I started out saying above, lower freight costs are ever more important for the promotion of trade. At the same time, as confirmed in this book, higher trade flows will also lead to further reduced freight costs, as they help to achieve economies of scale, increased competition and commercial incentives for investments in seaports. Policy makers are thus confronted with a potentially virtuous or vicious circle, and Wilmsmeier's book is an invaluable contribution to our better understanding of this fascinating topic.

Jan Hoffmann

Acknowledgements

I would like to express my sincerest thanks to Profesor Jürgen Deiters. My particular gratitude goes to Ricardo Sánchez, UN-ECLAC, who facilitated the access to the UN-ECLAC data, Dr Jan Hoffmann, UNCTAD, and Professor Margaret Grieco, Transport Research Institute, Edinburgh Napier University.

Further, I would like to thank the Friedrich-Naumann-Stiftung Foundation and the German Academic Exchange Service (DAAD) for supporting my research financially with funding from the German Federal Ministry of Education and Research (BMBF).

This book is dedicated to the memory of Captain Martin Sgut, a true mariner, dedicated and visionary man, and a good friend.

List of Abbreviations

BADECEL	Base de Datos Estadísticos de Comercio Exterior de América Latina y el Caribe (Database on external trade of Latin America and the Caribbean)
BAF	Bunker Adjustment Factor
BTI	Base de Datos de Transporte Internacional (International Transport database)
CAF	Currency Adjustment Factor
CARICOM	Caribbean Community and Common Market
CEPII	Centre d'études prospectives et d'informations internationales
CFR	Cost and Freight
CIF	Cost Insurance Freight
COMTRADE	Commodity Trade Statistics Database
CSAV	Compañía Sud Americana de Vapores
DEA	Data Envelopment Analysis
EC	East Coast
ECSA	East Coast of South America
FA	Factor Analysis
FCL	full container load
FDI	Foreign Direct Investment
FMC	Federal Maritime Commission
FOB	Free on Board
GDP	Gross Domestic product
GRT	Gross register tonnage
HS	Harmonized System
HSDG	Hamburg – Südamerikanische Dampfschiffahrts-Gesellschaft (Hamburg – South America Steamship Company or Hamburg South America Line)
IDB	InterAmerican Development Bank
IMF	International Monetary Fund
ISPS	International Ship and Port Facility Security

LA	Latin America
LAC	Latin America and the Caribbean
LAIA	Latin American Integration Association
LCL	Less than container load
LPI	Logistics Performance Index
LSCI	Liner Shipping Connectivity Index
LSNS	Liner Service Network Structure
MERCOSUR	Spanish: Mercado Común del Sur
NAFTA	North American Free Trade Agreement
NC	North Coast
NCSA	North Coast of South America
OECD	Organization for Economic Co-operation and Development
OLS	Square
PAF	Principal Axis Factoring
PCA	Principal Component Analysis
PFA	Principal Factor Analysis
SITC	Standard International Trade Classification
SQL	structured query language
TEU	twenty foot equivalent unit
THC	Terminal Handling Charge
TRI	Transport Research institute
TRQ	Tariff Rate Quotas
ULCC	Ultra Large Crude Carrier
UN	United Nations
UNCTAD	United Nations Conference for Trade and Development
UN-ECLAC	United Nations Economic Commission for Latin America and the Caribbean
UNOHRLLS	UN Office of the High Representative for the Least Developed Countries, Landlocked Developing Countries and Small Island Developing States
US	United States
USAID	US Agency for International Development
US$	United States Dollar
VLCC	very large crude carrier

WC	West Coast
WCSA	West Coast of South America
WEF	World Economic Forum
WTO	World Trade Organization

Chapter 1
Introduction

Setting the Scene

States and nations are redefining their place in the world at the present time in the wake of the economic, political and cultural transnationalization processes that have occurred in recent decades.

Each country, each region is seeking to recast its role and potential in accord with its geographical location, its history and the times. This positioning is, of course, conditioned by multiple factors, which include conditions of production, economic and political interests and transport-related issues especially. Maritime transport is the materialization of economic exchange in a globalized world. As a consequence, the performance of maritime transport as a derived demand through its organization, strategies and functioning has facilitated and potentially driven space-time compression and to a certain level affects the position of a country within the global market place.

Within this global situation, the region of South America and in a wider understanding Latin America, are particularly interesting cases. Maritime transport, the related infrastructural development, institutional reforms and the way the region imagines its place within the global trading pattern have been greatly changing in the last decade, driven by trade liberalization, economic development and globalization.

The intensification of intra-regional trade is a contingent part and result of trade liberalization and economic development in Latin America. This development brought quantitative and qualitative changes in trade relations and transport services. Transport services have been under constant pressure to accommodate these changes in the structure of demand. Being intrinsic parts of the distribution networks and markets, transport services present a mirror image of the structure and the direction of development of trade flows; however obstacles and barriers for the development of transport are drivers of inefficiencies within the system.

Aims and Objectives

Es genügt nicht, die rationalen Lösungen zu finden und darzustellen, sie müssen auch durchgesetzt werden. Die Wissenschaft kann der Wirtschaftspolitik nicht mehr bieten als rationale Leitbilder, die den widerstreitenden Kräften und der politischen Führung die Zusammenhänge ins Bewusstsein rücken. (..) Wir müssen uns nur darüber klar sein, dass das rationale Leitbild als solches niemals verwirklicht wird und dass der praktischen Wirtschaftspolitik nicht zufällig und gelegentlich sondern essentiell ein Element der Irrationalität eigen ist. Es ausschalten zu wollen würde aller soziologischen Erfahrung widersprechen und nichts anderes sein als Utopie. [Finding and presenting rational solutions is not sufficient, they need to be implemented. Science cannot offer more to economic policy than rational Leitbilder, which make the interrelationships known to disputing powers and the political leadership. ... We need to recognise that the rational Leitbild will never come true and that irrationality is not a random or sporadic but essential element of economic policy. Aiming to eliminate it (irrationality) is as shown from sociological experience nothing more than utopia.] (Predöhl 1958: 270 ff.)

Maritime transport is closely interconnected with the development of intra-regional (and global) trade flows. Maritime transport is not only a tool to bridge space, but has also shown to be an indirect driver of economic development processes with possibilities to consolidate, induce and interpose (Kumar and Hoffmann 2002, Voigt 1973: 8).

Kindleberger (1962) states that trade is only stimulated if the difference of distinct price structures in different countries is not eaten up by the costs to connect the two trading partners. According to Kindleberger (1973) two conditions for the realization of transport services apply:

- Technical bridging of space by the disposition of adequate mobile transport entities
- Economic bridging of space by a scheme of 'adequate' pricing

The realization of adequate technical transport services can result in transport costs at such an elevated level that the bridging of spaces becomes 'impossible'. This interdependence between these conditions leads to the question of market requirement.

In this respect transport costs have been considered as important components of market access barriers, but until recently they have been submerged in the discussion of tariff and other non-tariff barriers to trade.

With the extension of trade liberalization and the constant reduction and levelling of tariffs, transport costs have received growing attention. Increased competition between countries and globalization of production has driven tariff margins downward; consequently the relative importance of transport costs in the final price of traded goods has grown. Therefore low transport costs drive the international division of labour and give access to attractive markets (Skjølsvik et al. 2000: 78f). Francois and Wooton (2001) in line with Amjadi et al. (1996), argue that reducing shipping margins bears greater potential for countries in terms of competitiveness in globalized trade than further reductions of tariff rates.

Ninety-one per cent of Latin America's external trade by volume and 76 per cent in terms of value are carried by maritime transport (BTI 2010). Elevated shipping costs significantly impede competitiveness in trade for countries. In addition, transport costs are influenced by a number of factors and are far more volatile than other elements that impact on trade.

Consequently, important research questions arise as to what are the determinants of international maritime transport costs and to what level the structure of transport services and maritime industry as well as the performance and endowment of maritime and port infrastructure is reflected in these and contributes to elevated maritime transport costs.

Drivers of shipping costs have been identified in previous research, but an in-depth into the complexity and analysis of the evolution of shipping costs over time and their determinants which takes into account the changes in the shipping and ports industry remains to be developed.

The objective of the book is threefold:

- To identify and elaborate on the role of industry structures and strategies, institutions and geography in the formation of maritime transport costs
- To provide empirical evidence on the structure and complexity of determinants to international maritime transport costs
- To contribute towards conceptualizing policy areas which can influence international maritime transport costs in order to strengthen the region's competitiveness

A combination of factors in maritime transport in Latin America results in elevated transport costs to/from and within the region. This situation at varying levels reduces the competitiveness of Latin American (LA) countries in world trade. The integration of LA countries through bi- and multilateral trade agreements and the related gradual reduction and levelling of tariffs have led to a shift towards transport costs being one of the principal factors of competitiveness.

From the set objectives the following main questions emanate:

- How does research on the structure of international maritime transport costs contribute to the assessment of transport system functioning and inefficiencies?
- How do developments and strategies in the shipping industry shape maritime transport costs?
- Shipping lines decide on liner shipping network structures, thus if a country is peripheral or central within a network. Accordingly, the question arises in how far these networks determine the possibilities of trade and the 'distance' between markets?
- Is there evidence on the role of maritime industry structures i.e. competition and related international policies and their interrelation to the formation of maritime transport costs?
- Are specific maritime industry practices like the use of open registries reflected in maritime transport costs?

- What is the relevance of transport costs in a region striving for economic development, economic integration and cohesion?
- In how far does infrastructural endowment impact on maritime transport costs?
- What are the determinants of transport costs that can be proactively influenced by policy makers?
- External influences such as the development of charter rates, bunker fuel and external shocks, in this case the economic crisis in 2002, should also influence the general development of transport costs and have to be taken into account when comparing the development of transport costs over time. Therefore, the consistency over time of the estimated coefficients needs to be tested for commonly-accepted determinants of maritime transport costs.

Certain port characteristics and institutional efficiency and effectiveness, including aspects such as infrastructure development, port devolution and private sector participation can be influenced by governments. A so far neglected point is the impact of the effectiveness and efficiency of institutions and politics in converting plans into reality and facilitating market responses to changing environments.

However, the cyclical fluctuations of maritime freight rates as well as most of the determinants of freight rate levels on a given route are beyond the control of policy makers, since containerized trade is managed by international shipping lines that operate on a global scale. It seems important though to understand the market forces in order to identify the most effective responses for policy development.

The contribution of this book is twofold.

First, the author develops an in-depth analysis on the role and evolution of transport costs in international maritime trade and constructs a comprehensive panel data regression model of determinants of transport costs. The goal is to determine the influences of shipping lines strategies, maritime policy and port development over time and to identify the effect on competitiveness in international trade.

Second, the results are interpreted in the context of Latin American maritime trade and transport sector development and the impacts of developments in the shipping industry on transport costs and consequently the competitiveness of the region.

Structure of the Book

The research presented in this book constructs from four areas of evidence: theoretical, field work, institutional and empirical. The application of these areas also reflects in the sequence of discussion and the different strands are pulled together and integrated in the evaluation of the empirical evidence and the discussion of the research results.

The *theoretical evidence* is presented in Chapter 2. The chapter discusses, compares and evaluates relevant literature, concepts and theory in the disciplines of economic, trade and transport geography and economics, particularly maritime economics. An in-depth discussion is made on the position of this work within geographic research. The chapter culminates in the debate on the interrelationship between maritime transport costs and competitiveness in international trade and the definition of maritime transport costs and reflects on existing empirical research. In the final part of the chapter the author examines the question 'Who determines transport costs?' and introduces the basic concepts of economies in shipping.

Experience from field work has contributed significantly for the author to understand the complexity of the maritime and port industry and their manifold facets in the diversity of Latin American economic, social and institutional realities. During the course of the research the author worked in projects in 20 of the 33 countries in Latin America and Caribbean countries. Field work included evaluation of port development (e.g. Argentina, CARICOM states, Chile, Colombia, El Salvador, Paraguay, Peru, Uruguay, and Venezuela) and observing port privatization processes in Guayaquil, Ecuador. The field work allowed engaging with relevant actors from the public and private sector as well as at different levels of decision making. This direct engagement on the one hand enabled discussing specific problems and on the other hand offered the possibility to deepen expertise of known problem structures and to better understand the actual action and perceptive conditions.

The combination of *field work experience* and gathered *institutional evidence* set the foundations for the presentation and interpretation of the challenges in the region in relation to maritime transport, port development and international trade.

In Chapter 3 the theoretical discussion focusing on the complexity of determining liner shipping freight rates is underpinned with the field work experience. The author describes and evaluates the complexity of maritime transport costs determinants in five sections. These are: determinants of relation and geography, implications of cargo characteristics and trade structure, carriers, interfaces and regulatory and legal environment. The chapter closes by identifying the gaps in existing literature and mapping transport costs determinants in relation to the derived hypotheses for the empirical investigation.

The *empirical evidence* unfolds in Chapter 4. The chapter starts with a description of the used data sources and the author then introduces the International Transport Database (BTI) which forms the basis of information on international maritime transport costs. The database includes a collection of time series data on maritime trade flows and maritime transport services and industry, and ports. The statistical analysis of the data is presented in this chapter and is used for conducting factor analysis and econometric modelling. The chapter terminates with the definition of the econometric model used in the empirical analyses

Analysis of trade and transport determinants is realized in Chapter 5. Quantitative methods have been frequently used in transport sector research. They provide the possibility to visualize situations ex-post and to develop scenarios from these results. The study identifies the influencing factors for the current structure of transport costs in LAC and their development between 2000 and 2006.

Throughout the chapter a series of models is constructed which give insight into which factors influence maritime transport costs in the region.

Based on these empirical findings and their interpretation Chapter 5 combines the five areas of evidence to test for the hypotheses set out in Chapter 3.

The final Chapter 6 concludes the work summarizing and evaluating the research findings and reflects on the contribution of the provided evidence on research specifically in transport geography, maritime economics. Finally, future research areas emanating from the results presented in this study are presented.

Chapter 2
Theoretical Framework

Introduction

> Transport is a complex and increasingly prominent part of our lives. (Woudsma and Andrey 2004: 446)

Complexity is evident not only in the transport systems themselves, but in the multifaceted impacts these systems have on their environment. Research in the structures, functional relationships and influencing factors in international trade and especially in connection with maritime transport is at the heart of research in economic and particularly transport geography, but at the same time clearly depicts the interrelationship with neighbouring disciplines, in particular economics.

Transport facilitates *Raumueberwindung* while at the same time transport acts as a differentiator in space (*raumdifferenzierender Faktor*). Traditionally, transport geography discusses the relation between geography and trade and traditional theories discuss the influence of spatial organization using distance and transport costs as explanatory factors (Weber 1909, Christaller 1957, described in Schätzl 1998). Geography discusses the interrelationships between phenomena in a spatial setting and with the explanation of spatial patterns (Hoyle and Knowles 1998).

Regarding Pedersen (2001): 'Until the 1960s transport costs were generally seen as one of the main factors explaining the location of economic activities, and it was the central organising principle in most location theories. Until the early 1970s transport costs were among the most important explanatory factors in economic geography and theories of regional and industrial development.' Thoman and Corbin (1974) refer to transport costs as the limits to the spatial extent of the market. In this decade transportation and transport costs almost lost their relevance in the discussions and research in mainstream economic geography (Pedersen 2001). Consequently, transport as research topic, particularly freight transport basically disappeared from studies of economic and regional development during the 1970s and 1980s.

Pedersen (2001) further argues that 'Transport geography became a niche concerned with the transport system itself but with few linkages to economic and industrial development.' Transport costs were recognized as a condition for spatial dispersion and expansion of economic activity. However, the level of transport costs was regarded to have reached a level where any further decrease would not impact on the choice of location for production. Such argumentation becomes evident in publications like Taaffe and Gauthier (1994) and their overview of transport geography in the United States and is also illustrated in the discussion in the textbooks on transport geography by Hilling (1996), Simon (1996) and Hoyle and Knowles (1999). These books report on the 'traditional' transport/ development debate but almost neglect the interrelationship between and effects from the rapid changes in transport technology and market and spatial organization in freight transport. Standard textbooks on international restructuring, such as Dicken (1992), have no references to transport issues at all and Storper and Walker (1989) only have a single reference stating transport's lack of importance. The traditional focus on the movement of goods in research in transport geography, particularly in Germany, had somewhat shifted towards research in passenger transport (e.g. Hanson 1995, Hoyle and Knowles 1998).

The greater relevance of freight transport in the discipline was recently 'rediscovered' with the publication of '*Verkehrsgeographie*' in German geography research (Nuhn and Hesse 2006), Rodrigue et al. (2006) '*The Geography of Transport Systems*' and '*Transport Geographies: Mobilities, Flows and Spaces*' by Knowles, Shaw and Docherty (2008). Despite the fact that freight transport has emerged from its niche existence in transport geography research the progress and advances in research related to maritime transport and port development in the discipline despite their relevance for global trade is trifling. Nuhn and Hesse (2006) stress the importance for continued research in the relation between transport, trade and development particularly in peripheral regions and developing economies but discussions on transport costs remain linked to the traditionalist view as being principally a function of distance (Rodrigue et al. 2006: 44). Recent efforts by Ng and Wilmsmeier (2012) include a special Issue – *The Geography of Maritime Transport – Space as a Perspective in Maritime Research and Development* – where the editors gather contemporary studies on maritime transport that illustrate how geography, spatial theories and concepts offer important contributions to maritime transport research, and that experiences from the maritime sector can play significant roles to progress the current and future discussions and debates in contemporary issues within the geography discipline.

Trade, Economic Development and Trade Costs

Cost of international trade are the costs of transport and transaction related to the exchange of goods across national borders. These are a subset of all international transaction costs (see Figure 2.1). Anderson and van Wincoop (2004) state that economists, but also geographers, have relatively restricted knowledge on the magnitude, evolution and determinants of obstacles to international trade. Recognizing the various dimensions of transaction costs this work focuses on the costs of goods transfer and in this case particularly on maritime transport costs.

Early works on determinant of transport costs include Sampson and Yeats (1977) on OECD countries, Prewo (1978) on Latin America and Amjadi and Yeats (1995) on Latin America and Asia, Amjadi and Yeats (1995), Amjadi, Reincke and Yeats (1996) and UNCTAD (1995) on sub-Saharan Africa. All these studies

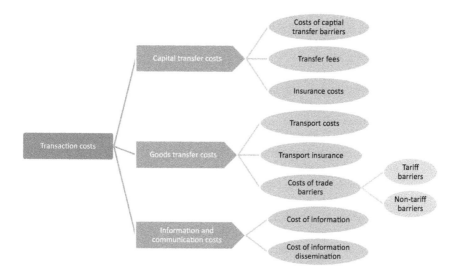

Figure 2.1   Transaction costs in international trade

Source: Amelung (1990), Kield Working Paper No. 423, Kiel: Institute of World Economics

document differences in shipping costs but do not directly estimate the underlying reasons and the relationship between export structures and economic development.

Despite the fact that production volumes have increased rapidly over the last decades and that final products are distributed and intermediate products are sourced globally the workforce producing directly for external markets has only changed marginally (e.g. Pedersen 2001). A main reason is that the growth in volume has been offset by the increase in production efficiency and technical innovation. This also implies that while transport costs for an individual product might have reduced, the global sourcing of intermediate products and the related transport of these, potentially means that the overall share of transport costs in the final product have not been reduced. This is also driven by the externalization of production and service functions that traditionally were delivered in-house. With increasing globalization these functions have moved and regrouped beyond local at national, international or global scale. In the process of this externalization transport, communication and storage costs have shifted from being internal to being part of the price of the externally sourced input.

Further, externalization incurs additional costs such as contract negotiation with suppliers, which can be significantly larger than the external transport and communication costs.

However, this does not reduce the importance of the local production environment (see e.g. Krugman 1996) as firms aim at minimizing their overall logistics costs, which include internal and external transport, storage and communications costs. Schmitz (1990) referred to the construct and working of private production and service enterprises and public infrastructures and services as collective efficiency.

Therefore transport costs today are an integral part of spatially dispersed production processes, and depending on the input requirements and complexity cannot be singled out as an isolated element, as they were in the old location theories (e.g. Thünen 1875).

Further, it needs to be recognized that transport costs might construct from the use of a sequence of transport modes within these production chains and as such are also related to other elements such as storage, packaging, forwarding, trade finance and insurance which are also part of these chains.

The relationship between transport and economic development must focus on the transport system as a whole and the way it is integrated into the processes of production, distribution and consumption. In this much broader perspective transport is now resuming a new importance as a factor structuring economic development.

In the literature a number of indications of such a renewed interest in the relationship between transport and development can be observed. It is evident in the increased focus on geography, space and agglomeration economies in the new economic growth and international trade theories (Krugman 1996), and in the increased focus on trade and services in studies of local as well as global development (see Pedersen 1998). But maybe it is most evident in more recent attempts to link transport and economic development at the macro level in studies of globalization (Janelle and Beuthe 1997) and of the long cycles which have often been explained by shifts in sources of energy and means of transportation (see e.g. Rodrigue, Comtois and Slack 1997). However, these different new approaches generally stop short of studying the increasing integration between transport, production and distribution taking place in the globalizing economy.

Transport costs are regarded as important because they affect economic growth through changing trade patterns. Naude (1999, p. 21) identified that for a country, the higher international transport costs, the more firms will have to pay for imported intermediate goods, and the less they will receive for their exports, *ceteris paribus*. Further, countries with higher international transport costs would be less likely to attract foreign direct investment (FDI) in export activities (Radelet and Sachs 1998). Additionally, relatively higher international transport costs would increase the price of all imported capital goods, which would reduce investment, the rate of technological transfer and thus reduce economic growth.

Transport costs play a fundamental role in the determination of the location of regional economic activities (see, e.g., Krugman 1991, 1998, Ottaviano and Puga 1998, Neary 2001). Characteristic assumptions in studies of regional activities in New Trade Theory and Geographical Economics are that transport costs are incurred in the goods shipped ('iceberg'), they are symmetric irrespective of the shipping direction, they are independent of the spatial organization of the economy and finally that transport costs are exogenous. Particularly the latter implies that transport costs are not set prices emerging from the interaction of supply and demand (Behrens and Picard 2011). The relevance of imbalances of trade flows and the role competition, whether perfect or imperfect particularly in container shipping are thus not considered.

Radelet and Sachs (1998) estimated a growth equation that includes shipping costs as an independent variable. Their results indicate that there exists a strong relationship between shipping costs and economic growth. Results further imply that doubling shipping costs are associated with slower annual growth rates by slightly more than one-half of one per cent.

Increased interest in the role of transport costs has developed with the progress of trade liberalization. The new interest is driven by economics research aiming at explaining differences in development particularly the relation between transport infrastructure development and economic development in various regions throughout the world (i.e. USAID 2007, Radelet and Sachs 1998, Hummels and Skibba 2002, Baier and Bergstrand 2001, Ghosh and Yamarik 2004, Limão and Venables 2001, Chasomeris 2005).

The main argument brought forward from the development banks, such as The World Bank, the InterAmerican Development Bank (IDB) and the Andean Development Fund (CAF) is that for the case of Latina America the current situation of elevated transport costs (for empirical evidence see e.g. Wilmsmeier 2003, Hoffmann et al. 2002, Wilmsmeier et al. 2009, Wilmsmeier and Martínez-Zarzoso 2010, Wilmsmeier and Sanchez 2010, Moreira 2009) leaves these economies at a disadvantage in comparison to other countries for exports as well as imports as also given in arguments from Chasomeris (2003) for the case of South Africa.

Transport costs are considered a friction to trade. The importance of international transport costs is an influencing factor of international trade and the perception of this importance of international transport costs have changed throughout time. In this respect international transport costs have been considered as important proxies for market access barriers, but until recently have submerged in the discussion of tariff and other non-tariff barriers to trade. In the 1990s discussion on transport and communication and their relevance in international trade reappeared in the mainstream of economic research. However, the focus shifted from pure transport issues to logistics. This focus has become an important element in analysing the organization and restructuring of the globalized economy. The relationship between production costs and transport costs has changed in recent years, and contrary to Glaeser and Kohlhase (2003) it is still far from zero. Elevated transport costs have been shown to significantly encumber international trade, and consequently a country's or region's competitiveness in international trade (e.g. Stopford 1997, 2009, Naude 1999, Fink et al. 2002, Limão and Venables 2000, Micco and Perez 2001, Wilmsmeier 2003, Wilmsmeier et al. 2006, Moreira et al. 2008; Wilmsmeier and Martínez-Zarzoso 2010, Wilmsmeier and Sanchez 2010).

International maritime transport costs in particular have been recognized as critical for economic development, as the overall reduction and levelling of tariffs results in the former gaining in relevance in trade.

> While liberalisation continues to reduce artificial trade barriers, the effective 'protection' from transport costs today is, in many cases higher, than the 'protection' envisaged by customs tariffs. IDB Annual Meeting 2001, Santiago, Chile. Cited in http://www.bcentral.com.ar/\Noticias\ (September 2008)

According to the World Bank (2001), transport costs outweigh tariff barriers in 168 out of 216 countries that are US trading partners. Micco and Perez (2001) show that in the cases of Chile and Ecuador, transport costs are more than twenty times greater than average tariffs.

The structures of transportation industry and production pattern are highly interdependent, not at the level of individual investments but at a broader national, international and global systemic level.

The constant restructuring of the global transport system therefore is likely to have a profound impact on the processes of globalization, not only in the industrialized and industrializing world, but especially in emerging regions such as Latin America.

> Space is no longer seen as a nested hierarchy moving from 'global' to 'local'. This absurd scale-dependent notion is replaced by the notion that what counts is connectivity. (Thrift 2004: 59)

Having said the above, the question on the impact of inefficiencies and shortcomings in the maritime transport chain and their effect on the overall sales price of a product becomes even more important.

Trade Costs

> By explicitly introducing costs of international trade (narrowly transport costs but more broadly, tariffs, non tariff barriers and other trade costs), one can go far towards explaining a great number of the main empirical puzzles that international macroeconomics have struggled with over twenty-five years. (Obstfeld and Rogoff 2000)

Trade costs can be broadly defined to encompass all costs encountered in getting a final good to a final user – other than the cost of producing the good itself. In general, an exporter or importer incurs trade costs at all stages of the trading process. This often starts with obtaining information about market conditions in a foreign market and ends with receipt of final payment for the traded good.

Frequently, firms serving the local market and willing to sell their product overseas are subject to costs of compliance with standards and technical regulations imposed by the importing country. As these costs would not be incurred if the goods were sold exclusively on the domestic market, they can be considered a trade cost. A similar framework applies to preferential trade agreements because preferential access to partners' markets requires compliance with rules of origin. These rules may involve, for example, adjustments to the intermediates mix or production process that often involve additional costs for producers.

In an extensive review of the literature on the sources of trade costs, Anderson and Van Wincoop (2004) estimate that trade costs for industrialized countries, on average, are equal to an *ad-valorem* equivalent of 170 per cent. The authors break down this estimate into three components: a 21 per cent *ad-valorem* equivalent for transportation costs, 44 per cent for border-related trade barriers, and 55 per cent for retail and wholesale distribution costs, as shown in Figure 2.1. It appears that trade costs have different magnitudes and patterns. This is true across countries and regions, as well as across sectors and goods. Available data suggest that the costs of trading a good for developing countries, including both international trade costs and domestic distribution costs, can be even larger than the costs of production. In addition, the ratio of trade costs to production costs is likely to be on average larger for developing countries than for developed ones because of the differences in physical infrastructure and business environment.

To illustrate the variability of trade costs across regional groups, Figure 2.2 shows the average costs of exporting and importing a standardized container by region, as reported by the World Bank's (2013) Doing Business report. The figures represent the official fees levied on a dry-cargo, 20-foot, full container load expressed in US dollars and associated with completing the procedures to export or import the goods. Costs include the costs of documents, administrative fees for customs clearance and technical control, terminal handling charges, and inland transport, and exclude tariffs as well as other trade-related taxes. Among the developing countries in the data set, those in Latin America oscillate close to average.

Portugal-Perez and Wilson (2009) provide a review of recent research presenting evidence of the impact of trade costs, with a focus on African countries, and highlight new data addressing the sources of trade costs. They classify trade costs into four broad groups:

- *Traditional trade policy barriers*, such as tariffs, quotas, or a combination of both (tariff-rate quotas, TRQ), and 'traditional' policy instruments, such as anti-dumping duties, countervailing duties, and safeguard measures.
- *Transport costs.*
- *Behind the-border factors*, such as governance, corruption, transparency, and the business environment have an impact on trading costs.
- *Specific preferential trade agreement factors*; preferential market access under preferential agreements is subject to the compliance of rules of origin. These rules may involve, for example, adjustments to the intermediates mix or production process that often involve additional costs for producers.

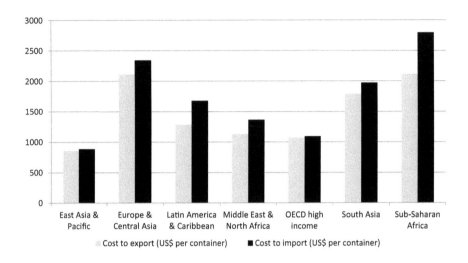

Figure 2.2   Costs of export and import procedures according to *Doing Business*, in US$ per container

Source: World Bank (2013)

Trade Facilitation

There is no exact and standard definition of trade facilitation. Trade facilitation can be broadly defined as the set of policies aiming at reducing trade costs. These policies can range from the simplification and standardization of customs procedures, to investment in physical infrastructure projects such as port improvements or road constructions. In an international environment of declining tariffs, trade facilitation has been at the forefront of policy discussions as the next key policy option to diminish trade costs for developing countries.

The relationship between trade flows and trade facilitation is complex, not only because a country's trade flows may change through its own trade facilitation reforms and through its trading partners' reforms, but also because of the multidimensionality and country-specific characteristics of trade facilitation. The meaning can vary depending on the issue at hand, country or region, and other factors. For instance, in a setting where the main topic concerns business logistics, trade facilitation can simply refer to various efforts to make customs procedures more effective. In a general sense, trade facilitation measures are usually associated with the simplification—and in some cases—the harmonization of trade regulations, both procedural and administrative, that may work as impediments to trade.

The World Trade Organization (WTO) has traditionally used quite a narrow definition, simply saying that trade facilitation is '[t]he simplification and harmonization of international trade procedures'. Another WTO definition states that trade facilitation is a 'wide range of activities such as import and export procedures (e.g. customs or licensing procedures), transport formalities, etc'. The latter symbolizes an important shift in how trade facilitation has been discussed in recent years. Instead of focusing exclusively on factors at the border – such as transparency of countries' regulatory environments – other 'behind the border' factors have begun to enter into the equation: such as professionalism of customs departments. As a result of this, focus also encompasses domestic policies. It is not all that uncommon that trade facilitation today refers to things like a country's general domestic trade environment. Importantly, due to the rapid integration of networked information technology in almost all aspects of the international supply chain, these services are frequently being incorporated into the definition as well.

Trade facilitation measures can be thought of along two dimensions: investment on 'hard' infrastructure (highways, railroads, ports, etc) and on 'soft' infrastructure (transparency, customs efficiency, institutional reforms, etc). A particular interest of this distinction resides on comparing the benefits and costs of investment or policy reform along both dimensions. Large investments in physical infrastructure projects to improve infrastructure quality alone do not necessarily lead to lower transport prices. Complementary steps in regulatory reform are also fundamental. The lack of competition along the different segments in the trade logistics chain, for example, can result in high mark-ups favouring cartels among logistic service firms. Corruption and interest groups capture can lead to regulatory barriers (such as market access restrictions, technical regulations, and customs regulations). Regulation in transport services can protect inefficient logistics operators and discourage the entry of more modern logistics operators with lower operational costs. Reform to dismantle cartels and enhance competition along different segments of the logistics chain is crucial to lower trade costs. In a more competitive environment, measures to improve physical infrastructure are likely to produce better results.

International development organizations such as the World Bank and UNCTAD, among others have focused on the importance of trade facilitation. The World Bank has put particular emphasis in trying to make trade facilitation issues easily understandable and to visualize performance of countries by developing the Doing Business Reports since 2004 (for details see: http://www.doingbusiness.org) and the Logistics Performance Index (LPI) (for details see: http://info.worldbank. org/etools/-tradesurvey/mode1b.asp). This effort goes hand in hand with the Reports from the World Economic Forum (WEF), e.g. Global Competitiveness reports (for details see: http://www.weforum.org) etc. These efforts try to make development comparable using country rankings. This challenging effort is developed based on a variety of methodologies, but mainly expert opinion. However, full empirical evidence is rare and when looking into the details of the reports surveys from earlier years are frequently reused in follow up reports. While the World Bank and WEF are aware of the limitations of their reports a significant challenge is that particularly developing countries take the results and refer to them without the necessary critical reflection. A more detailed discussion on particular indicators from these sources can be found in Chapter 1.

Empirical research assessing the impact of trade facilitation must address three issues: defining and measuring trade facilitation indicators; choosing an econometric methodology to estimate the impact of trade facilitation on trade flows; and designing a scenario to estimate the effect of improved trade facilitation on trade flows. Several regional studies have suggested the importance of infrastructure and institutional indicators on trade facilitation. Njinkeu, Wilson and Fosso (2008) analyse the impact of reforms in port efficiency, customs environment, regulatory environment and service infrastructure and find that improving port efficiency and infrastructure bring the most significant trade gains. Wilson, Mann and Otsuki (2005) showed important increases in trade from trade facilitation reforms in countries that have trade transaction costs above the average. Abe and Wilson (2008) explore institutional trade facilitation indicators and found that reducing corruption and improving transparency to lower trade costs would incur in significant trade and welfare gains.

Maritime Transport, Trade and Transport Costs

'Global economic integration relies upon efficient maritime transport' (Hoyle and Knowles 1998). Maritime transport being responsible for 80 per cent or 9 billion tons (UNCTAD 2013) of world trade is almost absent in transport geography research and if dealt with in textbooks the manner is rather descriptive (e.g. Hesse and Nuhn 2006, Hoyle and Knowles 1998). Given the relevance of the sector in globalization processes (e.g. Corbett, Winebrake and Energy and Environmental Research Associates 2008, Kumar and Hoffmann 2002), research in the functioning and geographical and economic implications resulting from the activities of the maritime and port industry should be expected to receive a greater attention in geographic research. Exler's work (1996) is one of the few numbers of works with a geographer's perspective on maritime transport during the 1990s. Exler analysed the role and structures of container transport in trade particularly focusing on maritime transport. In an effort to explain the 'constant contradiction between transport supply and demand, containerization and its spatial diffusion' Rodrigue, Slack and Comtois (1997) initiate a discussion on spatial cycles in maritime transport systems. Recently, more importance was given to maritime transport studies from a geographical standpoint (e.g. Wilmsmeier and Notteboom 2011, Rodrigue and Browne 2008, Notteboom 2002, Notteboom 2004, Notteboom and Rodrigue 2005, Notteboom 2006b, Notteboom 2009 among others). The following section discusses the current state of research in the interrelationship of trade, maritime freight rates and trade costs.

Maritime transport has been a key facilitator for globalization and particularly driven by technological developments i.e. the introduction of standardization through the use of container transport (for discussion on containerization and world trade see UNCTAD 2000–2008, Corbett, Winebrake and Energy and Environmental Research Associates 2008, Kumar and Hoffmann 2002, Exler 1996, etc). There is a close relationship between the development of maritime transport and world trade. The expansion of international trade has resulted in an increase in demand for transport services. This work relates specifically to developments in maritime container transport. Technological changes in sea shipping have led to considerable increases in capacities in sea transport and have thus vigorously spurred the expansion of world trade. Maritime trade predominantly takes places within the triad of North America, Europe and Asia (for detailed discussion see UNCTAD 2000–2008).

What are the Sources of Economies in Shipping?

In business, economies of scale are usually considered in relation to specific areas of the production process, which may be technical, managerial, marketing, finance, and risk. Economies of scale can also be produced when firms that need to cover similar routes operate their services together e.g. alliances. In the maritime industry different types of economies play a role.

Two types of economies of scale can be identified directly related to shipping. External economies of scale, where the unit cost depends on the size of the shipping company (or the trade volumes?), and internal economies of scales where the unit costs depend on the size of the individual transporting unit (ship, container, port, shipment).

In both cases economies of scale occur when long-run average production costs decrease as output increases. The high capital costs of ships are spread across a greater number of units (container) as more containers can be transported. If output increased by a factor of two, for example, the cost of production would increase by less than a factor of two.

A further possible source lies in the domestic trade infrastructure built up by each country. Ports (and the internal road or rail system necessary to reach them) tend to be large lumpy investments. If the fixed costs are large enough, increased trade scale will benefit the investing country directly and perhaps some of its trade partners, through lowered shipping costs.

Finally, scale economies may also operate at the level of the country pair and the trade route. The capacity of a modern ocean-going liner vessel is large relative to the quantities shipped by most exporters. Thus economies of scale may derive for shippers based on their volume of shipment.

Besides economies of scale economies of density and scope are of relevance and can be defined as followed:

> *Economies of density* Refers to the average costs of a firm as a consequence to an increase in production at an unchanged reach of the network. This means that a shipping company, in this case, increases its transported volumes without adding new ports of call to the routes. A firm that works with economies of density can fix its price for transport above the level of marginal costs, in order to avoid the entrance of new competitors to its market.

Economies of scope   In relation to maritime transport economies of scope means that the average total cost of production (service provision) decreases as a result of increasing the number of different services produced. For example the integration of door-to-door services and port terminal operation into the same company through vertical integration would result in lower transport costs than if three different companies (sea transport, port handling and road transport) handle the container along a transport chain.

As trade quantities increase it is possible to more effectively realize gains from different sources. First, a densely traded route allows for effective use of hub and spoke shipping economies – small container vessels move quantities into a hub where containers are aggregated into much larger and faster containerships for longer hauls (Hummels and Skibba 2002).

Understanding the concepts of economies in shipping, particularly economies of scale, are a prerequisite for the understanding of the maritime industry and for interpreting the empirical results in the context of this work.

Defining International Maritime Transport Costs

International maritime transport costs are part of trade costs. The term transport cost subsumes various different components of costs. The rather complex structure of this variable in international trade has for a long time put constraints on researching this topic. However, despite potential restrictions of existing research to address this complexity the investigation of the variable transport costs and its measurement has to start somewhere and according to Hummels (1999), it is sensible to begin in obvious places.

Before deepening the discussion, a distinction has to be made between transport prices and transport costs in order to avoid the usual confusion. This distinction is useful because prices may or may not reflect transport costs. Raballand and Macchi (2008) define transport prices as 'the rates charged by a transport company or a freight forwarder to the shipper or importer. Transport prices usually are the result of negotiated rates between the shipper and the transport service provider. Transport prices normally cover transport costs, the operator's overheads and profit margin.' Further in line with Raballand and Macchi (2008)transport costs are defined as 'the costs the transport operator incurs when transporting a cargo. In addition to vehicle operating costs, transport cost includes other indirect costs, such as flag registration, etc.'

In this work the term transport costs is used from the perspective of the shipper. This is equal to the transport price of the transport company

Based on the Oxford Dictionary, freight is 'Money charged for the carriage of goods from place to place by water.' According to the Encyclopaedia of Nautical Knowledge 'freight is a charge made by a carrier for transporting goods or merchandise'. In the container shipping practice, any amount paid to the carriers for the transportation of the container from the origin to destination is considered to be freight.

The ocean freight and hence international maritime transport costs is based on the cargo manifest. Historically, the ocean freight rates were categorized and divided by commodity, thus making the filing of rates extremely bureaucratic, and the same commodity could include a significant number of products. The target of this structure was differentiation of rates, thus the advancement of containerization freight of all kind (F.A.K.) means rates are more common and are applied for consolidated cargoes. These rates hypothetically do not discriminate between commodities. However, existing research suggests that discrimination of commodities in relation to the unitary value of the product (e.g. Wilmsmeier 2003, Hummels 2000, Wilmsmeier and Martínez-Zarzoso 2010). Reefer cargo is a notable case where higher costs through energy consumption and monitoring on-board while being shipped are levied as a premium.

International maritime transport cost for the purposes of this work is defined as the cost to the shipper to utilize a liner shipping service to transport his cargo between two points (ports). These are retrieved and analysed based on the actual charged ocean freight for a product x on the route between countries i and j as given in the cargo manifest. Making use of international standards, maritime transport costs can be defined using the Incoterms (see Box 2.1 and Figure 2.6). One of the main difficulties in analysing international transport costs is that of obtaining reliable and disaggregated data.

Box 2.1   INCOTERMS

FOB – Free On Board (named loading port): The classic maritime trade term. The seller must load the goods on board the ship nominated by the buyer, cost and risk being divided at ship's rail. The seller must clear the goods for export. Maritime transport only.

CFR – Cost and Freight (named destination port): Seller must pay the costs and freight to bring the goods to the port of destination, including all transportation, and miscellaneous charges to the point of debarkation from the vessel. However, risk is transferred to the buyer once the goods have crossed the ship's rail. Maritime transport only.

CIF – Cost, Insurance and Freight (named destination port): Exactly the same as CFR except that the seller must in addition procure and pay for insurance for the buyer. Maritime transport only.

Source: http://roberteyates.com/ry/incoterms/ (October 2009)

Previous research and publications to have attempted to directly or indirectly measure transport costs in international transport. Various authors used CIF/ FOB ratios as a proxy for transport costs (Radelet and Sachs 1998, Limão and Venables 2001, Baier and Bergstrand 2001). Micco and Perez (2001) analyse transport costs as 'the aggregate cost of all freight, insurance, and other charges (excluding import duties) incurred in bringing the merchandise from the port of exportation to the first port of entry in the importing country'. These authors used the availability of reported trade flows from customs: exporting countries report trade flows exclusively from freight and insurance (FOB), and importing countries report flows inclusive of freight and insurance (CIF). Hummels (2001) states that customs data typically only covers the international leg of transport, omitting port and inland charges. He argues further that international maritime transport costs only represent a third of total door-to-door shipping charges and are thus being restricted to analysing international door-to-door transport costs.

Hummels (1999, 2001) used data on transport costs from various primary sources including shipping price indices obtained from shipping trade journals (Appendix 2 in Hummels 2001); air freight prices gathered from survey data; and freight rates (freight expenditures on imports) collected by customs agencies in the United States, New Zealand and five Latin-American countries.

In addition to CIF/FOB ratios reported by the International Monetary Fund (IMF), Limão and Venables (2001) used shipping company quotes for the cost of transporting a standard container (40 feet) from Baltimore to sixty-four destinations. The authors recognized that the potential of generalization of their findings in the case of the 'Baltimore experience' might be restricted. Martínez-Zarzoso, García-Menendez and Suárez-Burguet (2003) used data on transportation costs obtained from interviews with logistic operators in Spain. They found import elasticities with respect to transport costs similar in magnitude to those found by Limão and Venables (2001) for the Baltimore case.

Micco and Perez (2001) used data from the U.S. Import Waterborne Databank (US Department of Transportation), where transport cost is defined as 'the aggregate cost of all freight, insurance and other charges (excluding US import duties) incurred in bringing the merchandise from the port of exportation to the first port of entry in the US'. Sánchez, Hoffmann, Micco, Pizzolitto, Sgut and Wilmsmeier (2002) analysed data on maritime transport costs obtained from the International Transport Data Base (BTI). They focused on Latin American trade with countries within the North American Free Trade Agreement (NAFTA).

The IMF established a database by using CIF/FOB ratios that covering a significant number of countries and years. They obtained the data from the United Nations Commodity Trade (UN COMTRADE) database and in some cases supplemented it with national data sources. The difference between the same aggregated flows reported from importer and exporter can be related to the transport costs including the insurance tariff for the freight. This methodology has however gained quite a few critics. IMF trade flow data in these publications has always been aggregated, thus just stating averages of transport costs over different products or product groups. Hummels (2000) argues that firstly the data sets are not collected from the same source and secondly, they are not disaggregated. In a subsequent work Hummels (2001) showed that importer CIF/FOB ratios constructed from IMF sources are poor proxies for cross-sectional variation in transport costs and such a variable provides no information about the time series variation. Hummels (2001) proved that due to high volatility of transport costs over the years, this data cannot be used to estimate time series variation. Ogueldo and Macphee (1994) also doubted the usefulness of CIF/FOB ratios from IMF sources as a proxy of transportation costs. Hummels and other authors therefore tried to work with data from primary sources such as shipping prices obtained from shipping companies, journals etc (see Martínez-Zarzoso, García and Suárez 2002, Wilmsmeier and Hoffmann 2006).

Hummels (2000, 2001) obtained the data on transport costs including indices of ocean shipping from trade journals. Conducting a survey he gathered data on air freight prices and freight rates which he collected from customs agencies in the United States, New Zealand and Latin-American countries (MERCOSUR plus Chile). The most direct approach is primary industry or shipping company information, which was subsequently applied by Wilmsmeier and Hoffmann (2008) for the case of the Caribbean and Gouvernal and Slack (2012).

Hummels and Lugovskyy (2006) compare aggregate and commodity-level bilateral CIF/FOB ratios to directly measured transport costs for the US and New Zealand and develop arguments why CIF/FOB ratios are not a perfect measure. Firstly, there are statistical difficulties, as importers may record the goods with more rigour to obtain higher tax revenues. Secondly, there are disagreements regarding the correct commodity classification of goods. Consequently, the export value sometimes exceeds the import value, which is meaningless. Hummels and Lugovskyy (2006) find that the matched partner CIF/FOB ratio is not suitable if one is interested in transport costs. One has to recognize the problems inherent to this kind of measurement. On the other hand, because of difficulties in obtaining better estimates for a wide range of countries and years, this data is still used by several researchers such as Bair and Bergstrand (2001).

Other authors like Martínez-Zarzoso et al. (2003) used data on transportation costs obtained from interviews with logistics operators in Spain. The most detailed and comprehensive data on transportation costs is available at the US Imports of Merchandise from the US Import Waterborne Databank (US Department of Transportation), used also by Hummels (1999) and Micco and Perez (2001). The US imports are reported at the ten-digit Harmonized System (HS) level by country of origin, mode of transport and entry port, by weight, and valued at FOB and CIF bases. Hummels, Lugovskyy and Skibba (2007), Kumar and Hoffmann (2002), Sánchez et al. (2003), Wilmsmeier et al. (2003, 2006) as well as Martínez-Zarzoso et al. (2002, 2003) used for their research the data from the International Transport Data Base (BTI). Data from the BTI for freight rates is given excluding loading costs. The main difference is that the IMF data report ratios and the BTI freight per tonne. Further, between these data and those reported by the IMF is that the

BTI data on imports at CIF prices and imports at FOB prices are obtained from the same reporting country. Since information is recorded by the same customs declarations, the data is more reliable than the IMF rates. 'For each maritime trade transaction, the value CIF declared to customs is the sum of the cargo's value FOB, the insurance costs, and the freight charges', states Wilmsmeier (2006). The BTI therefore allows differentiating between freight and insurance costs and thus any potential impact of insurance costs in the estimation of determinants.

Who Determines Freight Rates? Markets or Demand

Freight is the monetary value paid to a carrier for transporting and discharge of goods in a mercantile or recognized condition, ready to be delivered to the merchant.

The pricing of cargo movements is dependent on the forces of supply and demand, but as Branch (2008, p. 181) points out potentially more complicated than in the case of other industries. Transport is a derived demand for all transport modes and therefore affected by the elasticities of demand of the transported goods. For transport of goods/commodities it can be argued that the rates depend on the context of (Rodrigue 2009).

- Demand elasticity of goods/commodities transported.
- Ratio of transport costs to the costs of transported goods.
- The replaceability of maritime transport or of specific routes. Enterprises and individuals take decisions about how to route traffic through the transport system.
- Users have to negotiate or bid for transportation.
- Conditions (tariffs, salaries, locations, fuel costs) are changing constantly.
- Costs for gathering information, negotiating, and enforcing contracts and transactions.

The difference between costs and rates results in profit or deficit from the service provider. Rate setting in freight transportation is subject to a competitive pressure. Branch (2008) discusses that sea transport is affected by two types of competition, a) competition between carriers and b) competition between substitutes or alternatives for the particular product transported. Since shipping is a facilitator to global trade a ship owner on the one hand faces competition from other carriers on any particular routes and on the other hand also from shipping lines providing services to alternative supply regions of a same commodity.

On certain routes there might also be competition from rail, truck or air transport services. However, such competition is highly dependent on the product structure and the related modal affinity of a product, but also on the infrastructure endowment for any particular mode; the latter being decisive for the performance of one mode over the other.

The elasticity of demand for shipping services varies from one commodity to another. Under 'normal' market conditions the cost of sea transport in relation to the market price of goods is decisive (e.g. see discussion on unit values in Chapter 3, p. 35).

It needs to be mentioned here that it is necessary to differentiate between bulk, RoRo and container shipping markets, particularly because each one operates under different market conditions and within different frameworks (for definition of shipping markets see Stopford 2009, p. 345 ff.). This work only focuses on containerized cargo and liner shipping.

According to Branch (2008) 'the container rate structure falls into two divisions. In general container rates are negotiated between the shipper and the shipping line and reflect the trade, type of container, origin and destination, nature of cargo and potential volume discounts to shippers. A number of additional charges (Stopford 2009) might also apply CAF, BAF, port congestion charges, THC, terminal security charges (ISPS related) etc (for details see Stopford 2009; Branch 2008, p. 189). These charges are referred to as FCL. In the case where cargo from various shippers is consolidated in one container, usually negotiated through an agent, these rates are referred to as LCL.

Transport costs can be divided into fixed and variable (operating) costs (Rodrigue 2009). In the liner trade, once the decision to operate a liner service has been taken the major proportion of costs are fixed (Saggar 1970, p. 54) e.g. ship insurance, flagging, maintenance, crew wages, administration, port dues and fuel costs. The critical division is between port time and sea time. All cost items for the time a ship spends in port can enter into marginal costs; no cost items for sea time can enter marginal cost. The division of total costs between those incurred in port and those incurred at sea is of the order of 60:40 in liner services (Sturmey 1967, p. 192). Fixed costs vary in relation to route structure, but not in relation to the cargo carried.

The variable costs are chiefly those which vary with the amount and composition of cargo handled. This includes: cargo handling costs, cargo insurance, and other port costs beyond the GRT related ones. Heaver (2006) refers to Thorburn (1960) who states Biles (1923) findings that transport costs per ton and mile vary depending on the vessel size, speed and cargo loading and unloading rates. Yeats (1986) refers to Fasbender and Wagner (1973) who have been successfully explaining differences in liner conference freight rates for homogenous products through analysis of factors as distance, duration of voyage, stevedoring charges, differences in berth times, harbour facilities and quality of vessel deployed.

The rates are rarely set for the movement of cargo from A to B; they are normally for movement from A to ports in the range T to Z or for movement from the range A to F to the range T to Z. These ranges might be very wide in the geographic sense and may include ports widely different in type, with substantial differences in costs and significantly different distances from the port at which the journey began (Sturmey 1967, p. 191).

The important cost division is not between categories like handling charges, fuel and depreciation, but between costs in port and costs at sea (Sturmey 1967, p. 192).

Freight rate schedules are compiled with little regard to the actual costs for handling and carriage of the particular goods (Sturmey 1967, p. 193).

It would seem that the rate on any item might logically be composed of one constituent based on the time-cost of the ship's space occupied and another based on loadability. In practice, what the cargo will bear, bargaining between shippers and conferences, and accident are more important determinants to the individual rates than costs of carriage and handling.

The arbitrary nature of the schedule and the lack of any defined relation between cost and charge provide the scope for selective rate cutting (Sturmey 1967, p. 193). Only a minor proportion of voyage costs can be directly attributed to specific cargoes. In practice total costs are recovered via a pricing structure which is partly arbitrary. Still today it remains common practice to charge higher rates for high value cargoes and lower rates for low valued cargoes.

Laing (1977) stated that the highest rates for cargoes can be as much as twenty times the lowest (Davies 1990). This pricing structure has been applied by shipping conferences since they began over 125 years ago (for discussion on

---

Box 2.2   Traditional categorization of rates

Rate	Description
Alpha rates	Rates which, if the ship was fully loaded with such cargo would yield 'normal' profits or better to the shipowner, and where sufficient cargo of the type is available to prevent the idea of full loads from being patently ridiculous
Beta rates	Rates which, as above, would cover costs but yield less than 'normal' profits to the shipowner, and where cargo is available as above
Gama rates	Alpha or beta types rates where cargo volume never amounts to a shipload
Delta rates	Rates which would cover direct costs, but not total costs, irrespective of amount available. Rates which would cover the total costs of a casual entrant to the trade when sufficient cargo volume is available, the entrant not necessarily using a different type of ship or organization from that of the liner owner
Epsilon rates	Rates at which the shipowner would have been better off if he had not carried the cargo. Rates at which a ship such as a tramp or bulk carrier can add more to revenue than to costs by carrying available cargo

Source: S.G. Sturmey 1967. Economics and international liner services. *Journal of Transport Economics and Policy*, 1 (2), 190–203. Reproduced with permissions.

the concept 'What the cargo will bear' (WtCwb) see e.g. Faúndez, Perez, Sánchez and Wilmsmeier 2009 and Chapter 3, p. 35 for discussion on the unit values as determinants of transport costs). The explanation which relies on the structure of rates rather than the structure of costs can be referred to the particularities and economics of the shipping industry, particularly the strong relationship of rates to supply and demand.

The evaluation of the impact of supply and demand relationships on freight rates is based on the behaviour of supply and demand within the shipping cycles. The shipping cycle consists of a sequence of balances in the supply and demand of shipping services: the price and output behave cyclically. In a given period prices are above the equilibrium level, which means that supply in the following period will be higher than the equilibrium level. Once supply is above the equilibrium level, prices will be below that equilibrium level, and so on. The maritime cycle is a combination of price incentives and the typical inelasticity of supply within this market. The cycle originates from the lack of synchronization of ship production (changes in supply), in an environment of very dynamic and exogenous demand. When prices (freight rates) are low, there is less shipbuilding and increasing numbers of ships are scrapped. As demand increases and more transport services are needed, the supply (in terms of the number of ships and/or availability of effective transport capacity) cannot be adjusted rapidly, freight rates rise and shipbuilding begins again, which subsequently produces excessive supply and a lowering of freight rates (for explanation of shipping cycle in practice see Stopford 2009, particularly p. 107).

Evidence of International Maritime Transport Costs in International Trade

It is argued that globalization and trade as a result and cause of changing economic and technical frameworks has been driven by reduced transport costs, and the related impacts on the organization of trade flows require thorough analysis. An examination of the development of the share of freight costs in import values, however, does not suggest that transport costs continued to decline after 1990, while trade increased appreciably during this period (UNCTAD 2007 and Table 2.1 below). The price-driving effects of the increased demand for transport have evidently been compensated by the price-lowering technical progress that has clearly been made in the transport sector. While transport costs in international trade reduced overall (Laepple 1995), this reduction has neither been uniform over all modes, products and regions nor has it led to a reduction in the relevance of transport costs in international trade.

Table 2.1   Freight costs as percentage of import value

Country group	1990	2000	2004	2005
World total	5.3	5.0	5.1	5.9
Developed countries	4.4	4.3	4.7	4.8
Economies in transition	6.6	7.8	5.5	7.6
Developing countries	8.6	6.6	6.0	7.7
of which				
Africa	9.4	9.6	10.3	10.0
America	6.0	5.0	4.4	4.4
Asia	9.2	6.8	5.9	5.9
Oceania	9.5	9.5	10.0	9.6

Source: Calculations based on the UNCTAD Handbook of Statistics 2006/2007, IMF Balance of Payments Statistics and IMF Direction of Trade Statistics. Data in this table are not comparable to those published in previous issues of this publication owing to changes in sources and methodology. World totals include all countries, but regional aggregates for imports and their freight costs during recent years might be distorted because of slow reporting by some countries

The dynamic development of world trade is generally seen in relation to the progressive dismantling of national trade barriers which has taken place since the end of World War II, but particularly since the 1990s (see World Bank 2005). On a multilateral level, liberalization efforts have been concentrated for some time on tariff reductions. In Latin America custom tariffs were reduced from 43 percent in 1986 to 11 per cent in 1996. Through the reduction of state-imposed market access barriers other trade-inhibiting factors have gained in relative importance. Transport costs now constitute a far more serious trade barrier than tariffs. Since, generally speaking, the trade-inhibiting effects of transport costs are comparable to those of government trade barriers; it is not surprising that reductions in transport costs are regarded as a primary determinant in the increase in international trade (see e.g. Amjadi and Yeats 1995, Radelet and Sachs 1998).

When the oil price reached record highs in 2008, several trade analysts expressed concerns that this might revert the trend of globalization as it will lead to higher freight costs and thus encourage closer-to-home sourcing. Comparatively high costs of trade – i.e. the cost of transporting goods and moving them across borders – are a major obstacle to the trade performance of developing countries and prevent the full realization of the gains from expanding global trade opportunities. A growing literature has gathered empirical evidence of the negative impact of trade costs on a country's trade performance (Radelet and Sachs 1998, Amjadi and Winters 1997, Chasomeris 2005, Martínez-Zarzoso, Burguet and Menendez

2003 etc). Portugal-Perez and Wilson (2009) argue that economic performance of a country will be affected by elevated trade costs in different ways. According to these authors imported goods in countries will be sold at comparatively higher prices and thus will be accessible for fewer consumers. Domestic producers that require imported products when assembling their final product will be less competitive as the sourced inputs will be comparatively higher in price and thus also affect the final price of the product in a negative way.

Evidence on border costs shows that tariff barriers are relatively low across all countries. Weak infrastructure and institutions, however, can contribute to high trade costs along the logistics chain in developing countries (Portugal-Pérez and Wilson 2008).

Since freight rates until today are elevated for trade with developing countries, these face the burden of freight rates in their imports and exports. This is especially critical for their competitiveness in global production processes (Chasomeris 2005, Wilmsmeier and Sánchez 2009, Wilmsmeier and Hoffmann 2008).

Summary

In this chapter, the theoretical framework of the work is constructed and the work is set into context of recent developments in transport and economic geography. Investigation in maritime transport and particular maritime transport costs is an area that receives only little attention within geography research. As this work in its entirety combines in-depth analysis of empirical evidences with recent approaches in economic geography, it is also a response of geography research to the self-proclaimed new economic geography. The theoretic discussion on transport and economic geography is then set linked to research on maritime transport, trade and transport costs in relation to economic development.

Based on this discussion the concepts of trade costs, trade facilitation and in particular international maritime transport costs, fundamental to this research are examined. Following the examination of the theory underpinning maritime transport costs and their measurement, the chapter engages in the elemental discussion if markets or demand determine maritime transport costs. This theoretical framework chapter is closed by introducing key concepts of economies in shipping as a further foundation for the upcoming analysis.

Chapter 3
Determinants of Maritime Transport Costs – Defining the Dimensions of Complexity

Introduction

On the background of transport costs in international maritime trade this chapter investigates the theoretical background to explain the role of transport costs and their determinants in intra-regional trade in Latin America as a key factor for competitiveness in international trade.

To embed and analyse the current situation it is necessary review the theoretical discussions on the tripartite relationship between international trade, transport costs and the supply of shipping services.

Dimensions of Complexity

Recent research argues the fact that the *raumdifferenzierend* impact of transport costs has been reduced; thus, undermining the analysis of the role of transportation. Discourses on globalization, internationalization and free trade take transport services almost for granted and consequently give the topic little attention (Hesse and Rodrigue 2004, Holmes 2000). The effect of transport costs on trade is only residually recognized. The perception of transport

> … as a residual consequence – derived – of other processes or a mere 'space-shrinking' function. (Hesse and Rodrigue 2004)

loses out in understanding the role of transport and the diversity and differences particularly between developed and developing regions. The previous argument is also fuelled by arguments that transport costs have reduced to almost being irrelevant (e.g. Glaeser and Kohlhase 2003), while this might be true for trade within the triad or intraregional trade in Asia and Europe, evidence suggests differently for developing regions. One reason usually given for elevated transport costs in developing and peripheral regions is the lack of infrastructure development (e.g. Micco and Perez 2001, Limão and Venables 2001, Wilmsmeier et al. 2006).

Analysis of determinants of transport costs has been driven by economists rather than research in geography (e.g. Hummels 1999a, Micco and Perez 2001, Limão and Venables 2001). Recent works in the field of transport geography only briefly discuss the topic of international transport costs. Rodrigue (2009) gives a list of determinants

Table 3.1   Conditions affecting transport costs

Condition	Factor	Examples
Geography	Distance, physiography, accessibility	Shipping between France and England vs. shipping between France and the Netherlands
Type of product	Packaging, weight, perishable	Shipping coal Shipping flowers or wine
Economies of scale	Shipment size	A 747 compared to 737 (passengers) A ULCC compared to a VLCC (freight)
Trade imbalance	Empty travel	Trade between China and the United States
Infrastructure	Capacity, limitations, operational conditions	The Interstate
Mode	Capacity, limitations, operational conditions	A bus compared to a car
Competition and regulation	Tariffs, restrictions, safety, ownership	The European Union, The Jones Act

Source: http://www.people.hofstra.edu/geotrans/eng/ch7en/conc7en/table_conditionstransport. html (June, 2009). Copyright © 1998–2013, Dr Jean-Paul Rodrigue, Dept. of Global Studies & Geography, Hofstra University, New York, USA. Reprinted with permission

of international transport costs (see Table 3.1) and states that institutional effects should be analysed further. He does not provide any empirical evidence nor does he elaborate on the importance of each of the factors. Nuhn and Hesse (2006)

Gouvernal and Slack (2012) analyse freight rates of one global carrier for a period of three years on selected global routes. They argue that economic distance as a measure reveals spatial patterns different to physical distance and thus argue in line with Wilmsmeier and Hoffmann (2008) that physical distance is an imperfect proxy for maritime transport costs. Further Gouvernal and Slack (2012) follow the argument of Wilmsmeier and Hoffmann (2008) that developed economies seem to pay lower transport costs than developing economies.

Existing research has mainly been carried out using aggregated data, but with the availability of more detailed data sets a deeper and more differentiated level of analysis is possible (see discussion Chapter 2, p. 20).

The following discusses the state of the art in research regarding determinants of transport costs and develops an updated model defining the key categories of influencing determinants on maritime transport costs. This work is expected to particularly fill the gap of research on the role of liner networks in comparison to the role of distance, the effects of shipping industry and trade structures, but it also addresses determinants of ports infra- and superstructure.

The remainder of the chapter discusses and categorizes determinants of international maritime transport costs based on literature and thus develops a framework for determinants and identifies gaps in existing literature. The following categories are considered: Relation and geography, implications of cargo characteristics and trade structure, carriers, interfaces, the environment. Within each category hypotheses on the impact on international maritime transport costs are developed.

Relation and Geography

Distance

As confirmed by the literature distance is an obvious determinant of transport costs between trading partners. Traditionally transport costs were considered as a distance decay function. It is argued that transport costs increase between 20 to 30 per cent if distance doubles. Distance is argued to be the most basic component of transport costs, arguing that the greater the friction of distance the more difficult it is to trade. Thus, distance creates friction to trade, which can be expressed as geographical distance (km), time, economic cost, or used energy. However, this friction varies according to transport mode (Wilmsmeier 2003).

In literature the role of distance is discussed under two concepts involving maritime transport costs a) focusing on the importance of distance as a determinant of transport costs and b) the potential to use distance as a proxy for transportation costs in the analysis of trade.

A wide range of articles consider only proxies for transport costs in their estimated trade models. For instance, gravity models use distance between country capital cities as a proxy for transport costs (Anderson and van Wincoop 2003). Boulho and de Serres (2008) apply a gravity model framework developed on a panel data covering 21 OECD countries over 1970–2004 to show that, relative to the average OECD country, the cost of remoteness for countries such as Australia and New Zealand could be as high as 10 per cent of GDP.

These gravity studies have found that geographical distance is a crucial determinant of trade. However, geographical distance may represent a series of factors such as cultural proximity, a shared history, a perception of closeness and information costs rather than acting exclusively as a proxy for freight rates. Anderson and van Wincoop (2004) emphasize the need to obtain better transport cost measures and to use these measures to expand gravity models and to deal with the endogeneity of the transport cost variable.

Geraci and Prewo (1977) estimated a transport cost equation for OECD countries and found that using only distance as a proxy for transport costs may result in underestimating the sensitivity of bilateral trade flows to transport costs. Bergstrand (1985) demonstrates that distance is negatively related to trade and argues in line with Deardorff (1995) that distance is a crucial determinant for trade costs. Hummels (1999a) and Hummels (2001) estimated transport cost elasticity with respect to distance by transportation mode using US import data. Hummels (1999) estimates the elasticity of shipping and costs with respect to distance, and charts its evolution over time for air and ocean shipping over the period 1974–98. Hummels finds that the difference between costs associated with shipping comparable ocean/shipped commodities over a long (9000 km) route and a short (1000 km) route decreased by 27 percentage points from 1974 to 1998. His results also show that the distance coefficient of sea transport is higher than that of air transport. Hummels (2001) shows that increasing distance by 1000 km enlarges the probability of shipping manufactures 0.02 per cent. Limão and Venables (2001), Micco and Perez (2002) and Martínez-Zarzoso and Suarez-Burguet (2004) emphasized the role of the quality of transport infrastructure. Limão and Venables (2001) found that using distance alone explains only 10 per cent of the variation of transport costs; this is much lower than the approximately 50 per cent explained when infrastructure variables are included.

Kuwamori (2006), analysing transport costs within Asia finds evidence that transport costs increase about 29 per cent with a doubling of distance from the Philippines. Results from Sánchez et al. (2003) show that a 10 per cent increase in distance increase transport costs by 0.9 per cent. Further, Clark et al. (2004) find that doubling the distance between an export country and the US increases transport costs 20 per cent. In the case of South American countries a doubling in distance increases transport costs 16.5 per cent (UN-ECLAC, Bulletin FAL No. 191, July 2002).

The relevance of distance comparing different transport modes was analysed by Martínez-Zarzoso and Nowak-Lehman (2007), who find a significant relevance for road as well as maritime transport, with road showing a higher importance of distance. Wilmsmeier (2003) shows that a 1 per cent increase in distance raises air transport costs 0.148 per cent. The elasticity of distance oscillates around 0.15 for all road transport models. In the regression for maritime containerized transport a 1 per cent increase in distance signifies a 0.08 per cent raise in transport costs. The general consensus of the past studies is that distance plays a certain role in determining transport costs, but it does not sufficiently explain transport costs.

Nevertheless, the effect of distance on costs appears to have declined over time due to technological improvements, such as the introduction of containerization in maritime transport in the 1950s. So has the tyranny of distance (Blainey 1966) lost its impact on transport costs in maritime transport?

Recent research on transport costs, particularly international transport costs however has been driven by economists rather than geographers. Some (e.g. Cairncross 1997) proclaim the *death of distance* while others argue for a renewed relevance of distance within research in the denominated New Economic Geography. Kuwamori (2006) asks if distance really matters in the determination of transport costs and if distance is a significant factor, what is the magnitude of its impact?

Table 3.2   Distance measures

Distances	Operationalization
Euclidean distance	Km
Transport of travel distance	Km of costs
Time distance	Days, hours, minutes
Distances between regions	
Economic distance	Differences in Employment, income, productivity etc.
Administrative distance	Differences in: legislation, tariffs, rules, procedures etc.
Cultural distance	Objective differences in culture
Distances between people	
Affective	Expression of emotional connection
Cognitive	Estimation of physical distance (km) of location
Mental	Perception of the differences in conventions

Source: based on van Houtum (1999)

The role of distance as a separating factor or hurdle to trade thus remains to be answered. Traditionally transport costs were estimated calculating distance between two points A and B. Most of the literature on maritime transport costs has used point-to-point measures for internal and external distances. Point-to-point distances may give misleading estimates of the relevant geographic distance between and within geographic units as economies are not dimensionless points (Head and Mayer 2001). However, only in isotropic space is Euclidean space. Thoman and Corbin (1974) argue that the absolute scale of miles is often insignificant in the real world, but that operational distance measured as time or cost is more relevant. Limão and Venables (2000) show using the example of shipping costs from Baltimore to different destinations across the globe that geographic distance alone cannot explain price differences in freight rates.

The measure of distance in its pure statement seems to be simple, but many times it gets overlooked that there is more to the measure of distance than its *Euclidean dimension* mostly expressed in km. The measure of distance as crow-flight estimate is of course inaccurate for the factual analysis of interregional trade in Latin America, since the freight flows are bound to material transport linkages such as ports on the Panama Canal when moving between the different coasts. Distance as a measure gains a multidimensional aspect, if the influences on distance are considered. In reference to Houtum (1999) the following types of distance measures can be distinguished: Euclidean distance, travel, or transport distance, communication distance, time distance, economic distance, administrative distance, social distance, cultural distance, affective distance, cognitive distance and mental distance (see Table 3.2).

The *ascertained distances* can be categorized as economic and administrative distance, which will be partly reflected by variables for effects of integration. These can particularly be reflected in liner service network structures. Secondly, they can be defined as the time potential of time distance in the use of time.

Cognitive and mental distances are expressed as the individual efforts to overcome distance.

Cognition, uncertainty and identity are key words within anthropocentric approaches, flows of freight are conditioned by our perception and attitudes towards the destination as a social construct. Houtum (1999) uses three components of psychological personality to define anthropocentric constraints to freight flows: action, affection and cognition. These three different spaces can explain the perception of space by its users. One conclusion van Houtum (1999) got from a questionnaire on this topic was, that international orientation of entrepreneurs should be seen as a mental learning process. Internationalization for him starts in the home country and the entrepreneur matures in doing business on an international scale. Entrepreneurs, who have experience of cross border economic co-operation generally have a less negative perception of, and attitude towards, their partners in other countries, this could also be part of the explanation, why trade with countries outside the LAC region grows faster than within the region. Entrepreneurs from countries outside the region are the ones to co-operate in the regions' countries and weave trade connections with their home regions, while regional entrepreneurs are still in the learning process of doing international business. To facilitate this process the development of legislation, policies and material infrastructure shall be an important factor.

As regards the impact of distance, the gravity model would suggest that countries that are further away from each other will trade less (see for example Tinbergen 1962, Pöyhönen 1963 and Linnemann 1966). However, traditional gravity models ignore ascertained distance as potentially described by network structures (e.g. the regular shipping liner services configuration).

- Distance matters only indirectly in the determination of freight rates by shipping companies. Distance most likely is a proxy for voyage time related costs e.g. manning or fuel costs, but neither reflects market structures nor network configurations, which determine the ascertained distance in trade.

Maritime Corridors

Shipping lines charge different rates according to the features of the specific market in which the services are delivered. The ship is the same, but shipping lines tend to resist equalizing rates originating, say, from Chilean and Peruvian ports, called on the same route. However, being within the same corridor has potential benefits as services are usually concentrated for all trades.

Permeability of Borders

Borders play an important role (see also discussion on trade facilitation above, Chapter 2, p. 14). The permeability of borders might define if two ports located in two different countries compete for the same cargo. Further, in certain cases land transport might be an alternative to maritime transport on certain relations. Where this is the case the difference in the performance (i.e. time and cost) of the competing transport modes will have an impact on transport costs. Where such transport has to cross national borders, their permeability will have a significant impact on the land transport modes.

Cargo Characteristics and Trade Structure

Relationships of Weight to Measure and Value

In literature on the determination of freight rates in the shipping market unit and weight value have been perceived as important determinants of transport costs (Heaver 1973, Jansson and Shneerson 1987, Yeats 1986). Shneerson (1976) shows that the stowage factor and the unit weight give a reasonable satisfactory explanation of variations in freight rates. Moreover, he states that the 'stowage factor' is by far the greatest determinant of freight rates. Based on Canadian data, Bryan (1974) finds stowage and unit value significant in her regression, inferring that conferences and monopoly liners practice price discrimination. The latter can be seen as the scientific proof that shipping lines apply the policy of charging 'what the cargo will bear' (for discussion see Chapter 2, p. 24). Yeats (1986) argues that such practice in rate setting objectives counteract to progress in the insertion of developing countries in world trade and their economic development.

Palander (1935) maintains that transport costs are not regular but vary according to the weight, bulk, value, perishability of the product, mode of transport and distance. Radelet and Sachs (1998) find that countries will differ in their average CIF–FOB ratios not only due to differences in shipping costs but also due to differences in the commodity mix in external trade.

The influence of the unitary value of the product on ocean freight rates has to be interpreted in the context of the history and structure of shipping markets (see also Chapter 2, p. 22). Prices are a function of supply and demand. In this function the value of the product also determines the elasticity of the shipper to pay higher or even premium rates. Earlier works (Wilmsmeier 2003, Wilmsmeier et al. 2006, Martínez-Zarzoso et al. 2005, Wilmsmeier and Martínez-Zarzoso 2010 etc) all identify a relevance of the product unit value on transport costs.

Kuwamori (2006) reports that the impact of distance and weight value ratio is homogenous across the countries in his sample. Martínez-Zarzoso and Nowak-Lehman (2006) indicate a positive relationship between value-to-weight ratios and maritime transport costs. Sánchez et al. (2003) report that an increase of 1 per cent in the value per weight ratio of the carried merchandise generates an increase of 0.54 per cent in transport costs. For a sample of Latin American countries (UN-ECLAC 2002) a similar increase results in a 0.35 per cent rise in transport costs.

Wilmsmeier and Sánchez (2009) obtained results analysing transport cost determinants for containerized food imports to South America which show that a 10 per cent rise in the value of the commodity increases transport costs by around 7.6 per cent. These findings underline an interrelation between pricing strategies and product structures. This also depicts a circularity of influence from rising fob values, as e.g. the rise in food (FOB) prices will increase freight costs. The rise in freight costs will add to the price paid by the consumer on top of inflated FOB.

- Traditional pricing strategies referring to the unit value of cargo continue to play a significant role in the construction of international maritime transport costs.

Susceptibility to Damage and Loss

Containerization has produced standard units in terms of size, nevertheless the requirements for transporting goods vary and thus different types of container exists to satisfy these demands. Transport of refrigerated cargo has certain implications. The capacity to transport refrigerated or temperature controlled cargo depends on the number of plugs available on board a ship. Further, temperature controlled cargoes need a higher level of supervision on the journey, because a failure would result in the loss of the cargo. Besides the conventional reefer cargoes, containers with a controlled atmosphere, high humidity and ventilation exist. Márquez-Ramos et al. (2009) use a dummy variable for refrigerated cargo and show that a higher percentage of refrigerated cargo has a positive effect on the dependent variable (freight rate). Therefore, the variable has the expected sign, since freight rates are higher for products with special transport requirements.

- Special transport conditions and needs for certain types of cargo are reflected in the structure of international maritime transport costs.

Size of Shipment

Shipping lines discriminate between different types of shippers in terms of size. They also discriminate the charges between freight forwarders and direct shippers/ receivers. Finally they discriminate the size and scope of the company trying to approach customers who only work through tender offers which gives them the chance to establish strict logistic links.

Shipping lines also apply cumulative discounts, deferred premiums, and V.I.P. treatment. These options are a way to keep clients faithful to a company, when a certain volume is offered.

- The circumstantial evidence for investigating scale economies in shipping can be seen by examining freight costs for large versus small exporters.

Trade Volume

Transport demand is basically a derived demand from general economic activity at different geographic levels, regional, national, international etc. Accordingly, it is highly interrelated to the oscillation of economic development. Peters (2001) argues the existence of a positive interrelationship in the evolution of maritime containerized transport flows based on two pillars:

- the organic growth related to globalization, third party hiring, reduction of trade barriers, free trade treaties,
- the growth driven by technological change and new forms of organization, operation and using economies of scale.

Additionally, containerized transport volumes are driven by an induced growth originating from trade imbalances and the related repositioning of empty containers. The application of hub and spoke strategies is a further driver to induced growth.

However, recently, a number of studies have emphasized that transport costs may be endogenous. For example, Behrens et al. (2006) introduced the presence of density economies into a new economic geography model by assuming that unit shipping costs decrease with the aggregate volume of trade. Endogeneity of the transport costs is clearly also important for studies on international trade. For example, Anderson and van Wincoop (2004) stress the need to deal with this issue in studies of trade. There are a number of reasons why transport costs may be endogenous (for recent studies which discuss this issue, see Chowdhury and Erdenebileg 2007, Duranton and Storper 2008, Anderson 2008, UNOHRLLS 2013).

- Unit shipping costs decrease with the volume of trade due to the presence of density economies (as assumed by Behrens et al. 2006).

Trade Imbalance

> ... carriers operating full ships on one leg, but facing dwindling cargo volumes on the other, are likely to reduce rates on the light leg but attempt to cover those revenue losses by raising rates on the busy one ... . Haralambides (2004)

In this section, the relationship between transport prices and imbalances in transport flows in a two-region network is discussed, usually called the 'backhaul

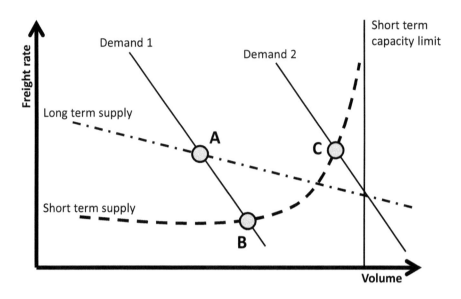

Figure 3.1   Short term and long term supply curves in shipping

Source: Author and Hoffmann

problem' (see, for example, Boyer 1998, p. 253). The figure below describes how ship utilization affects freight rates.

Theoretically, an imbalance in terms of trade volumes between two regions causes the transport price in one direction to exceed the price in the opposite direction when a positive proportion of carriers are required to return without paid cargo. One of the implications is that, *ceteris paribus*, unit shipping costs increase with the relative volume of trade between regions, implying that the transport costs increase with trade (as opposed to the assumption by Behrens et al. 2006).

When analysing the impact of 'volume' on freight rates, it is important to distinguish between a) short term versus long term effects (in the short term the supply curve slope is upward, in the long term economies of scale lead to a downward slope), and b) whether we have spare capacity in the short term or not (Figure 3.1).

In containerized trade, balance of trade flows is key in price setting from shipping lines. Shipping lines calculate the costs to move a container on a return trip basis, taking probability for empty positioning into account. When trade imbalance is negative, a country's imports exceed its exports and the greater the imbalance, the lower the freight rates will be for the country's exports; but if exports exceed imports, the larger the imbalance the higher the expected freight rates for exports will be. This divergence associated with the sign of trade imbalance occurs as a result of the freight rate price fixing mechanisms applying in the liner market.

Liner companies know that recurrently on one of the legs of the turnaround trip, the percentage of vessel capacity utilization will be lower, and therefore adapts its pricing scheme to the direction of the trip and to its corresponding expected cargo. Freight rates will be higher for the shipments transported on the leg of the trip with more traffic, as the total amount charged for this leg must compensate the relatively reduced income from the return trip, when part of the vessel's capacity will inevitably be taken up with repositioned empty containers. Excess capacity on the return trip will increase the competition between the various liner services, and as a result freight rates will tend to be lower. According to economic theory, imbalances in trade flows affect transport prices because (some) carriers have to return without cargo from the low demand region to the high demand region. Therefore, transport prices in the high demand direction have to exceed those in the low demand direction. The above situation that imports exceed exports (in terms of container volumes) applies to all Latin American countries' containerized trades.

In maritime containerized trade in Latin America imports exceed exports (in terms of container volumes. Shipping lines calculate the costs to move a container on a return trip basis, taking probability for empty positioning into account. When trade imbalance is negative, a country's imports exceed its exports and the greater the imbalance, the lower the freight rates will be for the country's exports; and *vice versa*.

However, in the case of containerized reefer cargo, exports of refrigerated cargo exceeds imports, which inverses the imbalance for these trades. The effect of this 'inverse trade balance' becomes obvious in regression results. These show that the import of reefer container is between 4.1 and 3.7 per cent less costly than that of standard containers (Wilmsmeier and Sánchez 2009). In the case of exports the opposite is the case (e.g. Wilmsmeier 2007). These results show that under the current situation the import of refrigerated cargo is favourable.

While imbalance is frequently recognized in the literature on maritime economics, particularly in relation to liner services (Stopford 2009), it remains discussed little in literature investigating the structure or maritime transport costs. Bennathan and Walters (1969) relate the imbalance on the transatlantic route to higher freight rates on the outbound e.g. due to competition with tramp shipping. Fuchsluger (2000) as UNCTAD (1997–2008) mention a relationship between trade imbalance of freight rates. Fuchsluger (2000) shows that transport costs paid by an importer on the Miami – Trinidad (Port of Spain) route are 87 per cent higher than the cost of a container in the opposite direction. In his reference year of 1998, 72 per cent of all containers from the Caribbean to the US were empty. Hoffmann and Harding (2003) state 'if the volume of sea-borne exports of containerizable cargo to a given country is half that of imports from that same country, it is estimated that the unit transport costs related to importing is around 19 percent less'.

Four studies examine the effect of imbalance in transport flows on maritime shipping empirically (Blonigen and Wilson 2008, Wilmsmeier et al. 2006, Márquez-Ramos et al. 2005, Clark et al. 2004). All of these studies assume imbalance is exogenous. Jonkeren et al. (2008) argue that transport costs are endogenous, based on textbook transport economics theory, saying that transport costs depend on imbalances in trade flows because carriers have to return to high demand regions without paid cargo. This implies that, *ceteris paribus*, unit transport prices positively depend on trade.

While trade imbalances *per se* cannot be altered, organization of the transport service market can reduce empty movements by information and equipment sharing, freight pooling, transnational cooperation of transport service providers.

- Liner companies know that recurrently on one of the legs of the turnaround trip, the percentage of vessel capacity utilization will be lower, and therefore adapt pricing schemes to the direction of the trip and to its corresponding expected cargo. Unidirectional excess capacity will increase the competition between the various liner services, and as a result freight rates will tend to be lower.

The Carriers

The development of liner shipping networks is primarily driven by the demand for containerized transport. The routing of containerized trade flows depends on the strategies of shipping companies and the demand of the shippers for specific service characteristics. As such, the location of a port or a region within the global liner shipping network is determined by the density of trade flows to and from a specific port or region. Shipping lines will determine their calling patterns and services structures in a region based on trade and port specific characteristics. The determinants taken into account are the number and dispersion of origins and final destinations, the density of cargo flows to and from these inland destinations and the existence of trade imbalances.

Based on these determinants, the service frequency (including the fixed days/hours of the week for departure/arrival), loading capacity of the transport equipment used, number of port calls per roundtrip and stops at intermediate terminals (transhipment/relay) are all determined (see Fagerholt 2004). Bundling is one of the key driving forces of container service network dynamics (Notteboom 2004). Different types of complex bundling networks (i.e. line-bundling, hub-and-spoke, triangular, pendulum, butterfly, etc) are used as an alternative to direct point-to-point container services. The advantages of complex bundling are higher load factors and/or the use of larger vessels in terms of TEU capacity and/or higher frequencies and/or more destinations served. The main disadvantages of complex bundling networks are the need for extra container handlings at intermediate terminals, longer transport distances and a higher dependency on service quality and synchronization. These elements incur additional costs and as such could counterbalance the cost advantages linked to higher load factors or the use of larger vessels.

Liner services have the common characteristic of most services that is, they are non storable and non-transportable, but the additional significant fact is that they

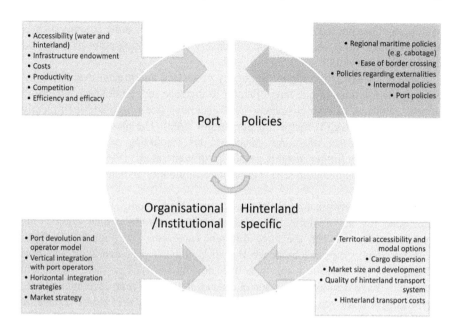

Figure 3.2   Determinants for liner service network configuration

Source: Wilmsmeier and Notteboom (2011)

are 'spatially unique' in the sense that transport between C and D is normally not a substitute for transport between A and B (Jansson 2001).

The design of individual liner services is often linked to other liner services of the same shipping line. Hence, shipping lines can have operational incentives to concentrate several calls in one or more hubs in a region. Cullinane and Khanna (1999, 2000) and Frémont and Soppé (2007) referred to the concentration of cargo at the level of liner networks of individual carriers. From a shipping line's perspective, the economies of scale in shipping, port operations and inland operations would favour a very limited number of load centres in a region. The advantages of concentrating cargo in only one or a few ports of call would be stronger at the level of a shipping line than at the port level, simply because not all carriers will choose the same load centres in their liner service networks.

Container lines operate in an increasingly competitive and market-driven environment caused by global tendencies of market concentration in the maritime industry. Therefore, besides lowering shipping costs, container carriers enhance services to increase quality. Such factors for service enhancement include high sailing frequencies, reduction of shipping time, and a high level of reliability. This aims to satisfy shippers' interests in the minimization of shipping and inventory costs and high reliability. The trade-off between customer demands and strategies of shipping lines has led to the development of a variety of calling patterns such as hub-and-spoke, relay, feedering, and direct services, including point-to point and line bundling services.

Shippers benefit from higher frequency of service and greater availability of capacity. The actions of one liner operator to increase service or space benefit all shippers, not just its own customers. This generates free riding and inefficiently low levels of service (Veenstra and Bergantino 2002). The literature on shipping networks and vessel operating considerations (including scale increases in vessel size) offers further insights, see e.g. Cullinane et al. (1999). In Figure 3.2, Wilmsmeier and Notteboom (2011) present a combination of determinants of liner shipping networks.

Based on determinants Wilmsmeier and Notteboom (2011) develop a framework for the evolution of liner shipping networks which depicts the interrelationship between the three different categories (see Figure 3.3). They argue based on empirical evidence that shipping network evolution and port development go hand-in-hand with the development of a trade route and historically have developed in a somehow parallel way. These developments are converging through vertical integration in the maritime and port industry. Specific trade route analysis also shows that in a 'penetration period' shipping lines try to develop new markets and aim for a global coverage (see Wilmsmeier and Sánchez 2009 for the case of South America). This is especially observable for small and medium-sized markets see e.g. Guy (2003) for South America. The authors find further evidence that shipping lines move towards consolidation in those markets, as the market size is not sufficient to allow the realization of economies of scale and density in a highly competitive environment. It can therefore be observed that shipping companies tend to create alliances or other forms of agreements to maintain market presence, but at the same time reduce risk levels and competition (see Chapter 3, p. 49 for detailed discussion).

Networks

Only a few studies so far discuss the effect of service levels i.e. frequency on maritime transport costs. Sánchez et al. (2003) find that a 1 per cent increase in the frequency or number of available liner services per month, serving a particular route and port, causes lower transport costs between 0.1 and 0.2 per cent. Wilmsmeier and Pérez (2005) find for the case of South America that a greater number of services lead directly to a greater volume of trade between partners. This brings economics of scale and at the same time *ceteris paribus* gives the transport service user a greater choice to ship his cargo. The study finds that a fourfold increase in the number of services (from five to 20) implies a reduction in transport costs of 12 per cent.

From an abstracted network point of view the degree of interconnectedness of linkages (liner services) related to a set of nodes (ports) is a fundamental question. The degree of connection between all linkages is defined as connectivity (Taaffe and

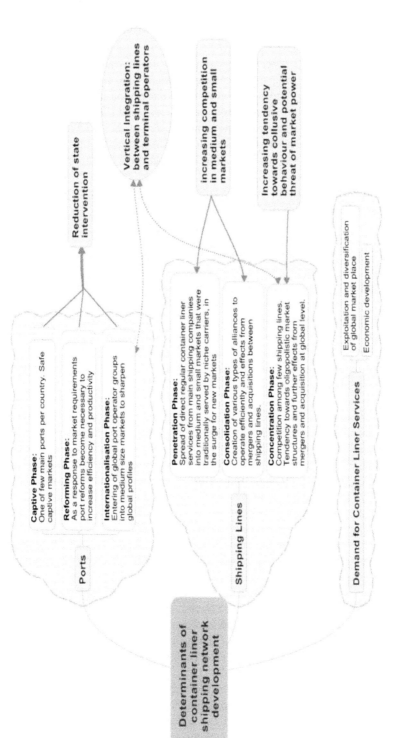

Figure 3.3   Shaping container liner network configurations

Source: Wilmsmeier and Notteboom (2011)

Gauthier 1973, p. 101). The concept of connectivity is most meaningful when a given network is either compared with other networks or its growth is viewed through time.

The use of connectivity measures allows the integration of the factor space in non-Euclidean and fluid frameworks and yields useful insights about the variability in convergence and divergence among places within a network (Janelle 1991). The author considers that liner service network structures can be used to explain ascertained distance and thus allow to reflect the importance of network structures on freight rates.

The search for an indicator to represent connectivity within a network has to consider the following aspects:

- measure network density
- indicators are either geographically or mode specific (in this case related to regular liner shipping networks
- improvement in connectivity cannot be unequivocally taken as an indicator of improvement in economic performance or welfare
- balance between links and nodes and the critical position of key hubs
- requirement of clear understanding of appropriate markets and threats posed by actors (opportunities/competitive threats)
- importance of competition between and within modes (in this case the liner shipping industry)

A number of variables describe connectivity in maritime transport. The before-mentioned variables on infrastructure endowment in ports and the characteristics of maritime services provide simple connectivity proxies, but do not reflect the system-inherent interrelations in the supply of transport services and transport infrastructure. The issue of connectivity and the impact on transport costs is here addressed in a broad sense, encompassing physical characteristics of the network, features of the services and cooperation of ship operators in conferences and strategic alliances. Port performance is essential for the efficiency and effectiveness of the maritime network. The functioning of the network and its structure involve complex interaction patterns that subsequently influence the cost of transport in the relation between two ports or regions.

Recent research has examined various aspects of maritime connectivity. Kumar and Hoffmann (2002), Marquez Ramos et al. (2006), Martínez-Zarzoso and Wilmsmeier 2010, Wilmsmeier and Hoffmann (2008) and Wilmsmeier et al. (2006) already incorporate measures of 'connectivity' into research on maritime transport costs. Angeloudis et al. (2006) and Bichou (2004) look at connectivity in the context of maritime security. McCalla et al. (2005) measure intermediacy and connectivity for Caribbean shipping networks and Notteboom (2006b) for seaport systems. Notteboom (2006a) also investigates the time factor in liner shipping services. UNCTAD (2006) developed the Liner Shipping Connectivity Index (LSCI) that measures direct connectivity between two countries and that is now available for the years 2006 to 2012.

Among the first Wilmsmeier (2003) and Wilmsmeier and Pérez (2005) analyse the effect of liner shipping network conditions on transport costs from different regions to South America. They show a decreasing effect of maritime services supply on transport cost and investigate to what extent the structure of the deployed fleet for directly connected regions contributes to the level of transport costs.

Wilmsmeier and Martínez-Zarzoso (2010) show in a panel data analysis (2000–2004) the relative importance of geographical distance and liner service network structure on maritime transport costs. The results indicate a significant effect of the liner service network structure (LSNS) on transport costs. The more central a trade route is located in the maritime liner service network the lower the average transport costs. This opens the important discussion on the 'cost' of being peripheral. The found elasticities show that the impact of being peripheral in the maritime network is higher than the impact of distance. Network peripheral countries pay higher prices for transporting their exports, especially when they trade with other peripheral countries. Countries that are both peripheral in the maritime network and distant from other export markets face higher freight rates. Location is an important issue in Latin America, given the insular geographic character of the Caribbean and given that countries on the west and east coast of South America are located at the endpoint of the global maritime liner shipping network. The development of a hierarchical network, with growing importance of transhipment centres in Panama, Callao (Peru) or Manta (Ecuador) and of some intermediary ports on the east coast in Brazil, might leave certain regions in even more peripheral positions.

Wilmsmeier (2009) integrates the impact of centrality in the empirical analysis using a 'transhipment connectivity index' which measures the centrality of a country within the global shipping network taking transhipment requirements into account. His results show, if a country can 'double' its centrality in the network, meaning a significant increase in direct liner services to a wider range of countries, transport costs can decrease up to 15.4 per cent. This important finding needs to be seen in the context of the influencing variables of liner network connectivity such as ship size and frequency, which are determined by the overall level of trade (see Chapter 3, p. 46), the geographic position and last but not least port infrastructure endowment and development options.

Additionally the results underline the fact that the position within the network has a more significant impact than the notion of distance which only expresses the geographical distance between the trading partners, but not the quality of liner shipping network to breach that distance.

The functioning of the network and its structure involve complex interaction patterns that subsequently influence the cost of transport in the relation between two countries. Conceptually, principle components analysis allows to calculate non collinear variables from the set of variables described above. This approach was introduced by Sánchez et al. (2003) and has been applied e.g. by Wilmsmeier (2003) and Hoffmann and Wilmsmeier (2008). Martínez-Zarzoso et al. (2011) and Marquez-Ramos et al. (2009) introduce the following variables in a PCA analysis:

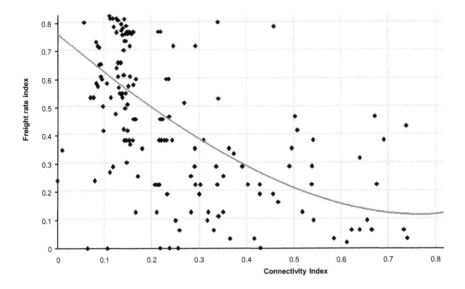

Figure 3.4   Relation between freight rates and connectivity in container shipping in the Caribbean basin, 2006

Source: Author

percentage of transhipment lines on that route, transit time, maximum and minimum number of calls on the route, distance between ports, number of services, time lag between shipping opportunities, vessel speed, fleet age, average capacity. They also include port infrastructure variables in their analysis (Chapter 3, p. 54).

The figure below exemplifies the reduction in freight rates with increasing connectivity, where connectivity is an expression of shipping possibilities, port infrastructure endowment and industry structure (for detailed discussion see Wilmsmeier and Hoffmann 2008).

- Liner Service Network Structure (LSNS) is an important determinant of international maritime transport costs. The position within a network describes the ascertained distance and thus has become increasingly important in identifying a country or ports position with the global shipping network. Particularly as hub and spoke network structures have been emerging and potentially impose significant deviations on actual cargo flows.

Capacities and Economies of Scale in Maritime Industry

The structure of capacity supply has also implications on transport costs, as greater demand allows for deployment of bigger ships and economies of scale and density.

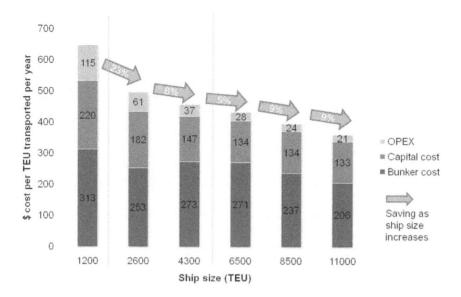

Figure 3.5   Container ship costs per TEU transported

Note: Calculation assumes 100 per cent vessel utilization
Source: Based on Stopford (2009)

Ships are a classic example of increasing returns to scale. To stress this point, McConville (1999) quotes Alfred Marshall:

> a ship's carrying power varies as the cube of her dimensions, while the resistance offered by the water increases only a little faster than the square of her dimensions.

Economies of scale at vessel level could also apply from technological advancements in the market. A continuous increase in vessel size is observed over recent years (Jansson and Shneerson 1982, Talley 1990, Lim 1998, Tozer and Penfold 2000, Cullinane and Khanna 2000, Lloyd's Register Technical Association 2002, Perrotti and Sánchez 2012). The largest container vessel built in 1968 had the capacity to carry 1,700 TEUs, this figure increased to 2,900 TEUs in 1980, 4,000 TEUs in 1990 and 8,000 TEU in 2004 and finally reached 18,000 TEU in 2013. Tozer and Penfold (2000) indicate that even if there are limits to scale economies, where further increases in vessel size provide only limited unit cost reductions, this inflexion point has not yet been reached. For example see figure below.

LAC is far from reaching the theoretical inflexion point of technical economies of scale of ship size due to the following restrictions (Wilmsmeier 2013):

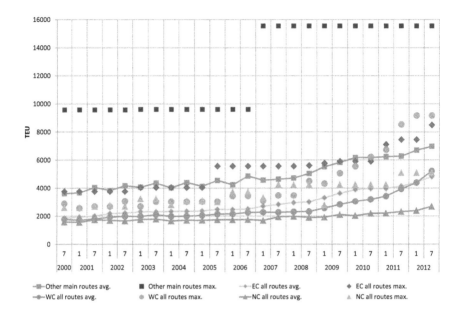

Figure 3.6   Evolution of vessel sizes in container trades to/from LAC

Source: Author based on ComPair Data various years

- Supply of shipping capacity is a function of the overall volume of trade, thus, only if certain levels of trade volumes are reached, technological economies of scale can be reached and makes the use of bigger ships economically sensible. Further, any transport entity, whether ship, train or truck only operates economically efficiently if a certain level of capacity utilization is used otherwise diseconomies of scale might result in higher transport costs. Further, from a logistics point of view smaller entities might not allow for significant economies of scale, but for higher levels of service frequency, which might be as or even more relevant in terms of market access, especially when thinking of trade in perishable food products.
- Infrastructure and superstructure bottlenecks restrict economies of scale, where trade volumes might be big enough for deploying bigger size ships, e.g. the Panama Canal, absence of gantry cranes in a number of ports (Guayaquil, Callao and Acajutla etc), draught of access channels (see Figure 3.6).

Analysis of transport costs shows that economies of scale are present in maritime transport (Wilmsmeier 2003, Wilmsmeier 2009). An analysis at shipments level for different product groups and modes illustrates that the greatest economies of scales are realized in transport products that are usually transported in bulk ships (Wilmsmeier and Sánchez 2009).

Following Bendall and Stent (1987) Wilmsmeier and Pérez (2005) introduce vessel specific variables, age of the newest vessel in each specific service, average capacity (in TEUs) and speed (in knots). It is expected that greater performance, higher speed, larger capacities and newer vessels will contribute to lower transport costs, due to higher productivity. These variables go beyond traditional measures of size that only capture economies of scale.

- Vessel specific variables are good proxies for technological economies of scale in shipping.

Maritime Industry Structure and Policy

The most anti-competitive form of market. (Bennathan and Walters 1969)

The pricing behaviour of shipping conferences has been investigated by Bryan (1974). Fink et al. (2002) find that private practices exercise a significant influence on maritime transport prices. They observe the impact of price fixing agreements and show that these are more decisive than co-operative working agreements.

Historically, shipping lines have tried to concentrate activities in accordance with other market players in certain points as they are aware of the benefits of economies of agglomeration. Early research from Koopmans (1939) and Tinbergen (1959), focused on the determination of shipping rates and the role of market structure in the different shipping markets. Deakin and Seward (1973), Heaver (1973) and Talley and Pope (1985) in their analyses of shipping conferences also relate to the effect of these on freight rates. Francois and Wooton (2001) point to a publication from Sjostrom (1992), who argues that the before-mentioned literature is inconclusive because of incorrect model specification.

This has given room for the development of hub and spoke networks, in which the hubs are nodes for high volume services to interchange cargoes and to transfer cargo to secondary routes. The concentration of flows in specific places has driven the development in two directions.

- On the routes where a shipping line cannot generate sufficient traffic to deploy its own ships, agreements (slot charter, vessel sharing etc) have become common to gain economies of density and scale through pooling.
- The more common strategy is the development of hub and spoke networks, where economies of densities are tried to be generated on specific legs of a route. This gives the shipping lines the possibility to maximize the use of economies of scale on the trunk routes and at the same time to generate economies of density on the secondary routes.
- The tendency of liner shipping companies to use these economies includes the risk that a market develops towards oligopolistic or even monopolistic market structures (see Figure 3.7). This is especially true for more peripheral markets with limited growth rates. Such 'quasioligopolistic' structures

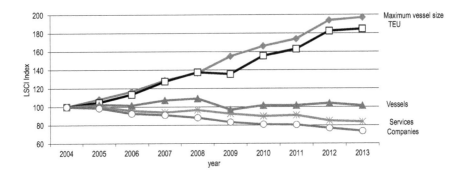

Figure 3.7   Trends in connectivity indicators. Index of country averages, 2004 = 100

Source: Based on Hoffmann et al. (2013)

can act as entry barriers to new competitors or only allow new entrants that form part of the existing alliances (Sánchez and Wilmsmeier 2011, Wilmsmeier 2013).

In the case of occurrence networks effects are most likely lost to the user of the transport service, because shipping lines will not pass on their savings. The dynamism and feedback loops of these consolidation processes also change the position of shipping lines towards ports in terms of negotiating the terms of usage, especially in competitive port environments. If a shipping company exceeds a certain market share in one port its negotiating position can divert into a situation where it can use market power. This again is especially true in smaller markets, but will not be discussed in depth here.

Carriers develop their wants to design service routes and itineraries for their ships as efficiently as possible, utilizing the available facilities. Furthermore, paths must be designed in such a way that the profit is maximized with regard to shipping the cargo.

Price setting in transport and logistics markets significantly depends on the level of effective competition. Competition in the transport markets depends on the size of the market and effective market regulation. Since existence of collusive behaviour, atomization and monopolies have potential impacts on price structures these are revised in the following.

Different strategies of shipping lines, the balance of power between shipping lines and shippers and constraints related to inland transportation have a potential impact on the development of maritime shipping networks. Moreover, strategic alliances between the port and the shipping industry, which have both been driven by strong concentration processes and vertical integration, have a profound influence on maritime network structure and also on the grade of integration of a region in the global maritime transport network. These developments have to a certain extent made port development dependent on network strategies of global players.

Commercial routes have different levels of competition and therefore different levels of monopoly power (higher or lower mark-ups). Monopoly powers can be sustained by either restrictive trade policies by government or by private anti-competitive practice (cartels). The former includes a variety of cargo reservation schemes, such as the UN Liner Code. The anticompetitive practices include primarily, but not exclusively, the rate-fixing practices of maritime conferences. Many trade routes are serviced by a small number of liner companies that have traditionally been organized in formal cartels called 'liner conferences'.

> A shipping conference is a group of two or more vessel-operating carriers which provides international liner services for the carriage of cargo on a particular route or routes within specified agreement or arrangement whatever is the nature, within the framework of which they operate under uniform or common freight rates and any other agreed conditions with respect to the provision of liner services. United Nations (1974: chapter 1)

It is an open question as to whether these companies successfully exert market power in pricing shipping services. Clyde and Reitzes (1995) examine shipping rates filed by ocean liner conferences with the FMC between 1985 and 1988. They look for evidence as to whether the rate structure in ocean shipping markets is based on costs, the exercise of market power by conferences, or the exercise of market power by firms in a manner unrelated to the conference system. They conclude that 'some aspects of the conference system may contribute to higher shipping rates, particularly when the conference has a sizable market share'. They also find that 'conferences do not act as perfect cartels maximizing the joint profits of their members'.

Some authors have used contestability theory to argue that the small number of participants is in no way indicative of their market power. Sjostrom (1988) suggests that these shipping conferences may exist, not as monopolizing cartels, but to ensure that shipping services are provided in a market in which there is no competitive equilibrium. However, this point has never been adequately addressed empirically, and at least one study (Fink, Mattoo and Neagu 2002) has found evidence that freight rates are sensitive to regulatory changes meant to constrain collusive behaviour by liner conferences. Supposing that freight prices do include significant monopoly mark-ups, it is possible that increasing trade quantities would lead to entry, and a pro-competitive effect on prices (Hummels, Lugovskyy and Skibba 2009).

Sánchez and Wilmsmeier (2011) analyse the evolution of competition and contestability on the East Coast of South America (ECSA) and the West Coast of South America (WCSA) between 2000 and 2008. They find that market contestability is 'impeded' by collusive behaviour and strong alliances among carriers, thus allowing market entrance only to strong global carriers.

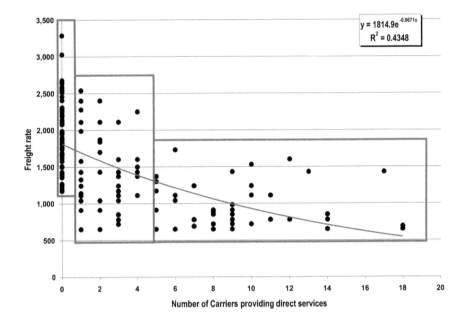

Figure 3.8   Correlation between freight rate and the number of carriers providing direct services, case of Caribbean Container Shipping, 2006

Source: Wilmsmeier and Hoffmann (2008)

Cabotage regulation in South America, especially on the ECSA, has lead to an evolution of service structures that use alliances among regional carriers and global shipping lines. The structure of capacity supply for ECSA Asia and Europe trade suggests that leading global carriers are using regional shipping lines to overcome the existing cabotage restrictions, companies as Alianca, CSAV Brazil and Maruba thus face the risk of being 'converted' into regional feeder operators (Brooks et al. 2013). While capacity supply has expanded between 2000 and 2012, effective competition has been reducing, suspicion of high entrance barriers and collusive behaviour among existing players in the market prevail since the market has seen almost no new entries to the market (Wilmsmeier 2013) (Figure 3.8).

Wilmsmeier and Hoffmann (2008) find for the case of the Caribbean that the number of liner shipping companies providing direct services between pairs of countries appears to have a stronger impact on the freight rate than does distance. For routes where there is no company providing direct service, i.e. where all containerized maritime trade involves at least one transshipment in a third country's port, freight rates in their sample range from US$ 1,170 to 3,290, with an average of US$ 2,056. For routes with one to four carriers providing direct services the reported freight rates range from US$ 650 to 2,250 with an average of US$ 1,449. If five or more competing carriers provide direct services, the freight rate ranges from US$ 650 to 1,730, averaging US$ 973. Statistically, the number of carriers explains around two fifths of the variance of the freight rate. Their empirical results support the hypothesis that competition between shipping lines makes shipping services less expensive for the shipper, i.e. oligopolistic market structures imply higher costs to shippers.

- International maritime transport costs are administered prices, which discriminated against weaker elements. If competition exists in a market, international maritime transport costs should be lower in comparison to routes with oligopolistic or monopolistic characteristics.

The Interfaces

Nodal situations change the spatial qualities of centrality and intermediacy enhance the importance and traffic level of strategically located hubs within transport systems (Fleming and Hayuth 1994).

In relation to the type of network structure (see Chapter 3, p. 42), a port selection is determined by multiple factors. An abundant literature has addressed the issue of port selection (Barros and Athanassiou 2004, Chou et al. 2003, Guy and Urli 2006, Lirn et al. 2004, Malchow and Kanafani 2001, Murphy and Daley 1994, Murphy et al. 1992, Nir et al. 2003, Song and Yeo 2004, Tiwari et al. 2003, Chang et al. 2008, Wiegmans et al. 2008, Notteboom 2009). Typical port selection criteria relate to:

- the port's physical and technical infrastructure (e.g. nautical access, terminal infrastructure and equipment, hinterland accessibility profile);
- geographical location;
- port efficiency (e.g. port turnaround time, cost efficiency);
- interconnectivity of the port (e.g. sailing frequency of deep-sea and feeder shipping services);
- reliability, capacity, frequency and costs of inland transport services;
- efficiency and costs of port management and administration;
- availability, quality and costs of logistic value-added activities; and
- strategic considerations of the shipping line concerned (e.g. market entry, strategies of alliance structure).

The need for more of a supply chain-oriented approach to port selection is echoed in recent work. Magala and Sammons (2008) argue that port choice is to be considered as a by-product of a choice of a logistics pathway. Port choice becomes more a function of the overall network cost and performance. The literature on port competitiveness, port competition and port selection offers more insights into the determinants of cargo shifts between ports; see e.g. Huybrechts et al. (2002).

Shippers make decisions about which ports to use on the basis of factors such as efficiency, proximity, service and reliability: 'customers want speedy access to ports, to deliver goods just in time'. Good inland transport links and proximity to major conurbations and distribution centres are further reasons to use specific ports. The cause for concern depends upon both the likelihood and potential impact of severe disruption to ports.

It is importance to analyse efficiency in three key dimensions that might affect the pricing of ports and in return international maritime transport costs:

- Allocative efficiency (relative input usage), may be affected because the goals of the governing entity (authorities or cities) may not coincide with economic efficiency. In the port context, inefficiencies arise because inputs are used out of proportion to their relative costs.
- Technical efficiency (overall cost minimization), concerns arise because the governing entity may not minimize costs given output.
- The rate of technical change or cost of innovation concerns arise because the form of governance may affect the rapidity with which ports respond to changing conditions in the shipping industry.

Wang et al. (2005, p. 7) compare technical and allocative efficiency at it reveals the relationship between productivity growth and technical change.

While allocative efficiency might be relatively high, as it maximizes the use of existing infra- and superstructures, the rate of technical change in the region is slow and has resulted in the prevalent technological gap in ports (see Wilmsmeier et al. 2013).

Port performance is essential for the efficiency and effectiveness of the maritime network. The functioning of the network and its structure involve complex interaction patterns that subsequently influence the cost of transport in the relation between two countries.

The relationships between port characteristics, port performance, port costs, and international transport costs are not at all straightforward (see for example Tovar et al. (2003) for a literature overview of cost functions in the port sector; Cullinane and Song (2002) on private sector participation in ports; Hoffmann (2001) on ports in Latin America; de Langen (2004) on maritime clusters and seaports; Beresford and Dubey (1990) on the competitiveness of trade corridors; Bichou and Grey (2005) on port terminology).

Port Infrastructure and Superstructure

Weigmann (1933) affirms that spatial distribution of transport infrastructure has a restrictive influence on mobility and competition, which leads to higher transport costs.

Port infrastructure endowment can be described by variables such as: number of cranes, maximum draught and storage area at origin and destination ports.

The interaction of these variables is decisive. By way of example a post Panamax gantry crane will not contribute fully to efficiency if the port access channel is too shallow for port Panamax ships.

Wilmsmeier and Hoffmann (2008) focus on port infrastructure endowment, which they describe by variables such as: number of cranes, maximum draught and storage area at origin and destination ports. The interaction of these variables is decisive. Installing ship-to-shore gantries, for example, may well lead to higher port charges to the shipping line. The line may still achieve an overall saving, because its ships spend less time in the port, or because it can change from geared to gearless vessels. This, in turn, will also lead to lower freight rates. However, a Post-Panamax gantry crane will not contribute fully to efficiency if the port access channel is too shallow for Post-Panamax ships. Better port infrastructure may improve efficiency, but this may be at a cost, i.e. it might actually increase port charges and consequently also the overall transport costs.

Port infrastructure endowment is one important part that contributes to port productivity and major works have investigated issues such as optimal berth length and utilization of quay cranes (for list of publications see Wang et al. (2005, p. 17). However, it should be kept in mind that development of port infrastructure is only worthwhile if the entire transport system benefits and not if only bottlenecks are shifted to another element within the system. Factors influencing productivity are physical, institutional and organizational. Physical limiting factors include the area, shape and layout of the terminal, the amount and type of equipment available, and the type and characteristics of the vessels using the terminal. Lack of cranes, insufficient land, odd-shaped container yards, inadequate berthage, inadequate gate facilities, and difficult road access are all physical limiting factors. Productivity must be considered in a system perspective for it to be of maximum value to industry. This is importance from a policy perspective, thus emphasizing the need for co-modality and multimodal visions in policy recommendations and guidance. All players should have an awareness of the entire system and beware of becoming its weak link.

In order to capture the correlation between the different port infrastructure variables Wilmsmeier and Hoffmann (2008) develop a 'port infrastructure endowment index' based on a set of descriptive variables, using principal components analysis. Their results reveal that the more harmonious the development of port infrastructure the lower transport costs.

Figure 3.9 shows the relationship between adequate infrastructure provision and freight rates for the case of the Caribbean (Wilmsmeier and Hoffmann 2008). 'Adequate' means that infrastructure variables such as draught, length of berth, storage area are configured in such a way that no bottlenecks are created and that all parts can be used without restrictions.

In order to capture the relevance of port infrastructure endowment as a determinant for transport costs this work, in line with Wilmsmeier and Hoffmann, develops 'port infrastructure endowment' variables using Principal Components Analysis (see Chapter 4, p. 83). Wilmsmeier, Hoffmann and Sánchez (2006) find

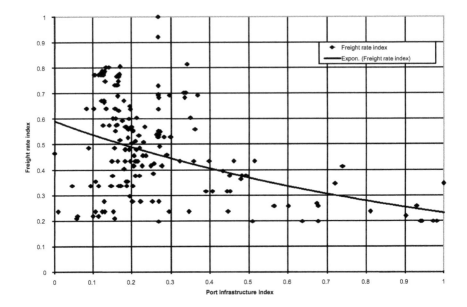

Figure 3.9   Relationship between infrastructure endowment and freight rates in the Caribbean basin, 2006

Source: Wilmsmeier and Hoffmann 2008

in their regression analysis that particularly the fit between the infrastructure in the exporting and importing country is relevant.

- A good fit between different components of infra- and superstructure in the importing and exporting port should have a reducing impact on transport costs as it facilitates better performance in port operations.

Port Productivity and Efficiency

An increase in terminal productivity is only worthwhile if the entire system benefits and not if only bottlenecks are shifted to another element within the system. Further, different definitions of terminal productivity according to the standpoint need to be considered:

- terminal operator: maximize profit per container
- port authority: increase annual throughout, avoiding building new until facilities are fully and efficiently utilized
- labour: increase union jobs and total cargo handled by its members
- carrier: minimize ship in-port time.

Limiting factors to terminal productivity are physical, institutional and organizational. Physical limiting factors include the area, shape and layout of the terminal, the amount and type of equipment available, and the type and characteristics of the vessels using the terminal. Lack of cranes, insufficient land, odd-shaped container yards, inadequate berthage, inadequate gate facilities, and difficult road access are all physical limiting factors.

Technical efficiency in Latin America is not exploited due to a lack of well trained personnel, lack of international standards and logistics systems and absence of infrastructure development from a system's perspective. However, positive examples like the port of Cartagena in Colombia exist. In Cartagena high emphasis is given to training of personnel, resulting in efficient and reliable terminal operations, at a terminal which is currently running at its capacity limits. The long-term training strategy and investment in human capital is paying back in this situation since it allowed developing innovative strategies in container storage management.

Theoretic quay productivity for different ship types and use of different types and combination of cranes is presented in Table 3.3. Better port infrastructure may improve efficiency, but this may be at a cost, i.e. it might actually increase port charges and consequently also the overall transport costs. Port privatization may lead to new investment, but it may also coincide with reduced public subsidies, leading to higher charges to port users. Shippers may be prepared to pay more for a

Table 3.3   Examples for theoretic quay productivity

Ship type	Feeder	Handy	Sub-Panamax	Post-Panamax
Capacity (TEUs/ship)	750	1 500	2 500	5 000
Average cargo carriage (TEUs/ship)	500	1 000	1 667	3 333
Loading vs. discharge (%)	67%	50%	33%	33%
Re-positioning (%)	10%	10%	15%	15%
Productive moves (TEUs/ship)	670	1 000	1 100	2 200
Total moves (TEUs/ship)	737	1 100	1 265	2 530
Hours/Ship				
– 2 ship cranes	37	55	63*	123*
– 1 ship crane + 1 mobile crane	26	37	42*	83*
– 2 mobile cranes	19	24	32	63
– 2 gantry cranes	17	25	28	54
Minimum time savings	11	18		
Maximum time savings	20	30		

faster and more reliable service, because overall transaction costs are not identical with the international transport costs. In spite of these diverse relationships, the empirical results presented by Wilmsmeier et al. (2006) are quite clear and straightforward: increases in port efficiency, port infrastructure, private sector participation and inter-port connectivity all help to reduce the overall international maritime transport costs.

Earlier works about the determinants of international waterborne transport costs that consider port efficiency, tend to work with proxies, such as GDP per capita, perception surveys, or infrastructure indicators (i.e. Global Competitiveness Report), and they all tend to work with data on the national rather than port level. Australian Productivity Commission (1998) uses some partial productivity measures.

Dollar et al. (2002) define the factors behind port efficiency as the activities that depend on port infrastructure, like pilotage, towing and tug assistance, or cargo handling (among others), but also activities related to customs requirements. They also state that efficiency, even timing, of many port operations is strongly influenced by customs (for potential impacts please see example below).

Wilmsmeier et al. (2006) estimate the impact of the perceived port efficiency of the importing and exporting countries' ports on international maritime transport costs. If the two countries of their sample with the lowest port efficiency improved their efficiency to the level of the two countries of the sample with the highest indexes, the freight on the route between them would be expected to decrease by 25.9 per cent.

Far more detailed research on port efficiency uses stochastic frontiers models or the Data Envelopment Analysis (DEA) (see for example Liu 1995, Coto, Baños and Rodriguez 1999 and 2000, Roll and Hayuth 1993, Martínez, Díaz, Navarro and Ravelo 1999, Tongzon 2001, Estache, Gonzalez and Trujillo 2001). The necessary information requirements to reach these measures tend to make a broad quantitative comparison difficult, and have – to the author's knowledge – not yet been linked to data on international transport costs.

Sánchez et al. (2003) analyse the impact of port efficiency using key variables on port productivity (waiting times, crane moves per hour etc). They identify a significant correlation between these measures. In order to be able to measure the impact of these variables they construct port efficiency measure using principal components analysis (PCA). They find that an improvement of the included port productivity characteristics has a significant impact on maritime transport costs. He brings evidence that port efficiency has an equivalent impact on international maritime transport costs as that for distance.

Example: Port congestion charges
A Port Congestion Surcharge went into effect on 20 February 2005 for all cargo carried into George Town, Grand Cayman. This charge was implemented as a result of the significant vessel delays incurred while berthing in George Town. These delays were creating significant increases in operational costs and also

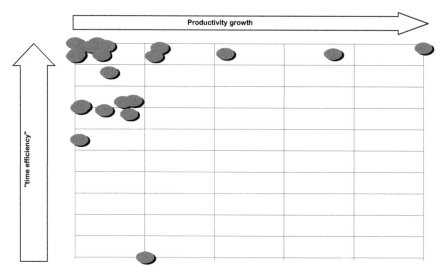

Figure 3.10   Scatter plot 'time efficiency' (Factor 1) and productivity (Factor 2)

Source: Processed from the Port Activity Survey, Austral University, taken from Sánchez et al. (2003)

impacting delivery time locally. These fees were implemented by the cargo ship companies. Caribbean Logistics has no control over these charges. The surcharge is estimated to have increased costs for deliveries around 20 per cent to Grand Cayman. The surcharge was lifted once the port resumed normal operations.

Due to the lack of uniform data input to measure terminal productivity, it is difficult to compare different terminals or to establish valid standards for terminal productivity. The only work related to the impact of port productivity and transport costs based on empirical data for a wide range of ports is Sánchez et al. (2003). Recently, new works have analysed the evolution of port productivity and efficiency in the region (Wilmsmeier et al. 2013, Morales Sarriera et al. 2013).

They identify two factors. The observation of the scatter plot below shows that a great share of the ports is working at the same level in regard to 'time efficiency' (Factor 1), while there are great differences in terms of 'productivity' (Factor 2) (Figure 3.10).

Container terminal productivity must be considered in a system perspective for it to be of maximum value to industry. This is important from a policy perspective, thus emphasizing the need for co-modality and multimodal visions in policy recommendations and guidance. All the players should have an awareness of the entire system and beware of becoming its weak link.

Example: Differences in productivity in the Caribbean
Caribbean carriers pooling data on island port productivity have uncovered wide scale disparity between facilities that use the same equipment. Over a period of eight months carriers of the Caribbean Ship Owners' Association have been sharing information on average moves per berth hour at selected island facilities. The port of Georgetown, Guyana, which uses only ship gear, is posting up to 19 moves per hour, versus other Caribbean ports using ship gear that handle just five moves per hour. Evidence was found that there is an island port using gantry cranes that does not match Georgetown's productivity with ship gear. The carriers' plan is for pooled productivity data to be extended to other ports in the Caribbean and Central America – and to be made publicly available on a regular basis.

Port container throughput: in recent studies container port traffic (container throughput) has been considered as an appropriate variable to measure economies of scale and port production (Wang, Cullinane and Song 2005). Economies of scale are also presented at port level. Larger volumes of containerized cargo loaded and unloaded at a port will enable the shipping lines to use larger container ships, as well as permitting the terminal operator to optimize the use of terminal equipment, infrastructure and stevedoring shifts. A more effective terminal can be expected to induce lower unit transport costs.

The empirical findings of Wilmsmeier et al. (2006) underline that we do not know if port improvements lead to lower freights because of lower port costs charged to the carrier, better services provided to the carrier, or both. What is clear, however, is that there is a clear measurable impact on international maritime transport costs. Increases in port infrastructure and private sector participation, too, lead to reduced maritime transport costs. Inter-port connectivity, also reduces transport costs, most likely because it allows for economies of scale, and also more competition among carriers. The elasticity for port efficiency is higher than the elasticity for distance; in fact, it is the highest of all the variables included in their research. Unlike distance, port efficiency can be influenced by policy makers. Doubling port efficiency at both ends has the same effect on international maritime transport costs as would a 'move' of the two ports 50 per cent closer to each other, i.e. reducing the distance between them by half.

Productivity growth and technical change can reveal important insights to policy makers; a slowdown in productivity growth, due to increase inefficiency or alternatively due to a lack of technical change may prompt different need for policy formulation. Slow productivity growth due to inefficiency may be attributable to institutional barriers to the diffusion of knowledge on innovations (Wang et al. 2005, p. 8). The origin of institutional barriers may be a lack of reform or institutional sclerosis.

- A more efficient port does not necessarily need to be less expensive. On the contrary, it may charge higher prices to the shipper and the carrier if it provides faster and more reliable services, or if it allows the shipper or the carrier to achieve savings elsewhere. Installing ship-to-shore gantries, for example, may well lead to higher port charges to the shipping line. The line may still achieve an overall saving, because its ships spend less time in the port, or because it can change from geared to gearless vessels. This, in turn, will also lead to lower freight rates.

- Efficiency increases as the scale of a container port increases. In other words, a large-scale container port is more likely to be associated with high efficiency than a small one.

Port Competition

Usually the container port industry in relation to the analysis of international maritime transport costs is analysed from a national perspective or the main port is regarded as representative. However, competition is one of the most important concepts when discussing market structure (Wang et al. 2005, p. 22). Different types of container port competition can be expected to have implications on maritime transport and its costs. In this work inter-port and intra-port competition are taken into consideration. Inter-port competition can be understood as the competition among different ports. The principal criteria to define inter-port competition is if they serve the same or overlapping hinterland e.g. the port of Valparaiso and San Antonio in Chile serve almost identical hinterlands (Sánchez, Wilmsmeier and Doerr 2008). Inter-port competition is a relatively new phenomena which has increased with container traffic growth and port devolution where many ports no longer enjoy the freedom by a monopoly or oligopoly (Wang et al. 2005, p. 23). These authors (p. 23) define the following forms of port competition in order of decreasing size of the geographic range of the competitive ports:

- Competition between whole ranges of ports or coastlines – e.g. North America Pacific and Atlantic coast lines; in the case of South America this type of competition exists in a very mild form for regions situated at the eastern foot of the Andes as they can be served either from Argentinean or Chilean ports.
- Competition between ports in different countries. This type of competition is prominent between Montevideo, Uruguay, Buenos Aires, Argentina and Rio Grande, Brazil.
- Competition between individual ports in the same country. This kind of competition can be found between Valparaiso and Chile, and a number of Brazilian ports.

One argument is that inter-port competition encourages efficiency of ports (for discussion on the case of Buenos Aires and Montevideo see Sánchez and Wilmsmeier 2006). However, some authors argue that inter-port competition also bears risks of overcapacity (e.g. Heaver 1995, Wang et al. 2005).

Intra-port competition was explained by Goss (1990) as follows: this [intra-port competition] does not necessarily mean that there should actually be a large

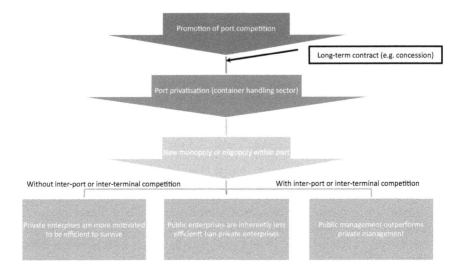

Figure 3.11   Privatization and port performance

Source: Author based on Wang et al. (2005, p. 30)

number of firms competing simultaneously: it means that the markets in question should be contestable, in the sense that entry is easy for a new firm, whose exit will also be easy if its efforts turn out to be unsuccessful.

This type of competition is necessarily related to port ownership and administration, because if a port is under the control of a public authority essentially no competition exists. Liu (1995) categorized ports by type of ownership or administration. Following Liu (1995) ports can be categorized as: a) a service port, if the port authority is responsible for the provision of all port facilities and services; b) a tool port if the public port authority provides the infrastructure and superstructure, while the provision of services is licensed to private operators; c) a landlord port, in while the domain of the port authority is restricted to the provision of the infrastructure, while investment in the superstructures and port operation is the responsibility of licensed private companies; and d) a private port if the provision of all of the facilities and services is left to the private sector.

Following arguments from Goss 1990, Heaver 1995 and Song et al. 2001 this work argues that port devolution in Latin America contributes towards encouraging competition among terminals. Wang et al. (2005) argue that the situation of inter-port competition, as a characteristic of current container port environment allows private enterprises to outperform their public counterparts. This stems from profit maximization and a higher proactive role of private operators (Figure 3.11).

Port Operator Models

> The most difficult task is, very often, the motivation of the whole port community and the establishment, among all parties including each docker in the port area, of a common consciousness of the port's development. The building of a third-generation port depends on the quality of the joint work of the community, government authorities, the municipality and even the people living in the city. (UNCTAD 1992, p. 21)

Institutional efficiency plays a key role in the devolution of ports. Time lag and institutional barriers to devolution processes impact on the efficiency and thus directly on the transport and logistics costs in a port and its integration to the hinterland.

Institutional factors include such things as port operator model, union work rules, import/export mix, container size mix, container availability, stow of arriving vessels, customs regulations, intermodal train scheduling, safety rules, and various requirements imposed on the terminal operator by the carrier. If there was one area whose effect on productivity we initially underestimated it was these institutional factors. The author's research indicates that the institutional factors, especially the requirements of carriers imposed on the terminal operator, are just as constraining as the physical factors.

Impact of port reform does usually have significant impact in the organization of ship handling processes. In the example of Cartagena, Colombia average ship waiting time reduced from 10 to zero days, and ship turnaround time reduced from 72 to 24 hours. The latter is a result of increased berth productivity reached by an increase of container movements per ship hour from seven to 52. At the same time reform allowed to reduce the time of cargo in the port to two days (avg.). These improvements were accompanied by a reduction of the Terminal Handling Charge (THC) from US$ 984 to US$ 224 (Kent and Fox 2005). However, a comparison of total ship costs for a port stay of a similar ship between Limon Moin, Costa Rica, and Cartagena, Colombia, revealed that the port of Limon Moin is cheaper than the port of Cartagena after reform. Such approach though has the flaw that the pure transport/port costs approach does not include the valuation of time. While the port of Limon Moin does seem to have a cost advantage of US$ 28 over the Cartagena, this advantage turns into the opposite when considering the value of time in the cost equation, leaving the Limon Moin with a US$ 111 higher cost per TEU than Cartagena (Kent and Fox 2005). This example shows that considering only transport costs and charges falls short in determining the impact of port development on logistics costs. Since time is a key determinant for food products the value of time can be considered even higher than those of a regular dry container.

> ... during the early years of the last decade, the government took measures to foster competition and efficiency in the port sector, one of which was to transfer the operation of public-owned infrastructure to the private sector. However, this

process was delayed several times, due mostly to political reasons, until it was completely stopped in 2001. (Source: Defilippi, E. 2004, p. 280 on the case of Peru)

Hoffmann (2002) and Wilmsmeier (2003) show the interrelation between the prevalent port operator model in a port and transport costs. They provide evidence that concise and proactive institutional and legislative frameworks allow for a response to devolution in the shipping market, as e.g. private sector participation in port infrastructure, which in return contributes to a reduction in transport costs.

The difference in terms of success in privatization in Latin America between the best and the worst case leads to a difference in the freight of less than 2 per cent. However, if the country with the lowest indicator had advanced as much as the country with the highest indicator on the exporting side, maritime freights for its exports would be expected to be 30.6 per cent lower (Wilmsmeier et al. 2006).

- Advances in port reform effectively reduce international maritime transport costs as it results in greater investment in infrastructure, higher productivity and thus improve port performance.

The Regulatory and Legal Environment

International Policy Framework

The present analysis also reviews the impact of sector development, satisfaction with privatization of public services and informality, because the authors consider these to be important factors of influence to pricing. Using the 'perceived competence of the logistics industry' as a proxy for efficiency in the transport sector, shows the expected results, stating clearly that the country with higher levels of logistics competence have lower transport costs of imports thus positively affecting food and all other containerized imports relieving the burden of transport costs. The 'satisfaction with the level of privatization of public services' shows comparable results as this indicator can be seen as a proxy for progress and reduced bureaucracy.

Recent research has focused on the channels through which institutions impact trade. For instance, Anderson and Marcouiller (2002) find that weak institutions act as significant barriers to international trade. Trade transactions are inherently risky due to, for example, imperfect contract enforceability that goes along with weak institutional regimes.

Nuhn and Hesse (2006) ask about the importance of physical and institutional infrastructure for creating regional disparities and their influence on trade flows (Carrere and Schiff 2003, Anderson and Wincoop 2004).

Finally clear evidence is given that the smaller the informal market, including informal payments, the more is positive, reducing the impact on transport costs.

These findings underline the significance of reform in a wider context which reaches beyond infrastructure but to all related institutions, as there exists evidence that those countries with the greatest progress in the areas are able to reduce the burden of transport costs on imports, which can reduce consumer prices, if passed on and in the best case alleviates the cost of food and other imported goods especially to the most price sensitive groups.

A further variable indicating the importance of functioning logistics systems for international transport costs is presented by 'frequency of shipments reaching the consignee within schedule', the models in the regression model indicate that higher reliability contributes significantly to reduced transport costs. Therefore evidence is given that good practice in the transport sector has positive implication for the burden of transport costs on imports. In the wider interpretation such functioning relies on knowledge and good capacity building in the transport sector that consequently allows for better planning and more efficient operation of transport services. It might be argued that better logistics systems can ease the burden of transport costs as the gains from efficiency are converted into monetary savings for the importer and in continuation for the final consumer.

Impact of Institutional Failures and Bureaucracy

Wilmsmeier (2009) reviews the impact of the logistics sector development and the impact of informality. In order to capture the impact of best practices, efficiency and quality in the logistics sector the authors use the 'perceived competence of the logistics industry' and the 'frequency of shipments reaching the consignee within schedule' as proxies. The results confirm that countries with higher level of logistics competence have lower transport costs of imports thus positively affecting food and all other containerized imports relieving the burden of transport costs.

The importance of functioning logistics systems for international transport costs is presented by 'frequency of shipments reaching the consignee within schedule'. Results from the analysis indicate that higher reliability contributes significantly to reduced transport costs. This underlines that good practice in the transport sector has positive implication for the burden of transport costs on imports. In the wider interpretation such functioning relies on knowledge and good capacity building in the transport sector that consequently allows for better planning and more efficient operation of transport services.

- A better logistics system can ease the burden of transport costs as the gains from efficiency are converted into monetary savings for the importer and in continuation for the final consumer.

Open Registries

One important characteristic of the liner shipping industry is the use of open registries. Open registry shipping is the practice of registering ships under flags of convenience (e.g. Liberia, Panama etc) in order to circumvent higher regulatory and manning costs imposed by wealthier nations. Open registry fleets have been growing continuously since 1950 and today about half of the world fleet is registered in open registries (Stopford 2009). Tolofari (1989) estimates that vessel operating costs for open registry vessels are from 12 to 27 per cent lower than traditional registry fleets, with most of the estimated savings coming from manning expenses. As far as the author knows only Wilmsmeier and Martínez-Zarzoso (2009) analyse the impact of the use of open registries on international maritime transport costs. Their findings show that open registry ships significantly reduce transport costs in intra Latin American trade. The negative impact on transport costs is consistent with small variations over the period 1999–2004. Wilmsmeier and Martínez Zarzoso's (2009) findings open further discussion on the role of flags of convenience, also raised by Hoffmann, Sánchez and Talley (2005). Their findings also imply that a shipper might take into account certain risks in using services that utilize flags of convenience to reduce their shipping costs. This tries to deepen the research using a longer period of time and a different geographic range of trade routes.

- The use of open registry flags is mirrored in reduced transport costs. The use of open registry vessel also is an indicator for free competition. When there are restrictions these may lead to both higher transport costs and the use of national flags.

Gaps in Literature

The discussion in this chapter shows that the common perception that transport costs are unimportant is wrong; they are neither small nor uniform across goods and transport modes. In the following empirical application of this work the author develops further evidence concerning the importance of transport costs. The author argues that the use of space and ergo sum distance as an explanatory factor for international maritime transport costs falls short in respecting reality, particularly when international transport costs are administered rates. So far strategy and structure of the maritime industry has been mentioned but seldom given high relevance in the analysis.

Existing results (Wilmsmeier and Hoffmann 2008, Marquez-Ramos et al. 2009, Wilmsmeier and Martínez Zarzoso 2010) underline the fact that the position within the network has a more significant impact than the notion of distance, the latter only expressing the geographical distance between the trading partners, but not the level of quality to breach that distance. This important finding needs to be seen in the context of the influencing variables of liner network connectivity such as ship size (Jansson and Shneerson 1982, Lim 1998) and frequency, which are determined by the overall level of trade, the geographic position and, last but not least, port infrastructure endowment and development options (Wilmsmeier and Notteboom 2011).

Consequently, it could be argued that the impact of the maritime network and services structures on maritime freight rates and consequently trade flows has traditionally been underestimated by the economic literature and requires further exploration.

In an environment where shipping lines are actively seeking out ways to reduce their costs, particularly by aiming for economies of scale and scope, this process results in a continued change in the structure of maritime industry and thus competitive conditions. The 'global' characteristics of the maritime industry also play a significant role particularly in developing markets and regions outside the main trading regions, due to the fact that concentration processes within the industry affect less developed markets (in terms of volumes) to a greater extent than the main markets.

The result is an extremely dynamic network that reinforces processes of agglomeration in some places, but at the same time provides an economic advantage that can improve the competitive position of a region in the global market. The relationship between ports and carriers in the context of this dynamic network can leave little doubt that the structure of transportation networks is an important variable for the structure of transport costs.

Consequently, the following questions arise: Why do some countries have higher transport costs than others? What are the main determinants of these transport costs? Can government policies affect these costs in order to improve the competitiveness of a country's industry in external trade?

Certain port characteristics and institutional efficiency and effectiveness, including aspects such as infrastructure development, port devolution and private sector participation can be influenced by governments. A so-far neglected point is the impact of the effectiveness and efficiency of institutions and politics in converting plans into reality and facilitating market responses to changing environments.

However, the cyclical fluctuations of maritime freight rates as well as most of the determinants of freight rate levels on a given route are beyond the control of policy makers, since containerized trade is managed by international shipping lines that operate on a global scale. It seems important though to understand the market forces in order to identify the most effective responses for policy development.

However, the full comparative advantages of improving infrastructure and networks can only be captured if this development is of comparable and equal level throughout the network. Changes and shifts in economic development can induce significant shifts in maritime transport service networks.

Existing literature usually focuses on particular issues. Since maritime and port industry are embedded in dynamic processes of supply and demand it seems necessary to address this dynamic by analysing the consistency of transport costs over time, which is so far only addressed by Wilmsmeier and Martínez-Zarzoso (2010).

At the same time the discussion in this chapter has provided evidence that traditional pricing mechanism prevail in the maritime industry. The author expects to be able to evaluate if traditional schemes of 'what the cargo will bear pricing ...' are being maintained over the period under study or if such concepts are traded against or overruled by other strategies.

In order to do so, the following analysis uses freight rates per ton and freight rates per measure can be calculated from the BTI disaggregated at five digit level SITC. The data covers the period from 2000–2006.

Mapping the Complexity of Transport Cost Determinants – a Summary

This chapter has sought to provide a solid definition of and justification for the chosen variables in estimating international maritime transport costs determinants. The scientific discussion in this chapter examines the complexity of the underlying determinants of international maritime transport costs in five main groups. The question on the role of distance as a determinant of maritime transport costs is addressed in depth and evidence is provided that the role of distance as a determinant might be overrated in existing studies. The discussion brings a wide range of proof on the complex interrelationship between certain determinants. The role of the shipping lines, their strategies and the structure was identified as a key area for research particularly the variables that form the elements of the liner shipping networks are discussed in detail. This discussion points out the representation of ascertained distance through the liner shipping network structure variables.

The role of port infra- and superstructure is emphasized and the potential impact of port devolution on maritime transport costs was pointed out. However, the theoretic discussion also accentuates the high correlation between the individual factors and the difficulty to capture the full complexity in an empirical analysis.

Based on this theoretical discussion of the theory underpinning the structure of maritime transport costs and the wide interrelations between the individual determinants, this chapter formulates 15 individual hypotheses. These hypotheses constitute important theoretical arguments for probing the structure of determinants of maritime transport costs in intra-Latin American trade. These hypotheses are empirically tested at a later stage of this work.

Following the plentiful discussion key influencing determinants of shipping costs can be categorized as presented in Figure 3.12. These findings set the framework for the detailed empirical analysis.

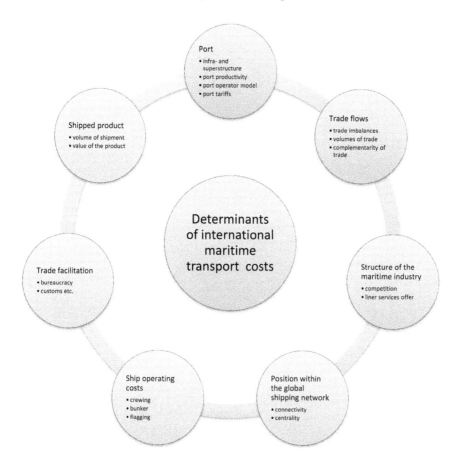

Figure 3.12 Key influencing determinants of maritime transport costs

Source: Author

Chapter 4
Empirical Analysis

Data Sources

Transport Costs and Trade Data

One of the main difficulties in analysing transport costs is that of obtaining reliable data (for discussion on data sources for international transport costs, see Chapter 2, p. 20). The data used for this work, collected, structured and tested for integrity by author, is based on a number of different sources. Works on international maritime transport costs are usually based on macro-level data pertaining to statistics on values and volumes of external trade, often disaggregated by transportation mode, and data on the flow of commodities. Government agencies are normally responsible for collecting this information.

The maritime transport costs, i.e. the variable this work attempts to explain, are taken from the International Transport Data Base (BTI). The BTI was created by UN-ECLAC's Transport Unit in 1999 as part of a research project (Fuchsluger 1999) with the primary objective of creating a database of commodity flows in the LAC region. The statistics are derived from the foreign Trade Data Bank for Latin America and the Caribbean (BADECEL), maintained by the Statistics and Economic Projections Division of UN-ECLAC. It represents information processed by each country's national customs service (for more information see Wilmsmeier 2003, Hoffmann et al. 2002, and Wilmsmeier et al. 2008).

The data include annual data on country basis from 1997 to 2010 and present all bilateral trade data for 12 LAIA countries. Evaluation of data for this research started with raw trade data provided for individual LAIA countries for the period 2000 to 2006. The raw data was then transferred into, consolidated and checked for integrity in a SQL database. This process also included the decoding and transforming of data sets. The full database only for maritime trade includes over 12 million individual datasets for external trade movement of LAIA countries. From these data only the data on maritime transport for intra-LAC trade was selected for this analysis. Data include:

- Mode of transport by which the merchandise leaves from or arrives in the country (i.e. maritime transport);
- Product: classified according to a) the harmonized system, and b) the Standard International Trade Classification (SITC), Rev 3, up to the five digit level;
- Country of origin, country or destination, exporting country;

- Tonnes (metric tons), in this context denominated as 'volume' per shipment;
- Value of exports FOB, imports FOB, and imports CIF (current US$) per shipment;
- Freight (current US$);
- Insurance (current US$);
- Port or point or entry (importing country);
- Flag of ship (country where ship is registered).

This work uses a subset of the BTI including data based on the following characteristics:

- Transport mode: Maritime;
- Time: 2000 to 2006;
- Exporting countries (22): Argentina, Belize, Brazil, Chile, Colombia, Costa Rica, Dominican Republic, Ecuador, El Salvador, French Guiana, Guatemala, Guyana, Honduras, Jamaica, Mexico, Nicaragua, Panama, Peru, Suriname, Trinidad and Tobago, Uruguay, Venezuela;
- Importing countries (7): Argentina, Brazil, Chile, Colombia, Ecuador, Peru, and Uruguay;
- Products: all products at SITC 5-digit level with affinity to containerization either dry or special containers.

This work attempts to portray the best estimate of the true movements of goods between Latin American countries. To achieve this, based on data as informed by the importing countries, this author builds his investigation on cargo flows from the 'country of departure'. In cases where this is not informed, the 'country of origin' is used instead, as the best approximation for the 'country of departure'. In most cases, country of departure and country of origin coincide, and it can be assumed that if a Customs declaration leaves the field for 'country of departure' empty, then this coincides with the information provided in 'country of origin'. This correction affects approximately 1 per cent of trade volumes.

Improvement in the estimation of transport margins must begin with the raw data. The BTI offers accurate transport cost data at the detailed commodity level. In difference to other databases freight and insurance are given as separate values and are not subsumed as when calculating the difference between CIF and FOB values. CIF, freight and insurance values are reported by the importing country and the fob values are reported by the exporting country. With the available differentiation of freight and insurance and product information it is possible to overcome problems presented when using CIF-FOB margins, which can represent discrepancies in the reported value of the merchandise rather than transportation cost for two reasons (for discussion see Chapter 2, p. 20): a) at a detailed commodity level the variation in the CIF-FOB is less extreme and b) the differentiation between freight and insurance allows for cross checking with the CIF-FOB difference.

Further certain procedures were used to reduce remaining problems associated with transport margins reporting. First all SITC 3 and 9 commodity group products were removed. In a following step all products were categorized regarding their affinity to containerization and the type of container, where applicable. Next, all observations, with the volume of shipment or CIF or FOB value of zero were eliminated from the database. Finally, all observations, which had a transport margin smaller than zero, were removed. Trimming the extreme observations in the freight/ton using a triple standard deviation to define the cutting point was done to improve accuracy.

The full data set includes 827,991 data points for international maritime trade transactions at SITC 5 digit level for 261 bilateral trade relations within Latin America and the Caribbean. For the regression analysis various subsets of the full data set are used. These subsets differ in the time span they cover or the cross-sectional composition.

Further Data Resources

In order to obtain further descriptive variables, which are estimated to present an influence on international maritime transport costs an extensive statistics literature research was realized to obtain the following data for the countries under study:

Trade Data for the total volume and value of total and bilateral trade are derived from import flows by country at the product level in the UN-ECLAC BADECEL database.

Distance The indicator used to measure distance, when used in model specifications, is the actual shipping distance between the ports in each country pair as calculated in nautical miles using commonly travelled shipping routes. This data is based on the CEPII data base.

Carrier and networks Data on the structure of liner shipping services (e.g. number of shipping lines, number of services, ship capacity, average speed and vessel size etc) has been obtained from ComPair Data and Containerization International (source: www.ci-online.co.uk). Data includes details from UNCTAD's Bilateral Connectivity Index and Transhipment Index.

Interfaces Data on port infrastructure endowment was obtained from Containerization International, World Shipping Services and individual ports.

Other Further data source include The World Bank (i.e. Doing Business, Logistics Performance Index and World Development Indicators, UN-ECLAC Statistics Division, World Economic Forum (i.e. Global Competitiveness Report).

Modelling the Complexity of Interrelationships

Factor Analysis

This work attempts to address the complexity of determinants of maritime transport costs. Being aware that many variables present high correlations and thus the use of individual variables traditionally restricted regression analysis.

Considering the variety of data available and relevant in the analysis of determinants of transport costs, the aim is to identify the independent influencing factors from this variety of data. In difference to previous research the following factor analysis allows the *discovery* of independent explanatory variables, thus permitting breaking down of some more complex structure.

This association should not obscure and indeed should help to make clear. The new variables offer a variety of interpretations and moreover a range of interpretations far beyond the apparent dimensionality of the data.

Factor analysis is part of the multiple general linear hypothesis family of procedures and makes many of the same assumptions as multiple regression: linear relationships, interval or near interval data, untruncated variables, proper specification, lack of high multicollinearity, and multivariate normality for purposes of significance testing

Factor analysis (FA) does not bring about variables explaining a particular phenomenon, but is seen as a statistical manner to isolate the variables most likely to constitute fruitful contributions to the study. Creating a set of factors to be treated as uncorrelated variables is one approach to handling multicollinearity when using the identified factors in such processes as multiple regressions.

Conceptually, the process to calculate factors from a set of variables merely consists of another measurement designed to capture the correlations among the correlations themselves. Correlation values can be shown to fall into certain broad clusters that can be explained as the manifestations of an abstract underlying dimension (Kachigan 1986). Correlation values of variables can be interpreted in three different causal ways (Backhaus et al. 2006). By way of example this can be as follows:

- The correlation between ship size and draught is that with increasing ship size the draught of the ship increases as well
- The correlation between ship size and draught is that with increasing draught ship size increases as well.
- The correlation between ship size and draught is dependent on a third factor behind both variables, i.e. this hypothetic factor is the reason for the existence of the correlation.

Factor analysis always uses the third interpretation. Only if a logical connection and dependency can be identified, factor analysis can be used.

The result is that a possible set of 100 variables might be aggregated to a much smaller set of significant principle components. Based on Backhaus et al. 2006, p. 268, the approach to run the factor analysis is used as follows:

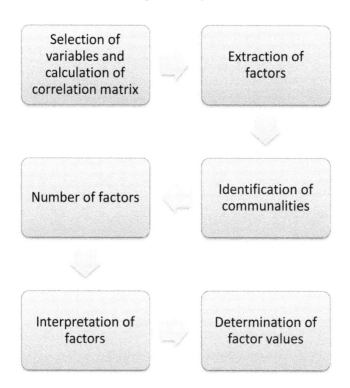

Figure 4.1   Factor analysis

Source: Author, based on Backhaus et al. (2006)

The correlation values allow understanding the relationships between pairs of variables. This also shows if variables can be interpreted as potential clusters. The correlation of a group of variables can be calculated using the following equation:

$$
r_{xm, xn} = \frac{\sum_{k=1}^{K} \left(x_{km} - \bar{x}_m \right) \times \left(x_{kn} - \bar{x}_n \right)}{2a \sqrt{\sum_{k=1}^{K} \left(x_{km} - \bar{x}_m \right)^2 \times \sum_{k=1}^{K} \left(x_{kn} - \bar{x}_n \right)^2}}
\tag{4.1}
$$

where:

x_{km} = values of variable m of object k (e.g. ports)

$$\overline{x}_m \quad = \text{average of variable m over all objects k}$$

$$x_{kn} \quad = \text{values of variable n of object k (e.g. ports)}$$

$$\overline{x}_n \quad = \text{average of variable n over all objects k}$$

In order to facilitate the calculation of correlations as part of the factor analysis, facilitate interpretation and to create a greater comparability of variables the raw data matrix is standardized. Standardization is done using the following equation:

$$z = \frac{x_{kj} - \overline{x}_j}{s_j} \tag{4.2}$$

where:

$$x_{kj} \quad = \text{value of the j-ed variable of object k (e.g. ports)}$$

$$\overline{x}_j \quad = \text{average of values of the j-ed variable all objects k}$$

$$s_j \quad = \text{standard deviation of j-ed variable}$$

$$z_{kj} \quad = \text{standardized values of j-ed variable of object k}$$

Based on the standardized data matrix the correlation matrix is calculated as follows:

$$R = \frac{1}{K-1} \times Z' \times Z \tag{4.3}$$

where:

Z' is the transposed matrix of the standardized raw data matrix Z.

In order to evaluate the acceptability of the correlation matrix the significance of correlation values, the inverse correlation matrix, Bartlett-test, anti-image covariance matrix and the Kaiser-Meyer-Olkin-Criteria are used (for detailed discussion on these evaluation possibilities see Backhaus et al. 2006).

The extraction of factors is itself a ranking process. The significance of factors is expressed as the percentage of the variance that they explain, resulting that a small number of latent variables is defined to account for most of the variation in the original set of variables. The extracted factors reflect the common and unique variance of the variables and may be seen as a variance with all components to reproduce correlations. Within the framework for factor analysis a number of extraction procedures have been developed. This work focuses on two approaches which are closely related to the determination of communalities: principal component analysis (PCA) and principal factor analysis (PFA).

PCA is the most common form of factor analysis. This procedure assumes that the variance of a variable can completely be explained through the extraction of factors viz. no rest-variance exists within the variables. The initial value for computation of communalities is set as, consequently, the communality of 1 is always reproduced completely, if as many factors as variables are extracted. In the case that less factors as variables are extracted the communality will be smaller than 1. The non-explained or rest-variance (1-communality) will be declared as *known level of information loss*.

PFA, also called principal axis factoring (PAF), assumes that the variance of a variable is always distributed in the components communality and rest-variance. The aim of the PFA is to explain the variance of variables to the level of the communalities. This means that the initial value when a estimating the communalities is set lower than 1. The real value of the communality can be influenced by the user based with regards to contents.

Identification of Communalities

Even though PCA and PFA are similar in their calculation methods, they are based on different theoretic models. The aim of the PCA is to create a comprehensive reproduction of the data structure using a minimum number of factors. Therefore no differentiation is made between communalities and rest-variance and PCA does not make any causal interpretation of the factors. In contrast, PFA aims at explaining the variance of the variables through hypothetical factors, which requires a differentiation between communalities and rest-variance. Correlations in this case are interpreted in a causal manner. Consequently, the differences become apparent in the interpretation of factors rather than the calculation methods.

By way of example the differences in the questions asked are:

PCA: How can the high loading variables on a factor be summarized through in a collective term (component)?

PFA: How can the cause be named, that is responsible for the high load factors of variables on this factor?

Factor loadings are the correlation coefficients between variables (rows) and factors (columns). Analogous to Person's r, the squared factor loading is the per cent of the variance in that variables are explained by the factor. To get the per cent of variance in all variables accounted for by each factor, the sum of the squared factor loading for that factor is build and divided by the number of variables.

Number of Factors

In order to determine the number of factors relevant to different comprehensibility, tests and algorithms can be used. Comprehensibility is not a strictly mathematical criterion, there is much to be said for limiting the number of factors to those whose dimension of meaning is readily comprehensible. Often this is the first two or three. One of the most common tests is the so called Kaiser criterion, dropping all components with eigenvalues below 1.0. The reason for the use of the Kaiser criterion is that a factor whose explanatory power of the variance is smaller than one, explains less of the variable than a single variable.

The Scree-test organizes the eigenvalues in a coordinate system in descending order, plots the components as the X axis and the corresponding eigenvalues as the Y axis and connects the points by a line. At the point where the difference between two factors is greatest the line forms an *elbow*. The Scree-test says to drop all further components after the one starting the elbow. Another way is to use the rule of keeping enough factors to account for a certain percentage of the variation. This method is not always unambiguous.

Interpretation of Factors

Once the number of factors is determined it is necessary to interpret the factors. This interpretation is done based on factor loadings. The user thus decides based on the cut off level for factor loadings (≤ 0.5). Obtained factor loadings are often hard to interpret, rotation methods serve to make the output more understandable. The sum of eigenvalues is not affected, but rotation will alter the eigenvalues of particular factors. In the following the Varimax rotation will be used. This is an orthogonal rotation of the factor axes to maximize the variance of the squared loadings of a factor on all the variables in a factor matrix, which has the effect of differentiating the original variables by extracted factor. That minimizes the number of variables which have high loadings of particular loadings. This rotation type makes it possible to interpret the results. Other rotation methods are quartimax rotation, equimax rotation, direct oblimin rotations and promax rotations (Kachigan 1986).

Determination of Factor Values

In order to be able to use the factors in the later regression analysis, the values of the factors for each object need to be estimated. This work uses regression analysis in order to estimate factor values.

The obtained and relevant selected factor values can be plotted against each other in a scatter plot. The number of principle components also reflects the number of dimensions expressed by the dimensions. In most cases it is easeful to only plot two variables against each other, to be able to interpret the results.

This work will use PCA in order to investigate the complexity of the determinants of transport costs. This is particularly developed in order to be able to capture the underlying complexity of the liner shipping network and port related determinants.

The next section outlines the used variable measures. In the cases the 'component-variables' are introduced the results from the PCA will be described. For all components the varimax-rotation is applied.

Specification of Variables

Dependent Variable: Transport Cost

The BTI distinguishes between the country of 'origin', which is where the good is made, and the country of 'departure', which is the country from where the good is exported during this particular trade transaction. This author uses the country of departure, which is of relevance for transport costs. The country of 'origin' would be of relevance if, for example, the level of customs duties had to be determined.

The freight rate data are disaggregated at five-digit Standardized International Trade Classification (SITC) level. This level of detail was chosen to avoid aggregation bias resulting from mixing heterogeneous product categories.

As mentioned in the previous section, the basic source of information is the BTI. The BTI gives information on the actual freight rates paid for the export of a certain good between countries i and j to a port p excluding loading costs. Using the level of detail available the author calculated the transport cost per ton and the transport cost per unit measure. The latter was calculated applying the stowage factors of individual products.

Stopford (2009, p. 575) refers to the relevance of stowage in container shipping and describes how stowage affects the balance of a ship and that differences in payloads of containers require compromise on the ship's loaded deadweight (he uses the difference of average payload in transpacific trades which varies between seven tonnes eastbound and 12 tonnes westbound per container). This author expects that stowage is thus included in freight. Earlier studies used transport costs per ton as the dependent variable (Wilmsmeier et al. 2006, Wilmsmeier and Martínez-Zarzoso 2009, Wilmsmeier 2003 etc). However, this measure ignores differences in measure (m^3) per unit shipped. The approach applied in this work will allow a) controlling for different unit measures and b) compare the empirical results for these two different independent variables.

One limitation of the data is that the series is annual, therefore, variations throughout a specific year cannot be allocated to a specific point in time and seasonality cannot be controlled. Nevertheless, until a more detailed time series data set becomes available, the BTI data will have to suffice.

In order to make the freight rate data comparable over time, the freight rate series and the product values are all deflated with the US GDP implicit price deflator. The use of the US GDP implicit price deflator can be used as an approximation for the national price deflators since all freight charges are paid in US$ and no other specific transport price deflators are available.

This work only analyses transport costs for containerized cargoes. The BTI does not provide information on whether the cargo was actually containerized or not. For the purposes of this work, the author selected a group of SITC codes at the three-digit level that are assumed to be in principle containerizable. Above all, those commodities that are usually transported as liquid or dry bulk (e.g. ores) are thus excluded from this research.

The dependent variable is described as: $Tcton_{ijkt}$ or $Tcmeasure_{ijkt}$.

Where: i is the port in exporting country I, j is the port in exporting country J, k is the individual product and t is the year of transaction.

See also Annex for a description of the data with respect to the number of observations, means, maximum and minimum values, and the standard deviation.

Independent Variables

Determinants of Relation and Geography

Distance   The maritime distance (D_{ij}) between the main ports of country i and country j is calculated in nautical miles. The expected sign of this variable is positive. The source is UNCTAD.

Maritime Corridor   This is a dummy variable ($MarCor_{IJ}$) defining if two trading ports in countries I and J are situated on the same maritime corridor. This variable is also expected to reflect the influence of the Panama Canal where movements between two corridors require the use of the Canal. The expected sign of this variable is negative.

Implications of Cargo Characteristics and Trade Structure

Unit value   Ratio of value to weight (in US$/ton) calculated for each specific export shipment. This variable ($UVal_{ijkt}$) as a determinant of maritime transport costs is expected to be positive, since goods with a higher value/weight ratio tend to choose transport services that offer a higher quality and better frequencies and speeds (Feo et al. 2003, Wilmsmeier 2003). Despite this fact, this variable is not correlated with other quality variables (i.e. frequency of services).

Refrigerated cargo   The variable ($Reefer_{ijkt}$) is a dummy variable that denotes the requirement to use reefer container for product k transported between ports in country I and J in year t commodities that require special transport conditions, such as refrigerated cargo, would incur greater transport costs. A positive sign is expected for this variable.

Economies of scale at consignment level   Volume of transaction ($ProdTradeVol_{ijkt}$) measured as total weight in metric tonnes of export flows of a specific containerizable product shipped between ports in country I to country J in period t. The expected effect on maritime transport costs is negative, since a larger volume of shipments are expected to relate to reduction in transport costs through economies of scale.

Trade imbalance   The BADECEL database also allows for estimating the imbalance of trade for containerized trades. The imbalances are adjusted for the different models depending on the subset of products used e.g. an imbalance in reefer products does not necessarily impact in imbalances of standard containers.

The trade imbalance in volume that influences the maritime transport costs correlates with the disequilibrium. It is calculated accordingly.

$$IMBAL_{I,Jt} = \frac{X_{I,Jt}}{M_{I,Jt}}$$

$IMBAL_{IJt}$ is the trade balance, where MIt is the imports of all containerized products k to country I in period t, and XIt is the exports of all containerized products k from country I in period t. The same is calculated for countries J. When trade imbalance is negative, imports exceed exports and the greater the imbalance, the lower the freight rates will be for exports; but if exports exceed imports, the larger the imbalance the higher the expected freight rates for exports will be. This divergence associated with the sign of trade imbalance occurs as a result of the freight rate price fixing mechanisms applying in the liner market. Imbalance is calculated in tons based on data from BADECEL at 3-digit SITC level for Latin American Countries in the period 2000–2006. The expected sign for the variable is either positive or negative depending if a country is the exporting or importing country.

The Carriers

TEU deployed   This is represented by the variable ($TEUdep_{IJt}$). This variable describes the capacity available in regular liner shipping services and is used as a proxy for total bilateral trade volume. The expected sign of this variable is negative.

Number of services   Describes the number of total direct services between countries I and J in year t. The variable is $NumServ_{IJt}$. The expected sign of this variable is negative.

Frequency   This variable ($FREQ_{IJt}$) reports the average time in days between two consecutive calls of vessels deployed in services between the port of origin i and destination j (according to the dates advertised in the regular liner schedules by each line). The variable is therefore expected to be negative and directly related to frequency. The effect of the number of days between service departures on the average service freight rate is uncertain: on the one hand frequency is seen as a proxy for service quality, as a more frequent port to port service reduces the shipper's overall transit time from door to door on average and increases its flexibility to programme its shipments. Hence, the impact of frequency perceived as quality on the freight rate will then be positive. On the other hand an increase in the number of days between service departures indicates lower competition between shipping lines. In this case, a longer time interval between departures will decrease competition and increase freight rates. The expected sign of this variable is negative.

Liner Service Network Structure   Data on liner service network structure includes the following variables fleet deployment, average ship sizes in services, capacity in services, number of shipping lines, and shipping opportunities between ports of country I and J have been calculated from liner schedules and Containerization International. The variable $LSNS_{IJt}$ is developed using PCA.

The concept is applied for two sets of variables a) variables describing the liner service network structure in 2006 including: number of ships, TEU, number of carriers, number of regular liner services and maximum ship size deployed between countries I and J; and b) variables describing the liner service network structure 2000–2006. This set includes: number of shipping lines, number of vessels deployed, number of services and capacity in TEU deployed between country I and J, as well as the average ship size in each relation IJ. The latter set of variables is slightly different, which results from the restriction in the availability of certain information for the whole period under study.

The construction of cluster variables including vessel specifications, acknowledges hypotheses 8 that *vessel specific variables are good proxies for technological economies of scale in shipping.*

Therefore if the LSNS variables prove significant hypothesis 8 can be accepted.

PCA LSNS 2006   The correlations between variables describing the liner shipping network structure as expected are high and ranged from –0.757 to 0.987. All five variables show high correlations. The Kaiser-Meyer-Olkin Test returns a sampling adequacy of 0.757 which is middling (for details see Appendix 8).

The PCA returned one component including all five variables, accounting for more than 89 per cent of the intrinsic variance of the data fulfilling the Kaiser criterion with eigenvalues over 1. The derived cluster variable is denominated 'Liner Service Network Structure ($LSNS_{IJ2006}$)'. The expected sign of this variable is negative.

PCA LSNS 2000–2006   The correlations between variables describing the liner shipping network structure as expected are high and ranged from –0.844 to 0.986 (Appendix 3, p. 143 ff.). All five variables show high correlations. The Kaiser-Meyer-Olkin Test returns a sampling adequacy of 0.68 which is middling (for details Appendix 3, p. 143 ff.).

The PCA returned one component including all five variables, accounting for more than 93 per cent of the intrinsic variance of the data fulfilling the Kaiser criterion with eigenvalues over 1. The derived cluster variable is denominated 'Liner Service Network Structure ($LSNS_{IJt}$)'. The expected sign of this variable is negative.

Competition   The number of shipping lines (Carrier$_{IJt}$) providing direct services between the main port of country i and main port in country j measured at one point in year t for the period 2000 to 2006 is a proxy for the degree of competition between lines offering the same service at a specific port, an increase in this variable would cause a decrease in transport costs. The source of this data is Containerization International. The expected sign of this variable is negative.

Quasioligopolistic market structures   A dummy variable that describes if four or less shipping lines provide regular liner services between country I and J. A small number of competitors is expected to increase due to collusive behaviour of shipping lines. The expected sign of this variable is positive.

The Interfaces

Port Infrastructure and Superstructure

Port infrastructure variables: number of cranes, maximum draught and storage area at origin and destination ports. The interaction of the three above-mentioned variables is considered an appropriate proxy for quayside operation performance.

Since one goal of the work is to identify the possible influence of port infrastructure endowment and port performance on maritime transport cost, important variables were gathered for 98 ports in Latin America and the Caribbean. These ports were also considered in the principal component analysis each one providing through their characteristics answers about variables which the author expected to be involved within port performance. To avoid concerns about over-parameterization and spurious correlations between multiple variables, the following approaches were utilized. Based on the variety of data three component groups through principal components analysis (PCA) were identified. The two groups of component variables obtained from the PCA are described below.

PCA 1   The correlations between the obtained port infrastructure variables from a set of 71 ports as expected ranged from –0.039 to 0.707. The eight variables show partly high correlations. The Kaiser-Meyer-Olkin Test returns a sampling adequacy of 0.70 which is middling (for details see Appendix 7, p. 153 ff.).

The first two components, account for more than 51 per cent of the intrinsic variance of the data fulfilling the Kaiser criterion with eigenvalues over 1.

The first factor, which accounted for more than 35 per cent of the total variance, incorporates the number of terminals, storage capacity, number of electric reefer points, total port area, and the number of berths, which could present a cluster measure for 'port infrastructure endowment' ($PORTINFPCA1_{i,j}$)

The second factor, which accounted for more than 15 per cent of the total variance, includes the following three dummy variables controlling for 24 hour operation: office hours, receive/delivery hours and quayside hours. This variable can be referred to as 'service level' ($SERVLEVPCA1_{i,j}$).

The original, unrotated principal components solution maximizes the sum of squared factors loadings, efficiently creating the set of factors. However, unrotated solutions are hard to interpret because variables tend to load on multiple factors. The Varimax rotation realizes an orthogonal rotation of the factor axes to maximize the variance of the squared factor loadings of a factor on all the variables. Consequently, it minimizes the number of factors, which have high factor loadings on any one given factor.

PCA 2 When further defining the model a second PCA was developed. The correlations between the obtained port infrastructure variables from a set of 96 ports as expected ranged from −0.234 to 0.707. The eight variables show mainly modest correlations. The Kaiser-Meyer-Olkin Test returns a sampling adequacy of 0.7 which is middling (for details see Appendix 12).

The first three components account for more than 62 per cent of the intrinsic variance of the data fulfilling the Kaiser criterion with eigenvalues over 1.

The first factor, which accounted for more than 33 per cent of the total variance, incorporates the number of terminals, number of berths, storage capacity, electric reefer points, and total area, which could present a cluster measure for 'infrastructure endowment' ($PORTINFENDOWPCA2_{i,j}$).

The second factor, which accounted for more than 16 per cent of the total variance, includes the following variables: pier depth and anchorage depth. This cluster variable can be referred to as 'port accessibility' ($QUAYACCESSPCA2_{i,j}$).

The third factor, which accounted for more than 12 per cent of the total variance, constructs from the variable access depth. This variable can be referred to as 'port accessibility' ($PORTACCESSPCA2_{i,j}$).

The original, unrotated principal components solution maximizes the sum of squared factors loadings, efficiently creating the set of factors in the table above. However, unrotated solutions are hard to interpret because variables tend to load on multiple factors. The Varimax rotation realizes an orthogonal rotation of the factor axes to maximize the variance of the squared factor loadings of a factor on all the variables. Consequently, it minimizes the number of factors, which have high factor loadings on any one given factor.

Productivity Economies of scale are also presented at port level. Larger volumes of containerized cargo loaded and unloaded at a port will enable the shipping lines to use larger containerships, as well as permitting the terminal operator to optimize the use of terminal equipment, infrastructure and stevedoring shifts. A more effective terminal can be expected to induce lower unit transport costs. The variable port throughput ($PortThrough_{i,j}$) is used as a proxy for productivity. The expected sign of this variable will hence be negative.

Port operator models Two dummy variables are introduced to describe prevalent port operator models in the period under study. The first one controls if both ports in transaction k are operated under a service port model ($ServicePort_{i,j,t}$). The expected sign of this variable will hence be positive. The second one controls if both ports in transaction k are operated under a landlord port model ($LandlordPort_{i,j,t}$). The expected sign of this variable will hence be positive.

Institutions and Regulation

Corruption   A country's degree of public corruption ($Corup_{I,J}$). The Corruption Perceptions Index score relates to perceptions of the degree of corruption as seen by business people and country analysts, and ranges between 10 (highly corrupt) and 0 (highly clean). The source is Transparency International. The expected sign of this variable will hence be positive.

Open registries   A dummy variable ($OpenReg_{ijkt}$) is introduced that describes the use of open registry flags for transporting product k between ports in country I and J in period t. The expected sign of this variable will hence be negative.

Note on Independent Variables

No theoretical model is complete enough to provide a full list of variables that may be important in the empirical investigation of many economic phenomena. The stylized model used in this research as departure point for analysis does not pretend otherwise.

Model Specification

When data are analysed for the purpose of studying a certain phenomenon, it is usual to begin with some assumptions expecting to be confirmed by the same data. This is the approach in the statistical hypothesis testing. On the contrary, the exploratory approach tries to find consistent patterns of regular relationships between variables, and in a subsequent stage, confirm them on new data sets. This exploratory approach advances through three specific steps:

- data exploration,
- pattern or relationships determination, and
- verification of findings on new data sets.

In order to determine the impact of the various identified determinants in this work in international maritime transport costs – considered as significant drivers to international trade competitiveness – an equation explaining such costs needs to be derived.

The work is based on a two stage approach, including a cross-sectional analysis of international maritime freight rates and a panel data regression analysis. The panel data varies from the cross-section regression in that it has double subscripts on its variables, i.e.

$$\gamma_{kt} = \alpha + X'_{kt}\beta + u_{kt}$$

with k=1,...,N; t=1,...,T   (4.4)

With k denoting international maritime transport costs of specific products and t denoting time. The k subscript denotes the cross section whereas t denotes the time-series dimension. The author uses a one-way error component model for the disturbances, with

$$u_{kt} = \mu_k + v_{kt} \tag{4.5}$$

Where: μ_k denotes the unobservable individual-specific effect and v_{kt} denotes the remainder disturbance. Note that μ_k is time-invariant and accounts for any individual transaction specific effect that is not included in the regression. In this case it can be referred to as the specific cargo transaction characteristics. The remainder disturbance v_{kt} varies with products and time and can be thought of as the usual disturbance in the regression.

A reduced form model of maritime freight rates for Latin American exports is used for the empirical analysis. It is assumed that exported commodities are produced in the country of export and then shipped, at a cost, to the import markets where the goods are sold. As a result of the shipping margin, the price paid by consumers in the destination exceeds the price received by producers. Since the shipping margin depends on competitive conditions in the shipping industry, similar to Clark et al. (2002) the shipping firms are assumed to be profit-maximizing identical firms and behave as Cournot competitors. Within this framework a simple constant-elasticity pricing equation can be easily derived from a fully specified general-equilibrium model (Francois and Wooton 2001). The pricing equation relates the cost in US$ of shipping one ton (or one m³) of cargo of commodity k (disaggregated at 5-digit level of the SITC classification) in year t from main port *i* in country *I* in Latin America to destination port *j* in country *J*, TC_{ijkt}, to the marginal cost of this service, mc (i,j,k,t), and a profit margin term, $\omega(i,j,k,t)$, ,

$$TC_{ijkt} = MC\,(i,j,k.t)\,\Omega\,(i,j,k,t) \tag{4.6}$$

The markup is a function of the elasticity of demand faced by liners companies operating regular services between country I and country J for product k. This can be written as follows:

$$tc_{ijkt} = mc(i,j,k.t) + \varpi(i,j,k,t) \tag{4.7}$$

where:

tc_{ijkt}: the cost of maritime transport per unit weight or measure of product k as transported between points i, I and j, J in log
i: port of departure in country I
j: port of arrival in country J

k: product defined at the five-digit SITC System level

ω: markup, in log

mc: marginal cost, in log

As can be observed in equation (4.7), both marginal cost and markup necessitate to be functions of factors dependent on the port of departure i, I and port j, J, the service and market characteristics between I and J, and the specific characteristics of product k. The factors as discussed in Chapter 1 specifically depend on determinants of geography and relation, cargo characteristics and trade structure, transport service and market structures, interface related variables (e.g. infrastructures and services) in origin, transit and destination countries, national and international institutional factors e.g. use of open registries and institutional failures and bureaucracy in departure and destination countries. Further, external factors such as the development of the charter market and oil prices, have an influence on transport costs. Assuming functional form in equation (4.7), the marginal cost equation is given by:

$$mc_{ijkt} =$$
$$\phi_k + \chi_t + \sum_n^1 \alpha_n GR_{ij} + \sum_n^1 \beta_n P_{ijkt} + \sum_n^1 \gamma_n Trade_{IJt} + \sum_n^1 \delta_n Network_{IJt} + \sum_n^1 \varepsilon_n Port_{i,j} + \sum_n^1 \varepsilon_n Inst_{I,J}$$

$$(8)$$
$$(4.8)$$

Where:

ϕ: is a dummy variable referring to product k

χ: is a dummy variable referring to year t

GR_{ijkt}: represents the group of variables describing geography and relations in between i and j in year t

P_{ijkt}: embodies the variables representing commodity k inherent characteristics in year t,

$Trade_{IJt}$: corresponds to variables of trade structure between i and j in year t

$Network_{IJt}$: denotes the variables related to regular liner service structures between I and J in year t

$Port_{i,j}$: variables describing port infrastructure, operation or performance in i or j respectively

$Inst_{I,J}$: symbolizes the group of variables related to international policy or national policies and institutional in I or J respectively

Further, following the formulation of Fink, Mattoo and Neagu (2002) and Wilmsmeier and Martínez-Zarzoso (2009) the potential effect of shipping company mark-ups is evaluated by using the following equation:

$$\psi_{ijkt} = \vartheta_k + \chi_t + \zeta_1 Carrier_{IJt} + \zeta_2 Agree_{IJt} + \zeta_3 Imbal_{I,J} \qquad (4.9)$$

Where:

ϑ_k: is product specific effect capturing the differences between products in transport demand elasticity. Transport demand elasticity results from the final demand of product k in country J.

$Carrier_{IJt}$: denotes the number of shipping lines offering services between I and J in year t.

$Agree_{IJt}$: existence of price fixing agreements on route IJ.

$Imbal_{I,J}$: imbalance of I or J respectively in containerized trade in year t.

Substituting equations (4.8) and (4.9) into (4.7) and adding an error term, the empirical model to be estimated is derived as:

$$tc_{ijkt} = \kappa_k + \chi_t + \sum_n^1 \alpha_n GR_{ij} + \sum_n^1 \beta_n P_{ijkt} + \sum_n^1 \gamma_n Trade_{IJt} + \sum_n^1 \delta_n Network_{IJt} +$$
$$\sum_n^1 \varepsilon_n Port_{i,j} + \sum_n^1 \epsilon_n Inst_{I,J} + \zeta_1 Carrier_{IJt} + \zeta_2 Agree_{IJt} + \zeta_3 Imbal_{I,J} + \mu_{ijkt} \qquad (4.10)$$

Where

$\kappa_k = \phi_k + \vartheta_k$ is a dummy variable κ_k summarizes the specific effects detailed in ϕ_k and $+\vartheta_k$

μ_{ijk} is the error term.

The full list of variables used is presented by groups in Table 4.1. The expected sign is given in the last column of the table.

Table 4.1   Independent variables used in regression models

Group	Variable	Description	m_n	Expected sign
GR_{ij}	D_{ij}	Maritime distance in nautical miles between principal ports in Latin American countries – ln		+
	$MarCor_{ij}$	Dummy variable if i and j on same maritime corridor		-
P_{ijkt}	$UVal_{ijkt}$	Unit Value (US\$/ton) – ln		+
	$Reefer_{ijkt}$	Dummy variable for reefer cargo		+
$Trade_{IJkt}$	$ProdTradeVol_{ijkt}$	Volume (tonnes) of product k traded between I and J in year t		-
	$ToTrade_{I,Jt}$	Total trade volume country I or J respectively		-

Group	Variable	Description	m_n	Expected sign
Network_{IJt}	Numserv_{IJt}	Number of services between I and J in year t – ln		-
	Freq_{IJt}	Monthly frequency of shipping services between I and J in year t – ln		-
	LSNS_{IJt}	Liner Service Network Structure – Cluster variable		-
	LSNS_{IJ2006}	Liner Service Network Structure – Cluster variable year 2006		-
	TEUdepl_{IJt}	Volume of TEU deployed between countries I and J in year t		-
$\text{Port}_{i,jt}$	$\text{PortIinfPCA1}_{i,j}$	Level of infrastructure development – Cluster variable (PCA1)		-
	$\text{ServLevPCA1}_{i,j}$	Level of service in port – Cluster variable (PCA1)		-
	$\text{PortInfEndowPCA2}_{i,j}$	Level of infrastructure development – Cluster variable (PCA2)		-
	$\text{PortQuayAccessPCA2}_{i,j}$	Quay access – Cluster variable (PCA2)		+
	$\text{PortAccessPCA2}_{i,j}$	Port access – Cluster variable (PCA2)		-
	ServicePort_{ijt}	Dummy for Service port operator model in port i and j in year t		+
	$\text{LandlordPort}_{ijt}$	Dummy for Landlord port operator model in port i and j in year t		+
	$\text{PortThrough}_{i,jt}$	Port throughput in TEU in port i and j in year t		-
$\text{Inst}_{I,Jt}$	OpenReg_{ijkt}	Dummy for use of open registry flagged vessel in transport of product k between i and j in year t		-
	PubCoru_{It}	Level of public corruption in country I in year t		+
	NumCar_{IJt}	Number of shipping lines offering services between I and J in year t		-

Table 4.1 *Continued*

Group	Variable	Description	m_n	Expected sign
	Carrier number $\leq 4_{IJt}$			+
	$Agre_{ijt}$	Price fixing agreements on route IJ		+
	$Imbal_{I,Jt}$	Trade imbalance of I or J respectively in containerized trade in year t		-/+

Source: Author

Explanatory Notes

- Interpretation of categorical variables not possible in the form β x category. Introduction of binary indicator variable for n − 1 categories, where n = number of categories. Selection of one variable as reference category. Interpretation of binary variables in relation to reference category.
- The results of the study have full value solely for the observations made in this work.
- This study focuses on containerized cargoes in intra LAC trade in the period between year 2000 and 2006.

Summary

This chapter described the use of Factor Analysis in the specific concept of Principal Component Analysis as a means to controlling the high level of correlation between the variables describing determinants of maritime transport costs and also to reducing the level of complexity.

A detailed description of the principle database BTI and the other relevant data sources is given. Evidence is given for the uniqueness of using the dataset in its disaggregated form and particularly the possibility to calculate freight per ton, excluding the insurance costs. Following, the dependent variable – maritime transport costs – and the independent variables are defined scientifically. This is a keystone in the analysis as it allows controlling the numerous inputs into the regression model.

Besides the definition of the variables, this chapter develops a transport cost model presenting the complexity of influencing factors as discussed in the previous chapters. The transport cost model is used for deriving estimates of transport costs determinants. The final version of the model in logarithmic form is used for estimating the cross-sectional and panel data as presented in the following chapter.

Chapter 5

Revealing the Complexity of
Maritime Transport Costs –
Empirical Results and Analysis

Introduction

This chapter describes the results of the OLS estimations for the defined transport equation. In equation 4.10 the dependent variable is the maritime transport cost per ton of exports on 261 trade routes within LAC. In order to explain the effect of single explanatory variables on transport costs the following sequence of models (see Figure 5.1) was estimated. In order to explain specific determinants of transport costs the regression analysis composes of two steps:

In a first step a set of models is only estimated for the year 2006 data. The data of determinants is the most complete and widest available for this year. The cross-sectional analysis allows identifying pattern and relationships determination based on the hypotheses derived in this work (see Chapter 1). As this analysis has not been performed with the 2006 data set before, this step also serves the verifications of previous findings (e.g. Wilmsmeier and Sánchez 2009, Wilmsmeier 2003, Wilmsmeier and Martínez-Zarzoso 2010, Micco and Perez 2001, Sánchez et al. 2003 etc) on a new data set. Further in comparison to earlier studies the geographical reach of the study is increased.

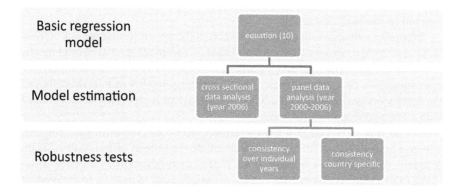

Figure 5.1   Model sequence

Source: Author

In a second step a set of models is estimated using panel data covering the period 2000–2006. The panel data analysis allows confirming the results found in the estimation for 2006 over time. This part of the analysis particularly focuses on revealing the consistency of determinants over time. This will also confirm the validity of the hypotheses for the period under study, and particularly the verification of Liner Shipping Network Structures as a determinant of maritime transport costs. Previously, this was only analysed by Wilmsmeier and Zarzoso (2009) for the period 1999–2004.

In the following the formulated hypotheses are discussed for both sets of models. The regressors are progressively introduced in the estimated models.

Maritime Transport Costs in Intra-Latin American Trade

This section gives an overview on the level and evolution of maritime transport costs in Latin America in the period under study.

Costs of maritime transport remained quite steady over the years and decreased significantly if compared to the price of other goods and services. The incidence of transport costs in the value of goods decreases (e.g. the freight of a barrel of crude drops from 25 per cent of the price of the barrel in 1960 to 5 per cent in 1990). The elasticity of demand falls resulting in greater negative effects of monopolies and collusion. Further, a paradox: the shipping service is less expensive but more important.

The usual argument about falling importance of transport, suffers from a number of problems:

First, although the average per unit cost of transport have been reduced, overall transport costs have generally not decreased, because the amount and length of transport have increased as rapidly as the unit costs have decreased. Thus in spite of reduced transport costs the size of the transport sector as a per cent of GDP has generally not decreased, and the availability of infrastructures and services has become increasingly important.

Secondly, although unit costs of transport and communication have decreased they have not decreased equally for all types of commodities and consignments, all types of communication and all origins and destinations. In fact transport and communication costs depend increasingly on the availability of infrastructure and the density of demand on specific links. Latin America is especially disadvantaged with a low and dispersed demand.

For an approximation of international transport costs, the difference between CIF and FOB values is usually used to estimate the burden of transport costs on products. Analysis of the relation of the freight costs (excluding insurance costs) to the FOB value reveals that the burden of freight costs in relation to the product value has actually been almost constant or even reducing for some product groups (e.g. food products). In a first approach the evolution of freight and insurance margins for containerized cargoes in intra-Latin American trade are depicted in

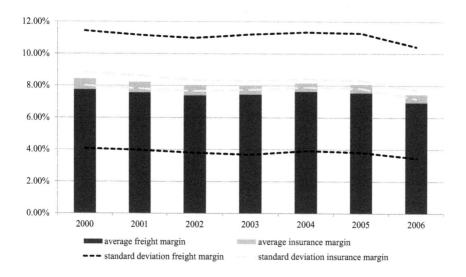

Figure 5.2   Evolution of freight and insurance margins, intra-Latin American trade, year 2000–2006

Source: Author, based on BTI 2000–2006

Figure 5.2. The average margins reduce from 7.87 per cent in 2000 to 6.75 per cent in 2006. Freight margins in the same period oscillated between 0.35 per cent and 0.42 per cent. The standard deviation amplitude of freight margins calculated at individual product level reduces about 1.5 per cent for freight and insurance margins. At first sight the impression is created that freight costs have reduced in the region. However, this impression is false. The reductions of freight margins originate from an increased average unit value and an only minimal reduction of freight per ton. Consequently, the use of margins needs to be handled carefully and with the necessary comments on the potential interpretations of findings. Wilmsmeier and Sánchez (2009) and Wilmsmeier (2009) found particular evidence for this phenomena and danger when analysing the evolution of international transport costs for food products.

In a second step the freight and insurance margins for different products groups are described (Figure 4.3). While insurance margins are relatively stable across all product groups, freight margins vary significantly across these groups. The stability of insurance margins originates from the high correlation between insurance costs and the product value. The figure therefore also underlines the problems mentioned in Chapter 2 with using CIF/FOB margins as the dependent variables in analysis of maritime transport cost determinants, particularly when using aggregated figures. One observation from Figure 5.3 is relevant as it hints towards the different susceptibility of product groups to changes in freight rates.

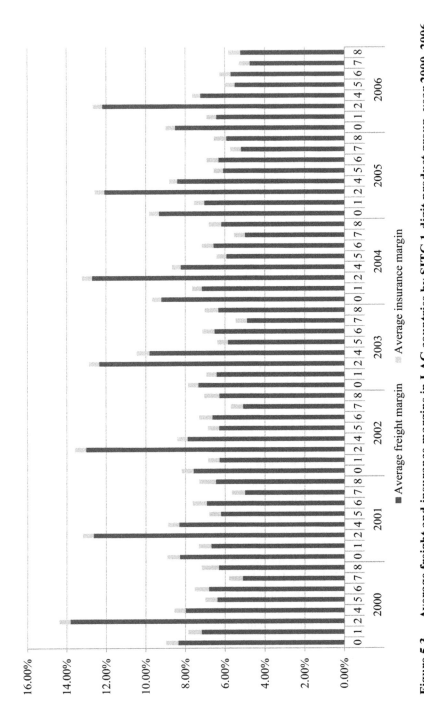

Figure 5.3   Average freight and insurance margins in LAC countries by SITC 1-digit product group, year 2000–2006

Source: Author based on BTI data 2000–2006

Especially, lower value goods have a higher margin of transport costs and therefore are likely to be more sensitive to changes in freight.

This first approximation underlines the need for more detailed analysis of the evolution of transport costs.

Freight margins and maritime transport costs per ton differ at country level for Latin American and Caribbean countries. Keeping in mind that the level of freight margin significantly depends on the structure of traded goods and therefore makes the numbers at aggregate level difficult to use for comparison, the figures vary in the average freight margin between 4 per cent (Anguilla) and 17.4 per cent (Argentina). For a detailed analysis of trade and transport profiles of Latin American countries please see Latin American Modal Split in International Transport – Year 2006 and Hoffmann, Perez and Wilmsmeier (2002).

The restriction of this type of aggregated data and analysis starts to show when analysing the average freight rates per ton. Average transport costs per ton over the period under study range from just over US$ 200 per ton to US$ 1100 per ton. The significant variation in the amplitude of the standard deviation hints at the significant variations depending on the product and composition of trade. In this case it relates to the differences in composition on exports to other LAC countries.

In order to be able to interpret the impact of transport costs on the competitiveness of Latin American countries and to understand the structure of these in more depth, analysis is required. Despite continued growth in maritime trade, deployment of bigger ships and port development average international maritime transport costs margins still exceeds those of other regions (Table 2.1). Detailed analysis is required in order to understand how far this general impression originates from the differences in the composition of traded products in comparison to other regions and further underlying determinants. In order to reach this the chapter elaborates on the complexity of international transport cost determinants.

Cross Sectional Data Analysis

Tables 5.1, Table 5.2 and Table 5.3 include the OLS estimation for the transport cost equation. Data are for 2006. The database includes 134,212 observations after incomplete data and outliers are excluded from the empirical analysis. Each observation corresponds to a given transaction, k. Hence the above mentioned number of observations refers to the variables TC_{ijk}, $ProdTradeVol_{ijk}$ and $UVal_{ijk}$. The dependent variable is maritime transport costs per ton of exports on 261 trade routes in 2006.

Distance and Liner Shipping Network Structures

In order to test for the relevance of Liner Shipping Network Structures (LSNS) in comparison to distance (Hypotheses 1 and 7) the first set of regressions (Table 5.2) includes only the variables D_{IJ} and $LSNS_{IJ2006}$ (Models A–C in Table 5.2)

Hypothesis 1 Distance matters only indirectly in the determination of freight rates by shipping companies. Distance most likely is a proxy for voyage time related costs e.g. manning or fuel costs, but does neither reflect market structures nor network configurations, which determine the ascertained distance in trade.

Hypothesis 7 Liner Service Network Structure (LSNS) is an important determinant of international maritime transport costs. The position within a network describes the ascertained distance and thus has become increasingly important in identifying a country or ports position with the global shipping network. Particularly as hub and spoke network structures have been emerging and potentially impose significant deviations on actual cargo flows.

These hypotheses can be tested by evaluating their individual explanatory value in the regression model and by observing and comparing the behaviour of the Beta coefficients. The obtained results show that Liner Shipping Network Structure explains 7.4 per cent of the variation of the dependent variable transport costs (Model A); whereas distance explains 9.4 per cent (Model C).

$LSNS_{IJ2006}$ is significant at the 1 per cent level and displays a negative sign, indicating that a greater number of shipping opportunities, services deploying bigger vessels, a greater number of deployed ships and of competing shipping lines reduces transport costs to a slightly lesser extent than geographical distance increases transport costs.

Geographical maritime distance between main ports is significant at the 1 per cent level and has the expected sign. Longer distances increase maritime transport costs. The estimated distance elasticity is 0.29 (Model C). A 10 per cent increase in distance, raises transport costs by 2.9 per cent. This is in line with elasticities found in earlier studies. Wilmsmeier and Martínez-Zarzoso (2009) find elasticities of 0.21 while Wilmsmeier et al. (2006) show elasticity as being slightly higher, between 0.33 and 0.38, for intra-Latin American maritime trade. Hummels (1999b) estimates the distance coefficient as between 0.2 and 0.3 for different commodities.

Liner Service Network Structure displays an elasticity of 0.26 (Model A). LSNS sustains its level of impact in the further models when additional variables are introduced. When both variables (D_{ij} and $LSNS_{IJ2006}$) are introduced into the model the Beta coefficients vary significantly. Further, modelling tests have shown that the Beta coefficients for the variable distance (D_{ij}) vary significantly. The author argues that the variable Liner Shipping Network Structure ($LSNS_{ij2006}$) might be a better variable to describe the relation between two trading partners as it measures ascertained distance – the impact of the position within a network. Ascertained distance can vary significantly from geographic distance (Janelle 1991). Consequently, the author argues that maritime distance is more likely a proxy for voyage time related costs e.g. manning or bunker costs or information barrier. However, as freight rates reflect administered prices the use of distance

Table 5.1   Regression results – Impact of liner shipping network structure, cargo characteristics and trade imbalance, 2006

Model	A	B	C	D	E
(Constant)	4.852	3.337	2.777	1.952	2.153
	(1748.168)	(145.393)	(145.072)	(128.615)	(134.263)
$LSNS_{IJ2006}$	–0.263	–0.141		–0.248	–0.238
	(–96.063)	(–43.421)		(–98.035)	(–93.929)
Maritime distance$_{ij}$ (ln)		0.214	0.292		
		(66.473)	(109.183)		
Maritime trade imbalance$_I$				0.001	0.001
				(10.898)	(8.395)
Maritime trade imbalance$_J$				–0.262	–0.272
				(–39.375)	(–41.396)
Unit value$_{ijk}$ (ln)				0.413	0.407
				(235.961)	(233.499)
Volume of shipment$_{ijk}$ (ln)				–0.078	–0.08
				(–76.513)	(–78.919)
Reefer$_{ijk}$ (dummy)				0.402	0.384
				(16.689)	(16.039)
Landlord port model$_{ij}$ (dummy)					–0.19
					(–35.439)
Open Registry$_{ijk}$ (dummy)					–0.009
					(–1.87)
R^2	0.074	0.109	0.094	0.466	0.472
F	9228.121	7001.037	11920.95	13860.54	14189.37
N	115 122	115 122	115 122	134212	134212

Notes: T-statistics are given in brackets. The dependent variable is the freight rate per ton of transporting good k from the exporting country I to the importing country J in natural logarithms. All explanatory variables, excluding LSNS, imbalances and dummies, are in natural logarithms. Models A–D were estimated by OLS. The estimation uses White's heteroscedasticity-consistent standard errors. Data are for the year 2006

as a proxy for time related costs might be biased. The decision as to whether to accept or reject the hypotheses 1 and 7 cannot be made definite at this point of the analysis, but has to be decided when interpreting the panel data analysis. This originates from the fact the LSNS is time variant in difference to distance and thus only if the significance and comparable impact on maritime transport costs of LSNS is consistent over time, the hypotheses can be accepted.

Implications from Trade Structure and Cargo Characteristics

In Models D and E variables describing the implications of trade structures and cargo characteristics are introduced. All models are significant at the 99 per cent level. Progressive introduction of explanatory variables (Table 5.7) increases the explanatory value of the model from 10.9 per cent (Model B) to 47.2 percent (Model E).

To test hypothesis 6 the results have to be interpreted for the exporting and the importing country individual, because a similar imbalance has different implications on costs depending on the point of view from the country.

> *Hypothesis 6* Liner companies know that recurrently on one of the legs of the turnaround trip, the percentage of vessel capacity utilization will be lower, and therefore adapt pricing schemes to the direction of the trip and to its corresponding expected cargo. Unidirectional excess capacity will increase the competition between the various liner services, and as a result freight rates will tend to be lower.

In Models D-K (Table 5.2 and Table 5.3) the trade imbalances for the exporting country I and the importing country J are introduced. Both variables are significant at the 1 per cent level and have the expected signs. In relation to the way the imbalance was calculated the sign is positive for the exporting country I (maritime trade imbalance$_I$) and negative for the importing country J (maritime trade imbalance$_J$). This finding confirms Hypothesis 6 that liner companies will adapt pricing schemes to the direction of the trip and to its corresponding expected cargo. Hinting at shippers in a country that is a net exporter will pay comparably higher rates for exporting containers than for imports. Freight rates will be higher for the shipments transported on a leg of the trip with more traffic, as the total amount charged for this leg must compensate the relatively reduced income from the return trip, when part of the vessel's capacity will inevitably be taken up with repositioned empty containers. Excess capacity on the return trip will increase the competition between the various liner services, and as a result freight rates will tend to be lower.

The empirical results show exactly this. In case the ratio between exports and imports doubles transport costs in the exporting country I increase 0.1 per cent. In case the ratio between exports and imports doubles in the importing countries transport costs to that country reduce between 15.4 per cent and 28.4 per cent depending on the estimate model. The stronger influence in the importing country is logical as shipping lines will try to attract more cargo to container deficit regions and consequently will offer greater rebates to shippers importing countries to this country in order to avoid empty movements. At the same time the relatively small increase in transport costs in the exporting country relates to the price elasticity of the shipper. Here the shipper already pays the full cost to transport his cargo and increases can only be moderate as the shipping company does not want to discourage exports either. In order to fully accept Hypothesis 6 the results need to be confirmed in the panel data analysis. This is because in the case of the cross-sectional every imbalance is only observed once and, therefore, the imbalance estimates might be influenced by random effects.

In order to test Hypothesis 2 the variable unit value is introduced into the model.

> *Hypothesis 2* Traditional pricing strategies referring to the unit value of cargo continue to play a significant role in the construction of international maritime transport costs.

The estimated coefficient of unit value variable is positive and highly significant. An increase of 10 per cent in the unit value of the merchandise carried generates a 4.1 per cent increase in transport costs. These findings are significantly lower than those of Micco and Perez (2001). A main reason for this is the difference in the dependent variable. The dependent variable used in this work is exclusive insurance costs. In works that use CIF/FOB ratios insurance costs are always included in the dependent variable. Micco and Perez (2001, p. 15) therefore include a dummy variable for products at the six-digit level in their regression. They refer to Feenstra's (1996) who shows that there is a large variation in unit values, even at 10-digit-level. Feenstra (1996) provides the example of unit values of men's cotton shirts in US imports. According to his findings unit values range from $56 (Japan) to $1 (Senegal). He argues that these differences in unit values lead to large differences in insurance cost per kilogram, even for homogenous products.

Recognizing that the dependent variable is free of the influence of insurance costs using this unique database, the findings in this work still indicate that the more expensive the product, per unit of weight, the higher the transport costs. Following the earlier discussion on the determination of freight rates and industry's strategies, this empirical evidence therefore confirms the Hypothesis 2 that traditional pricing strategies referring to the unit value of cargo continue to play a significant role in the construction of international maritime transport costs. In particular, if goods are of very high value, the freight rate may effectively be charged irrespective of weight and measurement on an *ad valorem* basis. This practice potentially impedes the competitiveness of export products particularly from developing countries, especially if this strategy is paired with other barriers to trade.

Furthermore, a dummy for cargo transported in refrigerated containers is introduced in order to capture cargo characteristics in the estimation (Models D–F, Table 5.2) as set out in Hypothesis 3.

> *Hypothesis 3* Special transport conditions and needs for certain types of cargo are reflected in the structure of international maritime transport costs.

The requirement to use reefer container has a positive effect on the dependent variable and the results show that refrigerated cargoes pay transport costs between 49.5 per cent (Model D) and 46.8 per cent (Model E) higher than non-refrigerated cargo. These findings are comparable to earlier studies (Hoffmann 2001, Wilmsmeier 2003, Martínez-Zarzoso et al. 2006; Wilmsmeier and Sánchez 2009, Wilmsmeier and Martínez-Zarzoso 2010). The higher transport costs can be explained by the energy use of reefer containers in comparison to standard containers, different handling requirements and the costs for monitoring during their voyage. Consequently, Hypothesis 3 is confirmed.

Finally, the reducing effect of economies of scale (volume of shipment) on transport costs are analysed to test for hypothesis in Models D–F (Table 5.1).

> *Hypothesis 4* The circumstantial evidence for investigating scale economies in shipping can be seen by examining freight costs for large versus small exporters.

A 10 per cent increase in the volume of a shipment implies a 0.78 per cent (Model D) reduction in maritime transport costs, indicating that shipping lines are likely to give lower freight rates to high volume shippers. These values oscillate between 0.74 per cent and 0.88 per cent in the further model estimations (Table 5.2 and Table 5.3). As this variation in the Beta coefficient also hints towards some interaction with other independent variables it can be interpreted that a certain variability in freight rates for a similar service, depending on the exported volume and underlines the existence of certain negotiation margins between agents, but potentially to a certain extent also depends on the direction of trade imbalances and/or the LSNS.

The Influence of Open Registries

> *Hypothesis 15* The use of open registry flags is mirrored in reduced transport costs. The use of open registry vessel also is an indicator for free competition. When there are restrictions these may lead to both higher transport costs and the use of national flags.

In order to test Hypothesis 16 a dummy variable, which takes the value of one if the cargo is exported by a ship running an open registry flag (for discussion on open registries classifications see Hoffmann, Sánchez, Talley 2005), zero otherwise, is introduced. The obtained result (Models D, Table 5.2) shows that exports on ships running an open registry flag are 0.9 per cent lower in costs than exports using ships of other flags. This result is lower than those obtained by Wilmsmeier and Martínez-Zarzoso 2010). They estimate lower transport costs between 3.4 per cent and 6.5 per cent for the period 1999 to 2004, if open registries are used. Hoffmann et al. (2005) questioned whether the system of open registries is unfavourable for developing countries. The empirical findings indicate that Latin American exporters benefit from open registries in terms of maritime transport costs, which might contribute to the competitiveness of their products in destination countries. The findings indicate that shipping companies pass some of their cost savings when using open registry flags as identified by Tolofari (1989) on to the shipper. However, the impact of open registries on maritime transport costs seems to have changed in comparison to the earlier years. This would confirm Stopford's statement (2009, p. 673) that:

> ... open registries have, in the main, fallen in line with regulatory practice and this form of ownership has become less controversial than it was a decade ago.

Consequently, an adoption in regulatory practice in open registry countries might also have resulted in a reduction in cost differences between different flag states. This assumption will be further evaluated in the panel data analysis.

However, the use of open registry vessel is also an indicator for free competition. When there are restrictions these may lead to both higher transport costs and the use of national flags. Thus in order to fully accept Hypothesis 16 the results from the panel data analysis will have to be considered.

The Influence of Interfaces

In order to test for the influence the impact of ports on maritime transport costs the two sets of complex variables derived from PCA (see Chapter 5 p. 223) describing the port infrastructure and superstructure are introduced into the equation. These variables are used to test for Hypothesis 10.

> *Hypothesis 10* A good fit between different components of infra- and superstructure in the importing and exporting port should have a reducing impact on transport costs as it facilitates better performance in port operations.

All models are significant at the 99 per cent level. Progressive introduction of explanatory variables (Table 5.2) results in explanatory values of the models between 47.2 per cent (Model H) to 49.2 per cent (Model F).

Following Wilmsmeier et al. (2006) and Wilmsmeier and Hoffmann (2008), who argue that the fit between infrastructure endowment and port operator model in the exporting and importing country is decisive as only this condition allows to realize an efficient use of equipment, variables for the importing and exporting country are introduced simultaneously (Model F, Table 5.2).

The results imply that ports with a greater number of terminals, resulting in intra-port competition, greater storage capacity and total port area and a bigger number of berths and reefer points, as described with the cluster variable "port infrastructure endowment" ($PortIinfCA1_{i,j}$) have a reducing impact on transport costs. These findings are consistent for the exporting and for the importing country.

Further, a high service level represented by 24 hour operations for offices, receive and delivery and quayside, described by the cluster variable "service level" ($ServLevPCA1_{i,j}$), also results in lower transport costs.

Table 5.2   Regression results – Impact of port infrastructure endowment, 2006

Model	F	G	H
(Constant)	2.959 (61.375)	2.094 (134.225)	2.133 (132.942)
$LSNS_{IJ}$	−0.243 (−96.447)	−0.223 (−102.88)	−0.25 (−73.117)
Maritime trade imbalance$_I$	0.001 (5.898)	0.001 (7.175)	0.001 (8.317)
Maritime trade imbalance$_J$	−0.005 (−0.495)	−0.247 (−31.722)	−0.282 (−33.191)
Unit value$_{ijk}$ (ln)	0.417 (228.708)	0.401 (236.981)	0.4 (235.548)
Volume of shipment$_{ijk}$ (ln)	−0.074 (−71.229)	−0.081 (−82.524)	−0.081 (−82.791)
Reefer$_{ijk}$ (dummy)	0.395 (16.784)	0.302 (13.511)	0.302 (13.544)
Port infrastructure endowment$_i$	−0.04 (−20.323)		
Port service level cluster variable$_i$	−0.228 (−39.524)		
Port infrastructure endowment$_j$	−0.084 (−34.197)		
Port service level cluster variable$_j$	−0.054 (−8.674)		
Port accessibility PCA2$_i$		−0.088 (−19.68)	−0.076 (−16.407)
Port infrastructure endowment PCA2$_i$		−0.008 (−4.501)	−0.006 (−3.228)
Quay accessibility PCA2$_i$		0.027 (10.872)	0.024 (9.493)
Port accessibility PCA2$_j$		−0.382 (−67.329)	−0.388 (−68.057)
Port infrastructure endowment PCA2$_j$		−0.11 (−60.258)	−0.1 (−47.593)
Quay accessibility PCA2$_j$		0.278 (81.088)	0.273 (79.361)
Service port model$_{ij}$ (dummy)		0.535 (50.172)	0.544 (50.85)
Landlord port model$_{ij}$ (dummy)	−0.35 (−23.203)		−0.115 (−10.275)

Model	F	G	H
R^2	0.492	0.472	0.472
F	9766.401	9213.478	.8569.579
N	134 212	134 212	134 212

Notes: T-statistics are given in brackets. The dependent variable is the freight rate per ton of transporting good k from the exporting country I to the importing country J in natural logarithms. All explanatory variables, excluding LSNS, imbalances and dummies, are in natural logarithms. Models F–H were estimated by OLS. The estimation uses White's heteroscedasticity-consistent standard errors. Data are for the year 2006

These findings provide important hints to the influence of port operation on ship voyage costs. The results for the first cluster variable indicate how port infrastructure allows for realizing economies in scale. Also if the number of terminals in a port increases the theoretical likelihood of intra-port competition increases, which is expected to have a reducing impact on maritime transport costs. Secondly, 24 hour operations contribute to a reduction of a ship's turnaround time in ports. This has a reducing impact on a voyage's port costs.

However, the first set of cluster variables omits the important influence of a port's water access depth, which defines the maximum size of ships calling in a port. By introducing the second set of cluster variables this issue is addressed (Model G and H, Table 5.2).

Confirming the results found using the first set of port cluster variables, these results suggest that ports with a greater number of terminals and berths, bigger storage capacity and total port area as well as a higher number of electric reefer points, as described by the variable "infrastructure endowment" ($PortlinfEndowPCA2_{i,j}$) imply lower transport costs.

Further, a greater depth of the access channel, described by "general port accessibility" ($PortAccessPCA2_{i,j}$), also has a reducing impact on maritime transport costs. It can be argued that this allows for using bigger ships and consequently for economies of scale.

Finally, the model results indicate a greater pier depth and anchorage depth have an increasing positive impact on transport costs ($PortQuayAccessPCA2_{i,j}$). This is interpreted that greater pier depth will require dredging activity in a port which is then levied on the port costs of a ship and potentially passed on to the shipper.

Beyond infrastructure endowment previous studies have discussed the influence of port reform on maritime transport costs (Hoffmann 2001, Wilmsmeier 2003, Wilmsmeier et al. 2006). Expectations are that the port devolution process from service to landlord ports, beyond investment in infra- and superstructure also results in improved port performance. Improved performance is in general associated with reduced costs as well. In the following hypothesis 13 is tested for.

Hypothesis 13 Advances in port reform effectively reduce international maritime transport costs as it results in greater investment in infrastructure, higher productivity and thus improve port performance.

The model captures the effect of port operator models by introducing two dummy variables: a) takes the value of one if the ports associated with transaction k are both landlord ports and zero otherwise (Landlord$_{ij}$ Dummy), b) takes the value of one if the ports associated with transaction k are both service ports and zero otherwise (Service port$_{ij}$ Dummy). Both variables prove significant at the 1 per cent level and have the expected sign.

According to the models (Model E, Table 5.2 and Models F and H, Table 5.3) maritime transport costs are between 12.2 per cent (Model H) and 41.9 per cent (Model F) lower if both ports are landlord ports.

The results for the service port dummy variable show exactly the opposite (Models G and H, Table 5.2) maritime transport costs are between 70.7 per cent (Model G) and 72.3 per cent (Model H) higher if both ports are service ports.

When both port operator dummy variables are introduced the model proves significant. This model allows interpreting the results that cargo transported between two service ports faces the highest charges in comparison to all other combinations and at the same time that cargo transported between two landlord ports faces comparably less transport costs in comparison to all other combinations. Consequently, the hypothesis can be accepted for the cross-sectional analysis of year 2006 data.

The Influence of Market Structures

In a further step the model is tested for the impact of market structures, particularly for the influence of competition between shipping lines.

Hypothesis 9 International maritime transport costs are administered prices, which discriminated against weaker elements. If competition exists in a market international maritime transport costs should be lower in comparison to routes with oligopolistic or monopolistic characteristics.

First a variable representing the number of carriers is introduced. The results (Models I–P, Table 5.3) show that the variable has the expected negative sign and is significant, implying that a doubling in the number of shipping lines has a reducing impact between 2.1 per cent (Model I) and 3.8 per cent (Model J).

Considering the findings from Wilmsmeier and Hoffmann (2008) that competition does not increase gradually a dummy controlling for oligopolistic market structures that takes the value of one if the number of carriers is equal or less than four and zero otherwise is introduced (Models K–P, Table 5.3). The variable proves significant and has the expected positive sign. In markets with four or less carriers providing services transport costs are between 18.4 per cent (Model K) and 21.3 per cent (Model N) higher. These findings entail the discussion on the impact of absence of competition on transport costs.

The use of these dummy variables only controls for direct services between the exporting and importing country. All trade relations used in this analysis have a minimum of one carrier providing direct services. Therefore an analysis on the impact of obligatory transhipment is omitted in this analysis. For a discussion on the impact of transhipment on maritime freight rates see Wilmsmeier and Hoffmann (2008).

With regard to the variables referring to agreements between liners companies, none of them turns out to be significant at 5 per cent for this dataset. For the positive and significant impact of fixed-pricing agreements and the existence of cooperative agreements see Fink, Mattoo and Neagu (2002).

In the Models (M–P, Table 5.3) cargo and trade specific as well as port related variables and maritime distance are introduced. The models are significant at the 99 per cent level and the explanatory value of the models increases. All variables, except the trade imbalance variables, maintain their expected signs. The change in the sign of the trade imbalance variables opens a discussion on the interrelationship between trade imbalances and market competition. As stated in the discussion on the impact of imbalance on maritime transport costs, it can be assumed that the level of competition will have a significant impact on the pricing strategy to smooth imbalances. However, this issue requires further investigation that is beyond the scope of this work.

Further Considerations

Beyond the presented results all models were estimated using the dependent variable freight rate per measure (see Chapter 3, p. 86). The assumption that the inclusion of the stowage factor in the dependent variable provides a better reflection of reality, proved only partly successful, even though the models proved significant, the explanatory power of the models was lower compared to the ones using the freight cost per ton as the dependent variable. Further, investigation in this direction would be useful. The author sees one reason for the shortfall in explanatory power that the stowage factors for certain products that are subsumed within one 3-digit SITC product group vary so strongly that the used average does impact negatively on the explanatory value rather than improving it. Therefore research with stowage factors at the 5-digit SITC level might prove better results, but goes beyond the scope of this study.

The analysis of determinants related to port efficiency is omitted since no satisfactory empirical data on port efficiency indicators is available to the years under study. The author would like to refer to Sánchez et al. (2003) and Wilmsmeier et al. (2013) who present the only works that analyses the impact of port efficiency based on a significant empirical of port productivity and efficiency measures in LAC. Using PCA cluster variables they show that

> ... The coefficient related to Factor 2, 'port productivity', is negative and significant at 1% showing that increasing port efficiency implies a reduction in transport costs; that is, the greater the efficiency at port level, the lower the transport costs.

Table 5.3 Regression results – impact of maritime industry structures, 2006

Model	I	J	K	M	N	O	P
(Constant)	5.349 (920.169)	3.463 (141.957)	4.174 (42.833)	4.197 (39.455)	2.866 (34.214)	2.908 (32.21)	2.921 (30.905)
$LSNS_{IJ2006}$						-0.029 (-2.613)	-0.019 (-1.672)
Maritime distance$_{ij}$ (ln)		0.234 (79.466)	0.27 (77.203)	0.273 (70.592)	0.174 (53.674)	0.163 (48.866)	0.168 (44.852)
Maritime trade imbalance$_i$				-0.001 (-5.624)	0 (-2.819)		-0.002 (-5.244)
Maritime trade imbalance$_j$				0.016 (1.345)	0.027 (2.751)		0.021 (2.091)
Unit value$_{ijk}$ (ln)					0.388 (202.855)	0.389 (199.259)	0.39 (199.347)
Volume of shipment$_{ijk}$ (ln)					-0.086 (-80.556)	-0.085 (-78.382)	-0.085 (-78.112)
Reefer$_{ijk}$ (dummy)					0.31 (13.79)	0.346 (14.393)	0.345 (14.355)
Port infrastructure endowment$_i$			-0.034 (-15.188)	-0.037 (-15.875)	-0.235 (-38.791)	-0.235 (-36.733)	-0.241 (-36.887)
Port service level cluster variable$_i$			-0.132 (-26.301)	-0.135 (-26.121)	-0.512 (-23.587)	-0.528 (-23.338)	-0.535 (-23.432)
Port infrastructure endowment$_j$			-0.096 (-12.962)	-0.103 (-13.664)	-0.022 (-13.039)	-0.014 (-7.494)	-0.016 (-8.41)

	(1)	(2)	(3)	(4)	(5)	(6)	(7)
Port service level cluster variable$_j$			−0.176 (−6.575)	−0.19 (−6.898)	−0.07 (−16.917)	−0.069 (−16.284)	−0.07 (−16.336)
Landlord port model$_{ij}$ (dummy)			−0.139 (−9.731)	−0.142 (−8.908)	−0.066 (−5.188)	−0.067 (−5.297)	−0.066 (−4.936)
Carrier number ≤ 4$_{ij}$ (dummy)			0.169 (14.179)	0.178 (14.285)	0.193 (14.233)	0.183 (13.946)	0.191 (13.759)
Number of carriers$_{ij}$	−0.038 (−94.501)	−0.021 (−46.842)	−0.006 (−8.524)	−0.006 (−7.584)	−0.089 (−12.846)	−0.065 (−4.006)	−0.075 (−4.583)
R2	0.07	0.117	0.128	0.129	0.463	0.457	0.457
F	8930.488	7860.887	2158.709	1730.83	8764.508	8035.111	6891.312
N	118 341	118 341	118 341	118 341	118 341	118 341	118 341

Notes: T-statistics are given in brackets. The dependent variable is the freight rate per ton of transporting good k from the exporting country I to the importing country J in natural logarithms. All explanatory variables, excluding LSNS, imbalances and dummies, are in natural logarithms. Models F–H were estimated by OLS. The estimation uses White's heteroscedasticity-consistent standard errors. Data are for the year 2006

The coefficient for Factor 1, 'time inefficiency' has the expected sign, although it is not significant at the 5% level.

The coefficient for Factor 3, which is based on just one variable – the average stay per vessel – appears to be irrelevant to transport costs. Ships may stay longer because the port is less efficient, but also because their operators choose so in order to move more cargo or benefit from other services.

Finally, models including total trade volumes between countries I and J and a variable measuring the level of corruption in the importing country did not deliver expected results and in the context of the complexity of variables did not prove significant.

Panel Data Analysis, Year 2000–2006

The results presented in Table 5.1 to Table 5.3 clearly depict the complexity and interrelationship of the different components of the determinants influencing maritime transport costs for the year 2006. The main hypotheses were accepted for the cross-sectional models. However, the validity of the results in terms of consistency over time requires a discussion based on the panel data analysis results presented in this section.

Tables 5.6 to 5.8 include the OLS estimation for the transport cost equation (10). Data are for the years 2000–2006. The database includes 822,100 observations after incomplete data and outliers are excluded from the empirical analysis. Each observation corresponds to a given transaction, k in year t. Hence the abovementioned number of observations refers to the variables TC_{ijkt}, $ProdTradeVol_{ijkt}$ and $UVal_{ijkt}$. The dependent variable is maritime transport costs per ton of exports on 261 trade routes.

The panel data analysis progresses in three steps. First, in order to evaluate the effects of single explanatory variables and to confirm the findings from the cross-sectional results obtained for 2006, the regressors are progressively included in the estimated models. Year-dummy variables are introduced to test for the change of maritime transport costs against the reference year 2006. All dummies display significant and positive t-values. The results of the panel data show that transport costs have changed significantly in comparison to the reference year 2006.

Second, in order to test the consistency of keystone determinants over time two Models are estimated for each single year (Table 5.6 and Table 5.7).

Finally, in order to test for the robustness, models are estimated concerning three cases of a single importing country, Brazil, Argentina and Chile.

The Relevance of Individual Liner Shipping Network Variables

The progressing introduction of explanatory variables (Table 5.5) delivers an increasing explanatory value of the model from 36.6 per cent to 44.4 per cent. For all models, the estimated parameters have the expected signs. In Models

A_{panel} to E_{panel} the explanatory variables follow a comparable pattern of the models presented in the previous section. The goal is to reflect the underlying complexity and to confirm the findings for the reference year 2006 from the previous section.

In this first group of models the number of trade relations and geographic reach is kept constant in comparison to the previous model. Given a restriction in the use of the Liner Service Network Structure ($LSNS_{IJt}$) variable due to lack of data, this variable cannot be calculated for all 261 trade relations. In order to overcome this restriction single variables describing network structures to capture the effect of liner network structure as proxies are introduced.

In Models A_{panel} to E_{panel} the variables 'Frequency of Services' and 'Number of Services' are introduced. The bivariate correlation between these two variables of –0.518 is acceptable for the modelling. Both variables have the expected negative sign. The results for 'Frequency of Services' show that a 10 per cent increase of frequency, this means adding 10 per cent to the number of possibilities to ship a product between country I and J, reduces freight rates per ton by 15.1 and 9.8 per cent. The estimated coefficients for this variable are very high, but set into context seem reasonable. By way of example increasing the average frequency from two possibilities to four possibilities per month would be equal to duplicating the offered ship capacity, which could only be sustained by a comparable increase in trade volumes. Changes in the number of shipping possibilities will thus only take place at very low percentage level.

Interpreting the results for 'Number of Services', a 10 per cent increase in the number of services reduces between 2.61 per cent (Model B_{panel}) and 0.94 per cent (Model C_{panel}). The strong variation in the Beta coefficient comparing Model B_{panel} and Model C_{panel} hints towards the discussed problem of multi-collinearity. This can be resolved with the use of cluster variables derived from PCA.

While developing and testing various models, the variable 'Maritime Distance' was also introduced, but when introduced and omitting the individual liner shipping network structure variable, 'Maritime Distance' showed low Beta coefficients and did not improve the overall fit of the model. However, since the variable cluster LSNS was replaced by two single variables that do not capture the full complexity of the Liner Service Network Structure, it is necessary to construct a model which allows for a direct comparison. This is further described on page 96.

The Impact of Trade Structures Over Time

In Models C_{panel} to E_{panel} the variable 'TEU deployed' is also introduced. It has the expected negative sign and is significant. The TEU deployed in a region is used as a proxy for market size of maritime transport in a specific trade region. According to the models, a 10 per cent increase in TEU deployed in a trade region has an average reducing impact on transport costs between 1.24 per cent and 1.45 per cent. This can be interpreted as economies of scale that are realized in larger markets.

Table 5.4   Regression results – basic model – panel data, year 2000–2006

Model	A_{panel}	B_{panel}	C_{panel}	D_{panel}	E_{panel}
(Constant)	3.664 (129.089)	3.813 (129.958)	4.376 (139.721)	5.053 (154.188)	5.187 (157.803)
Unit value$_{ijkt}$ – ln	0.467 (587.749)	0.469 (588.898)	0.418 (505.666)	0.412 (500.958)	0.409 (497.819)
Frequency of shipping services$_{IJt}$ – ln	−1.517 (−90.917)	−1.603 (−93.226)	−0.98 (−57.312)	−1.216 (−68.969)	−1.392 (−78.145)
Number of services$_{IJt}$ – ln	−0.245 (−61.164)	−0.261 (−64.301)	−0.094 (−22.734)	−0.121 (−28.861)	−0.146 (−34.331)
Reefer$_{ijkt}$ (dummy)		0.267 (24.561)	0.33 (30.988)	0.325 (30.767)	0.321 (30.588)
Open registry$_{ijkt}$ (dummy)		−0.039 (−19.152)	−0.033 (−16.58)	−0.027 (−13.511)	−0.011 (−5.472)
Volume of shipment$_{ijkt}$ – ln			−0.088 (−183.877)	−0.092 (−192.306)	−0.093 (−195.425)
TEU deployed (region)$_{IJt}$ – ln			−0.124 (−80.291)	−0.145 (−93.002)	−0.14 (−85.519)
Maritime trade imbalance$_{It}$ (exporting country)				0.006 (69.57)	0.006 (64.528)
Maritime trade imbalance$_{Jt}$ (importing country)				−0.07 (−56.255)	−0.092 (−63.497)
Dummy year 2000					0.222 (59.645)
Dummy year 2001					0.224 (62.597)
Dummy year 2002					0.265 (66.639)
Dummy year 2003					0.112 (34.211)
Dummy year 2004					0.193 (51.781)
Dummy year 2005					0.156 (47.658)
R^2	0.366	0.367	0.402	0.41	0.444
F	117191.147	70625.116	58434.378	46915.671	28999.522
Number of observations	608 344	608 344	608 344	608 344	608 344

Notes: T-statistics are given in brackets. The dependent variable is the freight rate per ton of transporting good k from the exporting country I to the importing country J in natural logarithms. All explanatory variables, excluding LSNS, imbalances and dummies, are in natural logarithms. Models A_{Panel}–E_{Panel} were estimated by OLS. The estimation uses White's heteroscedasticity-consistent standard errors. Data are for the year 2000–2006

In reference to the hypotheses set out in Chapter 4 this result confirms Hypothesis 5, using the deployed capacity as a proxy for trade volume.

> *Hypothesis 5* Unit shipping costs decrease with the volume of trade due to the presence of density economies (as assumed by Behrens et al. 2006).

In Models D_{panel} and E_{panel} (Table 5.4) the trade imbalances for the exporting country I and the importing country J are introduced. Both variables are significant at the 1 per cent level and have the expected signs. In relation to the way the imbalance was calculated the sign is positive for the exporting country I (maritime trade imbalance$_I$) and negative for the importing country J (maritime trade imbalance$_J$). As these results underline the findings in the previous section and show that the impact imbalance might be consistent over time. This confirms Hypothesis 6: that liner companies will adapt pricing schemes according to the direction of the trip and to its corresponding expected cargo.

The Impact of Cargo Characteristics

The results suggest that the unit value of the cargo has a significant impact on maritime transport costs. Models A_{panel} to E_{panel} indicate that a 10 per cent increase in cargo value per ton increases average maritime transport costs between 4.1 per cent and 4.7 per cent. These findings reflect that the principles of 'traditional' tariffs, where shipping companies distinguish between different commodities, are still used in the region. In particular, if goods are of very high value, the freight rate may effectively be charged irrespective of weight and measurement on an *ad valorem* basis.

A dummy for cargo transported in refrigerated containers is introduced in D_{panel} and E_{panel} (Table 5.4). The requirement to use reefer container has a positive effect on the dependent variable and the results show that refrigerated cargoes involve charges between 30.6 per cent and 39 per cent higher than non-refrigerated cargo. These findings are comparable to the findings for the reference year 2006 and confirm earlier studies (Wilmsmeier and Martínez-Zarzoso 2010), reflecting the higher costs incurred by reefer container due to different handling requirements and energy consumption on board (for discussion on LAC reefer trade see Vagle 2012, 2013).

Furthermore, the reducing effect of economies of scale (volume of shipment) on transport costs is explained by the results in Models C_{panel} to E_{panel}. For the period under study a 10 per cent increase in the volume of a shipment implies a 0.88 to 0.93 per cent reduction in maritime transport costs, indicating that shipping lines are likely to give lower freight rates to high volume shippers. This also points towards a certain variability in freight rates for a similar service, depending on the exported volume and underlines the existence of certain negotiation margins between agents.

The findings described above imply that Hypothesis 2, Hypothesis 3 and Hypothesis 4 can also be accepted for the full period under study.

The Influence of Open Registries

According to Hypothesis 15: Open registries involve lower costs for shipping lines and results for the year 2006 show that these are reflected with a reducing influence in international maritime transport costs. In order to test if this argument holds over time a dummy variable, which takes the value of one if the cargo is exported by a ship running an open registry flag, zero otherwise, is introduced into the model. The obtained results (Models C_{panel} to E_{panel} in Table 5.4) show that exports on ships running an open registry flag are on average 1.1 to 4.0 per cent lower in costs than exports using ships of other flags. Thus, the findings confirm a positive impact of open registries for intra-Latin American trade over time. Yet, robustness tests estimating models for very single year need to show in how far a change in the level of influence can be observed over time. The author also expects differences in the use of open registries and their impacts for individual countries, the latter potentially being influenced by cabotage restrictions and the overall level of coastal shipping.

Comparing the Impact of Liner Shipping Network Structures (LSNS) and Distance

In order to test the significance of the Liner Service Network Structure ($LSNS_{IJt}$) cluster variable over time, similar models to the ones presented in Table 5.5 were estimated. This requires using a data set with reduced geographical scope of 64 bilateral trade routes.

The variables introduced in Model F_{panel} (Table 5.5) are all significant at the 1 per cent level. As expected the variable $LSNS_{IJt}$ has a negative sign. The results indicate that an improvement in the Liner Service Network Structure through using bigger ships, at greater frequency, with a greater number of services and more ships can have a decreasing influence on maritime transport costs between 33.3 per cent and 36.6 per cent. These findings again underpin the relevance of liner shipping networks and the relevance of the combination of individual components as a determinant of transport costs for the complete period under study.

The other variables in the model display the expected signs and coefficients comparable to the earlier model estimations. However, two exceptions have to be addressed. The variables controlling for the influence of imbalance in the exporting and the year dummy variable for 2003 change their signs. Since the combination of trade relations is altered the author expects that country specific effects that are not controlled for lead to a change in the sign. These country specific effects require further investigation.

In Model G_{panel} (Table 5.5) the role of distance as an influencing factor on determinants of transport costs is tested. The model includes the same variables

Table 5.5 Regression results – comparing the impact of LSNS and distance – panel data, 2000–2006

Model	F_{panel}	G_{panel}
(Constant)	2.046	1.726
	(170.283)	(239.166)
Unit value$_{ijkt}$ – ln	0.398	0.400
	(343.232)	(573.810)
Liner shipping network structure LSNS$_{IJt}$)	−0.332	
	(−200.455)	
Maritime distance$_{ij}$ – ln		0.004
		(204.356)
Maritime corridor$_{IJ}$ (dummy)	−0.094	−0.280
	(−25.568)	(−126.057)
Reefer$_{ijkt}$ (dummy)	0.365	0.292
	(34.510)	(32.893)
Open registry$_{ijkt}$ (dummy)	−0.036	−0.062
	(−13.988)	(−35.968)
Volume of shipment$_{ijkt}$ – ln	−0.104	−0.086
	(−175.585)	(−216.536)
TEU deployed (region)$_{IJt}$ ln	−0.001	0.002
	(−18.313)	(27.390)
Maritime trade imbalance$_{It}$ (exporting country)	−0.003	−0.001
	(−86.311)	(−64.494)
Maritime trade imbalance$_{Jt}$ (importing country)	−0.009	0.014
	(−5.172)	(10.981))
Corruption$_{Jt}$	0.009	0.017
	(8.906)	(24.165)
Dummy year 2000	0.068	0.099
	(14.408)	(31.217)
Dummy year 2001	0.057	0.073
	(12.568)	(24.047)
Dummy year 2002	0.095	0.046
	(18.197)	(12.915)
Dummy year 2003	−0.036	−0.097
	(−8.554)	(−35.105)
Dummy year 2004	0.139	0.001
	(32.272)	(0.370)
Dummy year 2005	0.200	0.92
	(43.094)	(30.268)
R^2	0.543	0.460
F	26565.982	43725.645
Number of observations	357 706	822 100

Notes: T-statistics are given in brackets. The dependent variable is the freight rate per ton of transporting good k from the exporting country I to the importing country J in natural logarithms. All explanatory variables, excluding LSNS, imbalances and dummies, are in natural logarithms. Models F_{Panel}–GE_{Panel} were estimated by OLS. The estimation uses White's heteroscedasticity-consistent standard errors. Data are for the year 2000–2006 as Model F_{panel} (Table 5.6), but the variable $LSNS_{IJt}$ was replaced by the variable 'maritime distance'. The variable 'maritime distance' proves significant at the 1 per cent level and has the expected positive sign. However, the explanatory power of the model reduces to 45.9 per cent of the variance. Further, the estimated coefficient for distance is significantly lower than in previous studies (Wilmsmeier 2003, Micco and Perez 2001, Sánchez et al. 2003, Wilmsmeier et al. 2006, Wilmsmeier and Martínez-Zarzoso 2010).

Further, it can be observed that the other variables remain significant and present comparable Beta coefficients as in Model F_{panel}. One exception is the variable 'TEU deployed' showing an unexpected positive sign. The results presented in this section surmise that:

> *Hypothesis 1* Distance matters only indirectly in the determination of freight rates by shipping companies. Distance most likely is a proxy for voyage time related costs e.g. manning or fuel costs, but does neither reflect market structures nor network configurations, which determine the ascertained distance in trade.

and

> *Hypothesis 7* Liner Service Network Structure (LSNS) is an important determinant of international maritime transport costs. The position within a network describes the ascertained distance and thus has become increasingly important in identifying a country or ports position with the global shipping network. Particularly as hub and spoke network structures have been emerging and potentially impose significant deviations on actual cargo flows.

should be accepted.

The Consistency of Determinants Over Time

In a next step the consistency of determinants over time is tested, using two comprehensive models based on the findings in the earlier sections. Each model is estimated for each single year in the period under study in order to be able to compare the coefficient for the variables over time.

The first model (Table 5.6) particularly tests for the consistency of the Liner Shipping Network Structure cluster variable. The estimated coefficients for unit value, reefer, open registry, volume of shipment and maritime trade imbalance (exporting country) are very stable over time. The estimated coefficients for Liner Shipping Network Structure, maritime corridor, reefer and maritime trade imbalance (importing country) are displaying small variations. These variations potentially originate e.g. from restructuring in the liner network or changes in reefer trade, but cannot be explained further at this level of analysis. Particular restrictions are given by the fact that data are annual, thus seasonal effects within a

Table 5.6   Regression results – variation over time – liner shipping network structure (LSNS)

	2000	2001	2002	2003	2004	2005	2006	Beta variation
(Constant)	1.784 (57.549)	1.799 (54.157)	1.949 (62.788)	2.016 (77.329)	2.29 (90.114)	2.404 (74.898)	2.414 (90.91)	0.63
Unit value (US$/ton) $\ln_{ijk}$	0.428 (128.788)	0.424 (135.008)	0.421 (131.432)	0.409 (142.715)	0.38 (138.856)	0.382 (112.061)	0.366 (128.107)	0.062
Liner shipping network structure$_{IJ}$	−0.272 (−53.515)	−0.282 (−57.754)	−0.338 (−70.614)	−0.376 (−87.748)	−0.35 (−88.07)	−0.297 (−58.199)	−0.37 (−86.219)	0.104
Maritime corridor$_{IJ}$	−0.145 (−12.643)	−0.144 (−14.224)	−0.139 (−14.2)	−0.101 (−11.983)	−0.091 (−10.295)	−0.134 (−11.52)	−0.007 (−0.845)	0.138
Reeferijk	0.339 (11.311)	0.344 (11.791)	0.294 (10.245)	0.4 (15.912)	0.433 (16.968)	0.359 (11.867)	0.307 (11.391)	0.139
Open registry$_{ijk}$	−0.019 (−2.51)	−0.01 (−1.366)	−0.016 (−2.222)	−0.05 (−8.459)	−0.028 (−4.967)	−0.016 (−2.006)	−0.039 (−6.227)	0.04
Volume of shipment$_{ijk}$ ln	−0.107 (−61.215)	−0.102 (−61.373)	−0.108 (−66.008)	−0.103 (−72.513)	−0.097 (−70.662)	−0.1 (−58.798)	−0.106 (−73.412)	0.011
Maritime trade imbalance$_{It}$ (exporting country)	−0.001 (−17.879)	−0.003 (−20.42)	−0.002 (−24.346)	−0.003 (−33.142)	−0.003 (−40.451)	−0.003 (−29.447)	−0.005 (−47.679)	0.004
Maritime trade imbalance$_{Jt}$ (importing country)	0.041 (3.979)	0.072 (6.954)	−0.038 (−8.996)	−0.102 (−17.138)	−0.015 (−4.769)	−0.018 (−2.541)	−0.059 (−6.761)	0.174
R^2	0.575	0.563	0.580	0.560	0.512	0.514	0.501	
F	6216.703	6807.403	7457.782	9419.292	8961.343	5867.574	7964.537	
N	36 749	42 318	43 211	59137	68 361	44 453	63 477	

Notes: T-statistics are given in brackets. The dependent variable is the freight rate per ton of transporting good k from the exporting country I to the importing country J in natural logarithms. All explanatory variables, excluding LSNS and dummies, are also in natural logarithms. All Models were estimated by OLS. The estimation uses White's heteroscedasticity-consistent standard errors. Data are for the years 2000–2006

Table 5.7 Regression results – variation over time – individual liner shipping network structure variables

	2000	2001	2002	2003	2004	2005	2006	Beta variation
(Constant)	2.303 (33.93)	10.804 (64.009)	5.959 (59.39)	4.993 (46.211)	6.41 (112.065)	7.12 (86.518)	5.959 (105.916)	8.501
Frequency of shipping services$_{Dt}$	-0.405 (-9.503)	-5.229 (-54.591)	-2.374 (-43.605)	-1.868 (-34.751)	-3.741 (-93.503)	-1.989 (-53.336)	-2.194 (-63.992)	4.824
Number of services$_{Dt}$	0.019 (1.873)	-0.58 (-42.201)	-0.338 (-29.668)	-0.417 (-29.102)	-0.038 (-4.33)	-0.936 (-55.708)	-0.497 (-64.231)	0.955
Maritime trade imbalance$_{It}$ (exporting country)	0.002 (15.05)	0.003 (20.291)	0 (-0.158)	0.004 (14.924)	0 (7.266)	0 (1.417)	0.001 (14.016)	0.004
Maritime trade imbalance$_{Jt}$ (importing country)	0.174 (18.275)	-0.865 (-52.2)	-0.169 (-43.95)	-0.143 (-20.029)	-0.202 (-67.291)	-0.335 (-42.282)	-0.413 (-64.062)	1.039
Unit value (US$/ton)$_{ijk}$ ln	0.405 (183.452)	0.404 (199.872)	0.414 (201.34)	0.436 (259.852)	0.405 (241.162)	0.455 (225.77)	0.43 (257.776)	0.051
Volume of shipment$_{ijk}$ –ln	-0.099 (-82.051)	-0.087 (-78.239)	-0.091 (-81.059)	-0.073 (-78.53)	-0.065 (-70.961)	-0.063 (-56.03)	-0.065 (-68.677)	0.036
Reefer$_{ijk}$	0.298 (11.704)	0.333 (12.98)	0.362 (14.444)	0.495 (22.97)	0.473 (21.055)	0.384 (15.17)	0.332 (15.446)	0.197
Brazil (dummy)	0.106 (16.359)	0.181 (30.603)	0.248 (44.042)	0.332 (68.639)	0.417 (82.785)	0.317 (48.17)	0.292 (55.187)	0.311
Maritime corridor$_{IJ}$ (dummy)	-0.455 (-71.593)	-0.504 (-84.814)	-0.441 (-73.698)	-0.332 (-59.755)	-0.207 (-41.352)	-0.163 (-24.747)	-0.152 (-29.336)	0.352
R^2	0.483	0.488	0.492	0.459	0.418	0.445	0.425	
F	8589.101	10149.496	10049.712	12935.921	12220.619	8965.465	12220.174	
N	82729	95884	93323	137428	152967	100513	148692	

Notes: T-statistics are given in brackets. The dependent variable is the freight rate per ton of transporting good k from the exporting country I to the importing country I in natural logarithms. All explanatory variables, excluding LSNS and dummies, are also in natural logarithms. All Models were estimated by OLS. The estimation uses White's heteroscedasticity-consistent standard errors. Data are for the years 2000–2006 year cannot be captured. The latter would be particularly interesting in the case of reefer trades. All coefficients are significant at the 1 per cent level.

In order to overcome the above described restriction of only having a restricted geographic reach within LAC of 64 bilateral trade relations a further model was estimated. In this model the cluster variable LSNS is replaced by single liner service network structure variables (for comparison see Chapter 4, p. 82). This allows for testing the consistency of the results as presented in Table 5.4)

The second model (Table 5.7) in its estimation focuses on cargo characteristics and trade imbalances. The coefficients for maritime trade imbalance (exporting country), unit value and volume of shipment are very stable. However, high variations show in the Beta coefficient for frequency of shipping services, number of services, maritime trade imbalance (importing country), reefer (Dummy), Brazil (Dummy) and the maritime corridor (Dummy) show the weakness of the individual Liner Shipping Network Structure variables, which are not able to capture the complexity of the network and thus are weak proxies over time. All coefficients are significant at the 1 per cent level.

Robustness of the Model

A series of robustness tests follows. First, Model F_{panel} except the variables referring to the importing country is estimated individually for Brazilian, Argentinean and Chilean imports. To be precise, of the 822,100 that enter in the panel regressions, 36,815, 59,473 and 32,827 concern a single importer, respectively.

The results show that the year dummies for all countries are positive and statistically significant at the 1 per cent level. One exception is the year dummy 2002 for Brazil, which does not return significant.

The coefficient Liner Shipping Network Structures (LSNS) is significant at the 1 per cent level and shows the expected sign. Brazil shows the lowest coefficient and Chile the highest. One assumption could be that the service liner network structure is more strongly impacting on peripheral countries. The coefficient of the variable 'unit value' is significantly lower for Brazil than for the complete sample and Argentina and Chile, which might hint in differences in product structure of varying pricing strategies from shipping lines in the countries.

Results for the variable open registry are varying. This implies that use of open registry regulation impacts differently on countries. Particularly interesting is to observe the difference between Brazil and Argentina. The main between these two countries is that all Argentinean external maritime containerized trade is basically moved through the port of Buenos Aires, being the end points within the liner shipping networks on the ECSA routes. At the same time Brazilian containerized trade is moved through a significant number of different ports spread along its coastline adjacent to the country's economic and population centres.

In the ECSA market cooperation with regional partners, like Alianca, Maruba, Libra-Montemar is a key to success as only this type of alliance allows overcoming Brazilian and Argentinean cabotage restrictions, which is of high importance, considering the extensive coastlines of the two countries. CSAV operates a Brazilian sister company to overcome the challenge of cabotage restrictions in Brazil. A Maersk and HSDG group uses Alianca as the 'entry card' to capture intra Brazilian trade, since Buenos Aires is the last and only port of call in the calling pattern of that group an Argentinean partners is not decisive. Both strategies aim at overcoming restrictions to realizing economies of density in the trade. Observing the expansion of the market share of these groups in the different ECSA trades seems proof for success of this strategy (see also Brooks, Wilmsmeier and Sánchez 2013).

Following this line of argument it can be assumed that the strategies of shipping lines to overcome market restrictions have a positive (freight reducing) impact on transport costs in Brazil, as more open registry vessels are operating in that market. However, to conclusively analyse the impact of open registry a full sample of all the countries' maritime trade would need to be analysed, which seems a logical step in follow-up research to this work.

The coefficient for the variable 'volume of shipment' is slightly higher for Brazil than for the complete sample, Argentina and Chile, showing that Brazil is able to exploit economies of scale in transport more than other LAC countries.

Summary

This chapter has presented the empirical results from the regression analyses that form the heart of this research. The results were used to test the hypotheses set out in this work based on the theoretic discussions presented in Chapter 4. What differentiates this work from previous studies on this subject is that both cross-sectional and panel data have been collected and analysed at the level of individual products. Another distinguishing feature of the analysis presented is that it uses freight rate per ton exclusive of insurance costs as the dependent variable. A further main differentiator is that this work is developed through the 'geographical' lens, but instead of insisting on the geographical measure of distance as an influencing factor of maritime trade, recognizes, evaluates and proves the space transforming role of networks. Thus the work puts the shipping lines and shippers in the centre of the discussion, because it is their actions and strategies that construct the network that facilitates maritime transport and thus determines the 'economic distance' between two countries.

Recognizing the role of network structures and understanding their complexity and interdependencies has also permitted to use the concept of principal component analysis to capture this complexity and 'make it' manageable in regression analysis.

However, beyond these benefits the use of panel data analysis, by being aware of the restrictions of annual data, has permitted the comparative assessment of the consistency of the results obtained from the exploration of the data using regression analysis.

Table 5.8   Regression results – panel data, 2000–2006 – imports from LAC to Brazil, Argentina and Chile

Model	Brazil$_{panel}$	Argentina$_{panel}$	Chile$_{panel}$
(Constant)	2.794	1.164	1.097
	(80.774)	(38.325)	(30.975)
Unit value$_{ijkt}$ – ln	0.296	0.441	0.477
	(79.072)	(147.476)	(124.329)
Liner shipping network structure (LSNS$_{IJt}$)	–0.186	–0.321	–0.425
	(–60.335)	(–68.505)	(–93.172)
Reefer$_{ijkt}$ (dummy)	0.48	0.597	0.415
	(22.707)	(7.873)	(11.059)
Open Registry$_{ijkt}$ (dummy)	–0.053	0.019	0.019
	(–6.094)	(3.271)	(0.494)
Volume of shipment$_{ijkt}$ – ln	–0.169	–0.07	–0.109
	(–87.77)	(–48.595)	(–55.382)
Maritime trade imbalance$_{It}$ (exporting country)	–0.001	0.001	0
	(–7.348)	(2.67)	(–1.357)
Dummy year 2000	0.106	0.276	0.116
	(7.165)	(26.422)	(7.943)
Dummy year 2001	0.025	0.24	0.203
	(1.733)	(20.957)	(13.631)
Dummy year 2002	–0.002	0.134	0.109
	(–0.173)	(7.028)	(7.346)
Dummy year 2003	0.033	0.071	0.013
	(2.143)	(6.674)	(0.956)
Dummy year 2004	0.068	0.118	0.078
	(4.433)	(11.93)	(5.794)
Dummy year 2005	0.092	0.201	0.081
	(6.121)	(18.024)	(6.355)
R^2	0.477	0.447	0.615
F	2804.585	4012.973	4365.273
Number of observations	36 815	59 473	32 827

Notes: T-statistics are given in brackets. The dependent variable is the freight rate per ton of transporting good k from the exporting country i to the importing country j in natural logarithms. All explanatory variables, excluding connectivity and dummies, are also in natural logarithms. Models 1–4 were estimated by OLS. The estimation uses White's heteroscedasticity-consistent standard errors. Panel data are for the year 2000–2006

To summarize, the main findings of this chapter specifically include:

- As expected Liner Shipping Network Structure is a key determinant of maritime transport costs.
- Trade imbalance is an important influencing factor on freight in containerized maritime trade, however the level of impact relates directly to the level of competition on a specific route.
- Traditional pricing strategies based on the value of the cargo still seem to prevail in the region under study.
- Economies of scale in relation to the volume of shipment are reflected in lower transport costs for high volume shippers.
- Competition is a key influencing factor on maritime transport costs. In markets with oligopolistic characteristics (four or less active carriers) maritime transport costs are likely to be higher.
- The use of open registries is reflected in lower transport costs, this allows for two interpretations a) the savings from using open registries are partly passed on to the shipper and/or b) the use of open registries is a proxy for open markets, which potentially allows for greater competition.
- Distance is a determinant of transport costs, but its actual influence when controlling for liner shipping network structures is low.
- Good quality of port infrastructure in ports on either side of the trade relation reduces transport costs as it allows for economies of scale in shipping and higher performance in shipside port operations.
- If maritime trade takes place between two ports operating under the service port model transport costs are significantly higher as if the same transaction takes place using two landlord ports.

Chapter 6

Beyond the Role of Distance – Maritime Industry and Network Structures – as Determinants of Competitiveness in International Trade

Introduction

This chapter aims to summarize the work that has been presented thus far and, on the basis of the discussions, findings and conclusions drawn herein, suggest further research in this field, and to conclude with a final note on the relevance of this research for Latin America.

The following section summarizes the main research contributions of this work in the areas of geography and economic theory underpinning international maritime transport costs and the issue of methodological concepts.

Limitations of the research and possible further work based on the findings in this investigation are presented in the third section.

The work concludes with a final note on the implications of the findings for the competitiveness of Latin America in international trade.

Summary of Major Research Contributions

This work contributes to existing studies by virtue of its thorough investigation into two important areas: economic theory underpinning international maritime transport costs and the issue of methodological concepts in the reduction of complexity by using principal component analysis.

Contribution to Understanding the Complexity and Consistency of Determinants of Maritime Transport Costs Over Time

The role of international maritime transport costs in the context of reduced and levelled tariff rates in developing countries, in this case by the example of Latin America, deserves a comprehensive and rigorous theoretical and detailed empirical evaluation. Existing research fails to present definite insights to the underlying complexity of determinants of maritime transport costs in a comprehensive manner and usually focuses on single issues (e.g. port efficiency, competition) at a single point in time. Particularly, the consistency of determinants over time and the potential changes in terms of their relevance have received little attention. Against this background, the work has attempted to investigate the complexity underpinning international maritime transport costs from an economic geographical perspective. The work has been structured accordingly to achieve this primary purpose.

In Chapter 2, the theoretical framework of the work is constructed and the investigation is set in the context of recent developments in transport and economic geography. The chapter works towards the cognition that economic actors produce their own environments by transforming material and institutional conditions. In maritime transport the 'environments' materialize in the form of networks and infrastructures, and thus maritime transport costs can be understood as the symptoms of transforming material and institutional conditions. It was suggested that geographical economics fall short of understanding the geographical perspective as they deal with space as a container that confines and determines economic action, thus, this work is also a response of geography research to the self proclaimed new economic geography.

In the context of research on maritime transport, trade and transport costs and the relation to economic development, the work describes how freight rates are determined by economic actors and market conditions. Based on this discussion, the concepts of trade costs, trade facilitation and in particular international maritime transport costs were examined to reveal the relevance of maritime transport costs to competitiveness in international trade. Consequently, the author identified that the 'geographical' lens can contribute particularly to economic actors and policy makers understanding the structure of and causes influencing maritime transport costs.

Chapter 3 examines the complexity of the underlying determinants of international maritime transport costs in five main groups. The question on the role of distance as a determinant of maritime transport costs is addressed in depth and firstly evidence is provided that the role of distance as a determinant might be overrated in existing studies. The discussion brings a wide range of proof on the complex interrelationships between determinants. The role of shipping lines, their strategies and the market structure is identified as a key area for research. The variables that form the elements of the liner shipping networks are discussed in detail.

The function of port infra- and superstructure is emphasized and the potential impact of port devolution on maritime transport costs is pointed out. However, the theoretic discussion also accentuates the high correlation between the individual factors and the difficulty of capturing the full complexity in an empirical analysis.

Throughout the thorough discussion, the chapter illustrates how port development is to a great extent in the hands of policy makers in individual countries, while changes in the maritime liner shipping industry e.g. mergers and acquisitions, routing strategies etc impact the region's trade development in a way that largely transcends the countries' policy makers' influences. These discussions, which are based on theoretical, institutional and field work evidence, underpinning the structure of maritime transport costs and the wide interrelations between individual determinants, led to the formulation of 15 individual hypotheses.

Chapter 4 gives detailed descriptions of the principle database BTI and the other relevant data sources. The construction of the underlying database for this work is anything but the simple task it might appear to be. In fact, building a database on Latin American trade from raw data and constructing the necessary relational database structure in order to be able to combine different datasets is a sophisticated and laborious task. Not only must the data be collected and collated in a consistent and thorough manner which facilitates the subsequent analysis, but the results from the empirical analysis are only interpretable if the whole database complies with data integrity. Evidence is given for the uniqueness and superiority of using the dataset in its disaggregated form and in particular the possibility of calculating freight per ton, excluding insurance costs. Based on the theoretic discussions in the previous chapter, a transport cost model is developed that presents the complexity of influencing factors. This is a keystone in the progression of the investigation as the model sets the scientific form for estimating the cross-sectional and panel data regressions.

Chapter 5 presents a response to the originally formulated hypotheses in Chapter 3 by demonstrating the main empirical results from the regression analysis. In conclusion, it is found that maritime transport costs are significantly influenced by variables that result from decisions and interpretation of material and institutional conditions by economic actors interpreting. The role of network structures, trade imbalances, traditional pricing strategies, economies of scale from a shipper's perspective, competition and the use of open registries are identified as key determinants of maritime transport costs. Beyond these the role of port infrastructure, port service level and different port operator models is illustrated. Distance, too, is a determinant of transport costs, but its actual influence when controlling for liner shipping network structures is low.

These outcomes give evidence to the space transforming role of networks and the importance of economic actors' strategies as influencing factors on maritime transport costs. The results indicate a significant effect of the Liner Service Network Structure (LSNS) on transport costs. The more centrally a trade route is located in the maritime liner service network the lower the average transport costs. This opens the important discussion on the 'cost' of being peripheral irrespective of its geographical distance to trade partners. The elasticities found show that the impact of being peripheral in the maritime network is higher than the impact of distance. Network peripheral countries pay higher prices for transporting their exports, especially when they trade with other peripheral countries. Countries that are both peripheral in the maritime network and distant from other export markets face high freight rates. Location is an important issue in Latin America, given the insular geographic character of the Caribbean and given that countries on the west and east coast of South America are located at the endpoint of the global maritime liner shipping network. The development of a hierarchical network, with the growing importance of transhipment centres in Panama, and Callao (Peru) and of some intermediary ports on the east coast of Brazil, are altering the network position of certain regions. Evidence suggests that higher export transport costs imply a reduction in competitiveness in comparison to exporters in more central locations.

Thus this work puts the shipping lines and shippers in the centre of the discussion, because it is their actions and strategies that construct the network that facilitates maritime transport and thus determines the 'economic distance' between two countries. Further, the consistency of key variables is proven, which allow for comparing the role of determinants over time and could be used to project future developments. However, at the same time a definitive analysis of the issue of exploitation of monopoly profits by shipping lines and port efficiency could not be given. Research in that area requires more comprehensive and detailed data than that utilized in this work.

Recommendations for Further Research

This analysis for the case of Latin America, if proven in a wider geographical context, might constitute the starting point for a transformation in the understanding of transport costs. If Liner Service Network Structures are more significant in the determination of freight rates than geographic distance in maritime transport, the question that arises is how far can geographic distance really be used as a proxy for transport costs? Or rather, how could liner shipping network structures be used in trade analysis?

A major difficulty in conducting panel data analysis over this time span of seven years is obtaining data of comparable quality and geographic coverage. Without reliable and extensive data that is regularly updated, it is very difficult to undertake systematic analysis. LAC countries must define their data needs. The data used in this work are annual and thus face certain restrictions. The regression analyses identified year specific effects. However, these are difficult to interpret since the data structure in this work does not allow for the controlling for seasonality or specific impacts at certain points throughout a year.

Liner shipping is a global business and intra-regional trade is linked into the global liner shipping networks. Therefore, strategies of liner shipping companies will not only be related to a region, specifically intra-regional trade. Recognizing this, an important step would be to analyse maritime transport costs and their determinants in their entirety for a region. This means analysing the determinants of maritime transport costs taking into account all maritime trade transactions in Latin America or a particular country with the world. A first step in this direction has been done in this work by using the total trade imbalances for a country, instead of bilateral trade imbalances. However, in order to be able to conduct an analysis of maritime transport costs for Latin America taking into account all maritime trade relations, a number of data restrictions must be overcome and a thorough preparation of existing data is also necessary.

In LAC countries, where markets for detailed disaggregated data are not developed, there is an opportunity for private data providers to develop proposals on the types of information the private sector can supply to national agencies, among other roles. More importantly, the private sector should be proactive about the roles it could play. Some of these data are already being collected in most countries. However, a functional data system must be defined with input from all stakeholders, including cross-support from the private sector, with the ability to make at least some of this information publicly available on a regular basis.

A Final Note

There is a strong tendency in Latin America to look at the symptoms and not the cause of the problem. Javier Hurtado Mercado, IRUPANA, Latin America Business Summit 2002

Maritime transport is characterized by the complexity of the relationships that contribute to its configuration. Understanding what may affect those relationships can assist policy makers in their efforts to improve the efficiency of maritime transport systems and thus the competitiveness of the region. A challenge in Latin America is that when data are collected they remain unused, or they may not be collected in the first place.

A populist argument posits a lack of competitiveness in international trade in relation to maritime transport in explaining the lack of port efficiency. The results presented in this study show that port infrastructure and port devolution have a role to play as determinants of maritime transport costs, but are not the key factors. Governments in the region have yet to understand that maritime transport is a derived demand and that supply will follow demand. Concepts to construct new ports or expand ports as a measure in improving competitiveness will not yield the desired results and have been shown to be 'white elephants' (see Manta, Ecuador and La Union, El Salvador as the most recent examples) if the institutional culture of the country is not developed.

This work clearly shows that maritime transport costs, to a significant part, depend on decisions and strategies made by liner shipping companies in terms of network structures and competition, but also depend on the application of traditional pricing strategies using mark-ups related to the value of the cargo.

Thus the economic distance of a country's export products to its destination markets is determined by players in what is probably the 'most globalized' industry in the world. Shippers and policy makers need to understand that these players can hardly be regulated from a national perspective. However, this work also shows important points of potential leverage for shippers as they can exploit a favourable imbalance to their advantage. By way of example, freight costs for exporting cargo from a net importing country might be lower and can give a product the required margin to be competitive in external trade. Further, clear evidence is given that high volume shippers can exploit economies of scale, consequently coordination and organization between small- and medium-size shippers can also reduce their costs in maritime transport.

Even though not proven in detail, there is evidence of the exploitation of oligopolistic market structures in the form of collusion. This is an important issue to understand for policy makers, particularly those involved in port development and port reform, because continuing vertical integration in the shipping and port sector might result in situations where monopoly pricing and discrimination directly impact a country's shippers. This risk particularly exists for countries whose external trade is realized only through one port and/or where ports serve isolated hinterlands.

Finally, the clear evidence provided on the role of Liner Shipping Network Structures also points out the interdependency of countries in the way they are being served by maritime transport services. The shipping services on a route will always display a structure that fits the least developed obligatory port of call on a route. By way of example, if only one port on a route does not provide gantry cranes, but is an obligatory port of call due to its cargo volumes, the characteristics of the ships deployed on that route will be adjusted to that 'weakest' port or shipping lines will reroute services. This is a clear call for policy makers and port authorities in the region to strengthen transnational co-operation in order to improve the development of the whole system, focusing on the causes that put the region at risk of becoming peripheral and uncompetitive.

Appendix 1
Data Collection and Modelling in LAC Countries

The Current Situation

LAC countries do not have a systemic process of processing existing freight transportation data. For example, there is no freight database with origin destination matrices available to facilitate the orderly analysis of commodity flows. Moreover, coordination between the various governmental agencies involved in transportation can be improved. These agencies also lack the resources to engage in periodic releases of information to the public, while at the same time the private sector is concerned about the confidentiality of sensitive information such as the manifests data. Indeed, a number of private companies are dedicated to collect data from bills of lading in international transport (e.g. Manifiestos in Ecuador). These companies sell the data to interested private and public parties. In some cases, governments buy this information although interest is often mainly shown by the private sector. Specifically shipping lines use the data for capacity planning etc.

One could be suspicious that the private sector is not pushing for better and more comprehensive data. This, however, is not usual behaviour around the world. There is a long history in the transportation sector of keeping data secret. Therefore, the need of a public role to take on the responsibility of leveraging market forces by releasing information on freight rates, volumes, values, network links, etc. Despite all difficulties, however, countries like El Salvador have recently started to analyse customs data, after having found out that such data allow depicting and differentiating the international cargo flows at border crossings. If studied and analysed in detail these data can be used for modelling flows on international routes and thus can also contribute to the planning of installations of border crossings. In Argentina, simple tools like the logistics costs index published by CEDOL in Argentina have proven fully applicable in applied research for the benefit of industry.

Overall, government funded studies are hard to find or non-existent, freight analysis has been performed for the most part either by international cooperative agencies or for academic purposes. As can be seen from the survey of databases that follows, much remains to be done in the region.

Without reliable and extensive public and private data that is regularly updated, it is very difficult to undertake systematic analysis not only of existing costs and bottlenecks, but also of potential efficiency gains that could be achieved through proposed large investments such as regional logistics corridors. Among the data that are needed, it is essential they contain information on all of the inputs that are required for the proper functioning of the logistics system, such as commodity origin and destination, costs of transport, infrastructure availability, operations indicators, registry of users, among others. The need for these data as well as their reliability must be validated with input from all stakeholders, including cross-support from the private sector.

A first step to define data needs used in some countries is the establishment of a National Transportation Board. This entity is ultimately responsible for establishing research and data collection priorities and provides detailed instructions on a platform to grant immediate access to recent information to users while protecting the data confidentiality. This step could be implemented relatively fast and would not require expensive investments. Countries already collect trade and manifests data. Moreover, through Latin American Association of Foreign Trade (LAIA), many countries already report information on freight rate, transportation costs, and trip length, among other relevant variables. ALDAI, however, due to limited resources, neither currently analyses these data nor produces any reports. The United Nations Economic Commission for Latin America and the Caribbean (UN-ECLAC) has taken the initiative to use the LAIA data to produce a series of reports. However, as the complexity of domestic and international transportation networks continues to diverge in different directions for the countries in the region, it would be ideal if individual countries could clearly define their data needs and tools of analysis.

Data on Freight and Logistics in Latin America

Import Export Data

Countries in the region, as mandated by UN Agencies, have increasingly improved their capabilities to collect and release timely external trade data. Central banks in the region report customs information on imports from all exporting countries at the 6-digit Harmonized System level by transport mode (ocean, air). Data include origin, destination, freight and insurance costs, volume and values (FOB, CIF) of products and the transport mode, dutiable value, and calculated duty. They are usually available at the country level for the origin of the shipment.

Information on freight rates, transportation mode, and shipments destinations is not being processed, although countries collect this type of information to different levels of detail. A few countries publish some of the data on their national statistics institutions website. Example: Bolivia publishes data on modal split, transport flows through border crossings and multimodal transport chains for imports and exports. However, little research is done and published beyond descriptive analysis. The only source comprehensive overview on modal split and international trade in South America in terms of volumes (tonnes, and value) and expenditures on trade has been published by UN-ECLAC: a) International

Trade and Transport Profiles, year 2000, and b) Modal Split in Latin American International Transport, 2006. These statistical information sources are derived from the International Transport Database (BTI), which is based on detailed information received from BADECEL.

Customs Manifests

Customs agencies of the region's countries have an embedded interest in collecting these data. Often, they have outsourced these services to the private sector in response to their own inability to process the vast amounts of information. In addition to duties, customs manifests can provide very valuable information from a freight analysis perspective. Depending on the country, additional information in the customs manifests may include port of origin, port of destination, shipping and arrival dates, shipping carrier, customs clearance times, transportation mode, type of aircraft or vessel, among other variables. In contrast to progress made by countries processing trade data, with the exception of data on levies, which is assessed for fiduciary reasons, the remaining manifest data are ultimately lost. Although the private firms in charge of consolidating and digitizing data include this additional information in a series of files that they deliver to the governments, not much progress has been achieved by government agencies in analysing such information.

LAIA (Latin American Association of Foreign Trade)

This dataset includes international trade data for several years: 1990, 1995, 2000–2006). Data continue to be collected although they are not being processed. This dataset reports customs information for Argentina, Bolivia, Brazil, Colombia, Cuba, Chile, Ecuador, Mexico, Paraguay, Peru, Uruguay, and Venezuela. Data include import values from all exporting countries at the 6-digit Harmonized System level (over 5000 products) by transport mode (ocean, air, ground and other), costs of freight, insurance and import duties. Data are available at the country level for the origin of the shipment and at the port level for its destination. Not all the information is available for all countries in all years and the most notable missing data is freight rates for Mexico and Venezuela and tariff data for Ecuador, Bolivia, Mexico and Venezuela.

Despite the breadth of information LAIA's database has one shortcoming: it does not cover Central America and the Caribbean countries because they are not members of the organization. Although the LAIA dataset includes 12 countries from Latin America, only Brazil, Chile, Ecuador, Peru and Uruguay have data available for a wider range of variables.

UN-ECLAC Data

The source of information of these data is the International Transport Data Base (BTI) of UN-ECLAC. The BTI was created by UN-ECLAC's Transport Unit in 1999 as part of a research project on the determinants of international transport costs. At that time, existing trade data bases did not include transport related information. The statistics are derived from the Foreign Trade Data Bank for Latin America and the Caribbean (BADECEL), maintained by the Statistics and Economic Projections Division of UN-ECLAC. It represents information consolidated and digitized by each country's national customs service. BTI data is available for the period 2000–2012.

Table A1.1   Available data from BTI

Type	Description
Year	Year of trade movement
Informing country	Reporting country
Trade flow	Import or Export
Country of origin/destination	Name of country of origin (imports)/destination (exports)
Country of shipment/ reception	Name of country where the product was shipped from or to
SITC	Product classification
Volume of shipment	Volume of shipment in kilogram
CIF	Value CIF (current US$)
FOB	Value FOB (current US$)
Freight	Freight costs (current US$)
Insurance	Insurance (current US$)
Transport mode	See below *

Source: Wilmsmeier, Perez and Hesse 2009

In the further analysis the first aggregation level as stated in the Table A2 is used for the different modes of transport.

Table A1.2   Classification of transport modes

Code	Classification	Definitions	First aggregation
1	Deep Draft Vessel	Barges, ships, or ferries primarily operating in the high seas	
2	Shallow Draft Vessel River	Barges, ships, or ferries operating primarily on rivers and canals	Waterborne
3	Shallow Draft Vessel Lake	Barges, ships, or ferries operating primarily on lakes	
4	Airborne	Commercial or private aircraft	Airborne
6	Rail	Any common carrier or private railway	Rail
7	Truck	Private and for-hire trucks	Truck
5	Postal	Delivery services, packages, and other small shipments that typically have low weight, or for which the weight or value is not necessarily registered	
8	Pipeline	Movements of oil, petroleum, gas, slurry etc by tube	Other modes
9	Other	Any mode not specified above	
0	Not declared	Mode of transport not reported by the reporting country	Not declared

Source: UN-ECLAC, based on data concept from BTI

Data on Caribbean Countries and Central America

An attempt to develop an international trade database comparable to LAIA's was undertaken in the Caribbean based on an UNECLAC initiative, data was collected and pooled until 2004, but then the effort was discontinued. In Central America regional data is presented by COCATRAM for maritime transport as in the other regions empirical research based on this data in limited.

Brazil's Data

Brazil has started developing programmes to collect different types of freight data – Secretaria de Indústria e Comércio Exterior (SECEX), which is part of the Ministry of Indústria e Comércio Exterior. As with similar government agencies in other countries SECEX is in charge of processing trade data. In addition, the Secretaria de Transportes do Governo do Estado de São Paulo has undertaken the

Origin Destination Survey on a sporadic basis, while the Instituto Brasileiro de Geografia e Estatística is in charge of the Annual Industrial Survey.

US Data of Interest: US Waterborne Databanks

The US Department of Transportation, Maritime Administration, dataset reports customs information on US maritime imports and exports from all and to all trading partners at the 6-digit Harmonized System level. Data include customs import value, cost of freight, insurance and other charges (excluding US import duties), shipping weight, and per cent of containerized shipped weight. Data are available at the port level for the origin of the shipment and at the port level for its destination.

US Data of Interest: Imports of Merchandise

The Census Bureau's database includes information for roughly 17,000 'products' (10 digit level, HS system), on imports (value and weight), tariff revenue, transport costs (freight plus insurance), by mode and district of entry (air and ocean) for all exporters to the US. The Waterborne databanks reports the same type information, but limited to ocean shipping and includes information on port of origin and port of entry.

Appendix 2

Average Freight and Insurance Costs per ton and as Margins of CIF Prices for Exports from Latin American Countries to LAIA Countries, 2000–2006

Table A2.1

Year	Country	Freight/ton	Insurance cost/ton	Freight margin	Insurance margin
2000	Antigua and Barbuda	120.37	7.26	7.57%	0.46%
2000	Argentina	474.84	74.35	7.81%	0.39%
2000	Aruba	234.06	8.48	13.80%	0.13%
2000	Bahamas	1 029.31	28.49	12.23%	0.09%
2000	Barbados	386.58	11.06	10.91%	0.32%
2000	Belize	1 497.40	39.84	25.08%	0.53%
2000	Bermuda	200.15	48.01	5.97%	0.09%
2000	Bolivia	637.74	198.40	9.04%	0.37%
2000	Brazil	439.46	72.61	6.50%	0.57%
2000	British Virgin Islands	826.90	318.93	6.49%	0.32%
2000	Cayman Islands	609.11	268.11	10.74%	0.34%
2000	Chile	238.04	24.53	8.07%	0.44%
2000	Colombia	282.58	39.80	6.60%	0.57%
2000	Costa Rica	573.06	29.80	11.50%	0.39%
2000	Cuba	444.73	46.53	15.44%	0.90%
2000	Dominica	385.89	68.48	5.48%	0.49%
2000	Dominican Republic	745.81	35.19	18.74%	0.55%
2000	Ecuador	228.33	10.98	8.21%	0.37%
2000	El Salvador	536.99	41.89	20.26%	0.45%
2000	French Guiana	7 761.82	116.44	16.27%	0.86%
2000	Grenada	247.55	19.68	3.08%	0.23%

Table A2.1 *Continued*

Year	Country	Freight/ton	Insurance cost/ton	Freight margin	Insurance margin
2000	Guadeloupe	609.96	0.00	13.57%	0.00%
2000	Guatemala	419.41	20.37	10.80%	0.33%
2000	Guyana	103.85	12.14	15.35%	0.61%
2000	Haiti	523.82	43.76	22.50%	0.20%
2000	Honduras	392.71	56.47	17.66%	0.75%
2000	Jamaica	332.02	32.70	11.13%	0.90%
2000	Martinique	1 021.05	0.00	36.04%	0.00%
2000	Mexico	663.68	43.68	8.52%	0.37%
2000	Montserrat	331.47	13.07	5.45%	0.21%
2000	Netherlands Antilles	569.80	21.03	7.93%	0.21%
2000	Nicaragua	415.71	28.70	17.67%	0.46%
2000	Panama	3 130.26	59.76	8.09%	0.31%
2000	Paraguay	339.12	8.35	13.26%	0.16%
2000	Peru	253.33	33.41	7.73%	0.48%
2000	Puerto Rico	647.50	51.09	11.30%	0.30%
2000	Trinidad and Tobago	2 271.49	8.24	15.23%	0.19%
2000	Turks and Caicos Islands	58.98	0.84	9.96%	0.12%
2000	Uruguay	683.42	298.91	7.20%	0.40%
2000	Venezuela (Bolivarian Republic of)	887.46	116.77	8.50%	0.44%
2000	Virgin Islands, US	349.57	68.07	15.89%	0.20%
2001	Antigua and Barbuda	745.92	1.08	10.18%	0.14%
2001	Argentina	373.69	61.92	7.15%	0.40%
2001	Aruba	206.11	6.68	18.34%	0.20%
2001	Bahamas	924.71	37.10	7.44%	0.23%
2001	Barbados	372.62	28.40	18.33%	0.37%
2001	Belize	843.40	10.51	20.23%	0.20%
2001	Bermuda	271.94	120.84	5.02%	0.33%
2001	Bolivia	163.08	16.52	11.47%	0.46%
2001	Brazil	685.19	120.29	6.79%	0.52%
2001	British Virgin Islands	869.28	268.71	6.79%	0.28%
2001	Cayman Islands	556.90	222.26	9.03%	0.34%
2001	Chile	260.28	35.87	7.70%	0.46%

Year	Country	Freight/ton	Insurance cost/ton	Freight margin	Insurance margin
2001	Colombia	278.37	42.11	7.32%	0.61%
2001	Costa Rica	581.24	28.29	12.57%	0.35%
2001	Cuba	308.51	21.05	16.13%	0.45%
2001	Dominica	641.68	102.54	9.97%	0.71%
2001	Dominican Republic	535.68	44.44	14.15%	0.85%
2001	Ecuador	276.60	16.25	7.44%	0.34%
2001	El Salvador	415.67	37.60	12.60%	0.42%
2001	French Guiana	22.14	0.00	28.80%	0.00%
2001	Grenada	429.35	26.21	7.42%	0.48%
2001	Guadeloupe	173.01	0.00	10.49%	0.00%
2001	Guatemala	577.13	21.11	14.15%	0.44%
2001	Guyana	331.93	13.48	18.05%	0.52%
2001	Haiti	197.42	78.34	9.83%	0.59%
2001	Honduras	442.51	42.54	24.65%	0.46%
2001	Jamaica	974.11	122.45	10.57%	0.73%
2001	Martinique	1 076.41	0.00	38.95%	0.00%
2001	Mexico	530.50	46.37	8.10%	0.36%
2001	Montserrat	60.05	6.83	5.07%	0.58%
2001	Netherlands Antilles	450.13	18.13	11.39%	0.12%
2001	Nicaragua	438.66	495.80	12.05%	0.45%
2001	Panama	275.92	39.79	7.95%	0.33%
2001	Paraguay	601.81	14.29	10.25%	0.13%
2001	Peru	664.35	143.69	7.55%	0.54%
2001	Puerto Rico	1 139.46	83.77	8.48%	0.47%
2001	Saint Lucia	19.13	0.00	28.49%	0.00%
2001	Saint Pierre and Miquelon	287.66	10.49	7.81%	0.14%
2001	Suriname	288.09	0.07	16.28%	0.03%
2001	Trinidad and Tobago	539.67	176.45	14.26%	0.30%
2001	Turks and Caicos Islands	57.78	0.00	9.51%	0.00%
2001	Uruguay	651.85	240.38	6.98%	0.31%
2001	Venezuela (Bolivarian Republic of)	387.38	40.82	9.04%	0.46%
2001	Virgin Islands, US	407.93	156.72	13.96%	0.38%
2002	Anguilla	327.83	0.00	2.63%	0.00%

Table A2.1   *Continued*

Year	Country	Freight/ton	Insurance cost/ton	Freight margin	Insurance margin
2002	Antigua and Barbuda	290.97	0.00	10.08%	0.00%
2002	Argentina	377.12	48.62	8.15%	0.39%
2002	Aruba	363.99	8.20	21.69%	0.19%
2002	Bahamas	569.73	32.43	10.48%	0.41%
2002	Barbados	1 307.57	196.73	6.16%	0.39%
2002	Belize	400.66	292.05	4.73%	1.73%
2002	Bermuda	281.34	719.73	4.70%	0.53%
2002	Bolivia	166.51	27.08	8.15%	0.43%
2002	Brazil	430.42	52.43	7.42%	0.44%
2002	British Virgin Islands	927.04	366.44	6.24%	0.37%
2002	Cayman Islands	532.44	196.50	7.21%	0.29%
2002	Chile	210.51	25.91	7.73%	0.42%
2002	Colombia	203.41	44.85	5.47%	0.57%
2002	Costa Rica	419.69	61.54	8.40%	0.35%
2002	Cuba	394.52	15.61	21.17%	0.50%
2002	Dominica	156.53	28.88	2.96%	0.55%
2002	Dominican Republic	510.17	82.35	16.99%	0.78%
2002	Ecuador	218.27	24.11	6.39%	0.41%
2002	El Salvador	344.81	1 945.10	15.78%	0.48%
2002	French Guiana	175.64	3.26	25.04%	0.22%
2002	Grenada	3 640.14	84.11	11.69%	0.66%
2002	Guatemala	250.56	21.88	12.16%	0.48%
2002	Guyana	79.17	4.23	19.90%	0.28%
2002	Haiti	239.49	2.20	12.62%	0.15%
2002	Honduras	532.78	38.32	20.92%	0.64%
2002	Jamaica	240.00	14.92	13.28%	0.45%
2002	Martinique	1 217.21	0.00	36.16%	0.00%
2002	Mexico	496.72	37.08	7.12%	0.34%
2002	Montserrat	237.15	6.29	21.10%	0.20%
2002	Netherlands Antilles	456.11	6.20	6.08%	0.08%
2002	Nicaragua	1 169.44	220.15	19.90%	0.67%
2002	Panama	271.19	30.31	7.37%	0.27%

Year	Country	Freight/ton	Insurance cost/ton	Freight margin	Insurance margin
2002	Paraguay	286.35	28.81	11.06%	0.38%
2002	Peru	697.01	82.33	6.35%	0.44%
2002	Puerto Rico	1 130.25	44.02	15.42%	0.40%
2002	Saint Kitts and Nevis	527.52	84.47	5.32%	0.85%
2002	Saint Pierre and Miquelon	595.57	63.17	6.04%	0.64%
2002	Saint Vincent and Grenadines	80.75	1.69	4.95%	0.91%
2002	Suriname	248.24	88.83	5.03%	1.53%
2002	Trinidad and Tobago	355.50	8.07	13.73%	0.25%
2002	Turks and Caicos Islands	134.65	35.92	8.96%	0.55%
2002	Uruguay	1 322.31	257.97	8.08%	0.27%
2002	Venezuela (Bolivarian Republic of)	228.33	19.48	8.30%	0.43%
2002	Virgin Islands, US	212.17	26.42	6.26%	0.31%
2003	Antigua and Barbuda	477.29	10.01	9.20%	0.15%
2003	Argentina	355.39	40.49	8.74%	0.36%
2003	Aruba	247.65	15.20	12.89%	0.48%
2003	Bahamas	703.62	28.01	8.92%	0.27%
2003	Barbados	584.74	359.13	12.93%	0.59%
2003	Belize	494.30	619.55	6.52%	2.83%
2003	Bermuda	228.42	55.69	4.28%	0.24%
2003	Bolivia	188.23	20.07	9.03%	0.25%
2003	Brazil	408.59	46.34	7.08%	0.42%
2003	British Virgin Islands	563.95	412.38	8.00%	0.37%
2003	Cayman Islands	568.89	234.68	8.06%	0.22%
2003	Chile	192.84	20.89	7.34%	0.40%
2003	Colombia	212.36	40.84	5.48%	0.48%
2003	Costa Rica	485.76	46.77	7.97%	0.40%
2003	Cuba	293.19	16.98	19.27%	0.57%
2003	Dominica	392.02	76.63	8.59%	1.11%
2003	Dominican Republic	1 021.10	76.57	21.27%	0.54%
2003	Ecuador	202.20	32.59	5.40%	0.40%
2003	El Salvador	570.89	46.91	16.60%	0.52%
2003	French Guiana	24.46	0.18	35.06%	0.30%

Table A2.1 *Continued*

Year	Country	Freight/ton	Insurance cost/ton	Freight margin	Insurance margin
2003	Grenada	326.50	53.67	4.85%	0.46%
2003	Guatemala	1 466.13	45.82	11.47%	0.32%
2003	Guyana	81.31	1.84	37.44%	0.32%
2003	Haiti	136.95	132.78	6.37%	0.28%
2003	Honduras	194.72	11.09	18.09%	0.42%
2003	Jamaica	263.71	27.36	12.68%	0.40%
2003	Martinique	1 182.38	0.00	25.82%	0.00%
2003	Mexico	365.60	30.67	6.30%	0.33%
2003	Montserrat	200.00	0.00	62.50%	0.00%
2003	Netherlands Antilles	534.21	18.56	8.19%	0.13%
2003	Nicaragua	388.49	72.38	8.22%	0.60%
2003	Panama	180.51	21.29	7.21%	0.28%
2003	Paraguay	358.16	60.07	11.51%	0.92%
2003	Peru	315.11	61.73	6.19%	0.41%
2003	Puerto Rico	673.22	37.64	12.94%	0.34%
2003	Saint Kitts and Nevis	326.89	0.00	7.64%	0.00%
2003	Saint Vincent and Grenadines	626.92	6.83	7.02%	0.23%
2003	Suriname	316.67	222.22	21.29%	0.40%
2003	Trinidad and Tobago	312.31	13.21	10.46%	0.23%
2003	Turks and Caicos Islands	778.62	0.89	9.42%	0.17%
2003	Uruguay	609.03	137.47	7.09%	0.22%
2003	Venezuela (Bolivarian Republic of)	179.14	13.69	8.16%	0.31%
2003	Virgin Islands, US	244.92	10.07	7.49%	0.15%
2004	Anguilla	130.71	12.59	4.91%	0.54%
2004	Antigua and Barbuda	458.75	49.08	12.97%	1.09%
2004	Argentina	395.95	47.43	8.46%	0.40%
2004	Aruba	190.43	6.22	11.83%	0.37%
2004	Bahamas	991.69	62.16	5.30%	0.32%
2004	Barbados	293.91	21.98	12.05%	0.54%
2004	Belize	1 100.67	5.03	8.23%	0.05%
2004	Bermuda	220.87	28.28	6.98%	0.09%

Year	Country	Freight/ton	Insurance cost/ton	Freight margin	Insurance margin
2004	Bolivia	160.61	10.16	9.43%	0.29%
2004	Brazil	1 519.75	95.18	7.08%	0.47%
2004	British Virgin Islands	466.40	13.31	11.69%	0.12%
2004	Cayman Islands	461.54	103.03	10.25%	0.16%
2004	Chile	352.00	50.26	9.23%	0.51%
2004	Colombia	226.43	42.64	5.32%	0.50%
2004	Costa Rica	487.79	34.90	9.50%	0.36%
2004	Cuba	267.81	48.36	21.60%	0.53%
2004	Dominica	177.87	57.27	1.70%	0.28%
2004	Dominican Republic	373.33	19.31	25.10%	0.47%
2004	Ecuador	240.99	52.35	5.96%	0.51%
2004	El Salvador	616.87	21.11	15.05%	0.72%
2004	French Guiana	28.46	0.01	22.85%	0.01%
2004	Grenada	226.90	32.04	4.80%	0.60%
2004	Guadeloupe	202.81	19.65	5.83%	0.43%
2004	Guatemala	298.40	19.39	11.61%	0.40%
2004	Guyana	49.71	1.31	45.21%	0.33%
2004	Haiti	651.14	28.98	26.97%	1.20%
2004	Honduras	178.55	10.08	18.32%	0.40%
2004	Jamaica	287.68	42.99	10.41%	0.56%
2004	Mexico	732.09	139.66	6.05%	0.42%
2004	Montserrat	313.25	12.05	34.21%	1.32%
2004	Netherlands Antilles	743.07	41.82	6.39%	0.13%
2004	Nicaragua	354.29	18.56	13.47%	0.42%
2004	Panama	206.29	35.85	7.21%	0.38%
2004	Paraguay	474.51	26.24	23.39%	0.26%
2004	Peru	402.04	63.74	6.97%	0.43%
2004	Puerto Rico	632.74	60.37	12.28%	0.46%
2004	Saint Kitts and Nevis	1 060.45	44.54	10.61%	0.45%
2004	Saint Lucia	13.13	0.02	64.36%	0.11%
2004	Saint Pierre and Miquelon	80.40	4.90	6.22%	0.38%
2004	Saint Vincent and Grenadines	1.87	0.97	3.75%	1.93%
2004	Suriname	32.50	0.00	14.23%	0.00%

Table A2.1 *Continued*

Year	Country	Freight/ton	Insurance cost/ton	Freight margin	Insurance margin
2004	Trinidad and Tobago	279.52	15.54	11.24%	0.33%
2004	Turks and Caicos Islands	42.89	2.32	9.61%	0.23%
2004	Uruguay	1 419.82	279.58	7.47%	0.35%
2004	Venezuela (Bolivarian Republic of)	238.81	23.94	7.62%	0.36%
2004	Virgin Islands, US	3 930.34	392.59	8.76%	0.51%
2005	Antigua and Barbuda	279.55	25.75	7.02%	0.61%
2005	Argentina	557.21	71.63	7.26%	0.38%
2005	Aruba	383.19	10.61	14.84%	0.59%
2005	Bahamas	541.88	29.12	6.06%	0.21%
2005	Barbados	373.66	93.58	8.19%	0.31%
2005	Belize	644.83	23.67	9.24%	0.30%
2005	Bermuda	374.37	51.06	4.74%	0.13%
2005	Bolivia	212.59	42.41	9.51%	0.43%
2005	Brazil	860.11	100.51	6.83%	0.45%
2005	British Virgin Islands	634.55	85.17	12.51%	0.15%
2005	Cayman Islands	517.99	113.46	9.36%	0.17%
2005	Chile	374.87	57.68	8.38%	0.53%
2005	Colombia	418.54	69.95	5.95%	0.52%
2005	Costa Rica	1 387.32	92.34	8.41%	0.47%
2005	Cuba	328.50	39.61	10.15%	0.44%
2005	Dominica	386.26	41.58	1.80%	0.12%
2005	Dominican Republic	292.54	38.12	18.89%	0.34%
2005	Ecuador	291.26	48.29	6.11%	0.52%
2005	El Salvador	400.07	23.14	10.50%	0.42%
2005	French Guiana	32.94	0.07	19.26%	0.04%
2005	Grenada	213.08	53.00	3.05%	0.78%
2005	Guadeloupe	945.86	58.75	15.78%	0.42%
2005	Guatemala	394.32	60.19	8.15%	0.57%
2005	Guyana	97.81	0.63	59.99%	0.14%
2005	Haiti	179.72	4.35	16.10%	0.81%
2005	Honduras	1 363.43	406.57	23.87%	0.56%
2005	Jamaica	859.90	84.96	11.39%	0.79%

Year	Country	Freight/ton	Insurance cost/ton	Freight margin	Insurance margin
2005	Martinique	62.20	0.53	40.60%	0.10%
2005	Mexico	519.74	54.20	6.38%	0.41%
2005	Netherlands Antilles	237.85	15.26	6.12%	0.11%
2005	Nicaragua	235.30	13.11	13.35%	0.60%
2005	Panama	310.78	40.45	7.91%	0.37%
2005	Paraguay	309.87	12.42	15.51%	0.36%
2005	Peru	536.78	79.05	6.09%	0.40%
2005	Puerto Rico	602.44	60.39	13.80%	0.40%
2005	Saint Kitts and Nevis	67.53	5.76	6.03%	0.51%
2005	Suriname	90.31	1.75	25.77%	0.31%
2005	Trinidad and Tobago	268.60	18.75	11.43%	0.33%
2005	Turks and Caicos Islands	23.97	0.00	9.26%	0.00%
2005	Uruguay	762.24	118.98	7.89%	0.29%
2005	Venezuela (Bolivarian Republic of)	408.44	83.71	6.18%	0.43%
2005	Virgin Islands, US	484.68	41.23	11.80%	0.58%
2006	Antigua and Barbuda	202.69	14.84	5.97%	0.23%
2006	Argentina	481.14	78.39	6.88%	0.41%
2006	Aruba	505.19	19.08	18.98%	1.35%
2006	Bahamas	709.72	196.21	7.20%	0.42%
2006	Barbados	2 997.81	23.72	7.01%	0.28%
2006	Belize	400.24	13.35	19.57%	0.35%
2006	Bermuda	243.98	1.43	3.35%	0.02%
2006	Bolivia	296.40	14.77	12.51%	0.23%
2006	Brazil	467.59	66.17	5.80%	0.43%
2006	British Virgin Islands	514.48	154.92	8.72%	0.18%
2006	Cayman Islands	441.64	150.37	8.55%	0.20%
2006	Chile	365.54	54.53	7.50%	0.48%
2006	Colombia	332.80	58.75	5.26%	0.41%
2006	Costa Rica	508.73	58.03	8.62%	0.32%
2006	Cuba	275.88	20.82	20.33%	0.34%
2006	Dominica	647.59	29.29	4.58%	0.28%
2006	Dominican Republic	382.14	23.30	12.01%	0.37%
2006	Ecuador	864.24	403.74	6.34%	0.51%

Table A2.1   *Continued*

Year	Country	Freight/ton	Insurance cost/ton	Freight margin	Insurance margin
2006	El Salvador	487.19	19.63	19.67%	0.41%
2006	French Guiana	41.14	0.22	25.47%	0.15%
2006	Guatemala	290.60	55.85	10.37%	0.56%
2006	Guyana	141.57	4.19	33.59%	0.33%
2006	Haiti	138.47	18.15	14.79%	0.97%
2006	Honduras	564.05	32.81	21.81%	0.65%
2006	Jamaica	1 018.56	51.57	16.08%	0.49%
2006	Martinique	299.86	15.31	27.75%	0.74%
2006	Mexico	928.39	53.65	6.06%	0.41%
2006	Netherlands Antilles	496.90	13.34	8.26%	0.24%
2006	Nicaragua	241.65	59.38	14.58%	0.74%
2006	Panama	254.80	51.23	7.02%	0.38%
2006	Paraguay	488.58	50.01	13.26%	0.48%
2006	Peru	347.40	51.84	6.12%	0.40%
2006	Puerto Rico	576.39	38.90	16.46%	0.30%
2006	Saint Vincent and Grenadines	673.88	71.62	3.31%	0.24%
2006	Suriname	166.01	23.87	12.48%	0.65%
2006	Trinidad and Tobago	538.52	18.35	16.37%	0.31%
2006	Turks and Caicos Islands	870.84	94.24	5.80%	0.63%
2006	Uruguay	647.48	92.16	6.54%	0.34%
2006	Venezuela (Bolivarian Republic of)	252.26	21.88	9.00%	0.27%
2006	Virgin Islands, US	498.55	49.32	8.52%	0.47%

Source: Author based on BTI 2000–2006
Notes: considers only containerizable cargo, excludes SITC 3 and SITC 9. Where insurance costs equal 0 insurance costs are included in freight

Factor Analysis Liner Service Network Structure (LSNS), 2000–2006

Table A3.1   Correlation matrix[a] LSNS 2000–2006

		Shipping lines	Number of vessels	Number of services	Average vessel size	Capacity deployed TEU
Correlation	Number of shipping lines$_{IJt}$	1.000	.900	.974	.868	.922
	Number of vessels$_{IJt}$	.900	1.000	.959	.844	.986
	Number of services$_{IJt}$	.974	.959	1.000	.863	.977
	Average vessel size$_{IJt}$	.868	.844	.863	1.000	.882
	Capacity deployed TEU$_{IJt}$	.922	.986	.977	.882	1.000
Sig. (1-tailed)	Number of shipping lines$_{IJt}$		.000	.000	.000	.000
	Number of vessels$_{IJt}$	.000		.000	.000	.000
	Number of services$_{IJt}$	.000	.000		.000	.000
	Average vessel size$_{IJt}$	.000	.000	.000		.000
	Capacity deployed TEU$_{IJt}$	.000	.000	.000	.000	

Note: a. Determinant = 4.56E-006

Table A3.2   Inverse of correlation matrix LSNS 2000–2006

	Number of shipping lines	Number of vessels	Number of services	Average vessel size	Capacity deployed TEU
Number of shipping lines$_{IJt}$	53.848	−10.146	−88.166	−13.942	58.831
Number of vessels$_{IJt}$	−10.146	42.392	20.501	7.276	−58.895
Number of services$_{IJt}$	−88.166	20.501	167.081	23.151	−122.656
Average vessel size$_{IJt}$	−13.942	7.276	23.151	8.650	−24.577
Capacity deployed TEU$_{IJt}$	58.831	−58.895	−122.656	−24.577	146.388

Table A3.3   KMO and Bartlett's test LSNS 2000–2006

Kaiser-Meyer-Olkin measure of sampling adequacy		.679
Bartlett's test of sphericity	Approx. Chi-Square	4861483.007
	Df	10.000
	Sig.	.000

Table A3.4   Communalities LSNS 2000–2006

	Initial	Extraction
Number of shipping lines$_{IJt}$	1.000	.932
Number of vessels$_{IJt}$	1.000	.943
Number of services$_{IJt}$	1.000	.977
Average vessel size$_{IJt}$	1.000	.847
Capacity deployed TEU$_{IJt}$	1.000	.974

Note: Extraction method: Principal component analysis

Table A3.5   Total variance explained LSNS 2000–2006

Component	Initial Eigenvalues			Extraction Sums of Squared Loadings		
	Total	% of Variance	Cumulative %	Total	% of Variance	Cumulative %
1	4.673	93.461	93.461	4.673	93.461	93.461
2	.192	3.847	97.308			
3	.117	2.342	99.650			
4	.015	.290	99.940			
5	.003	.060	100.000			

Note: Extraction method: Principal component analysis

Table A3.6   Scree plot LSNS 2000–2006

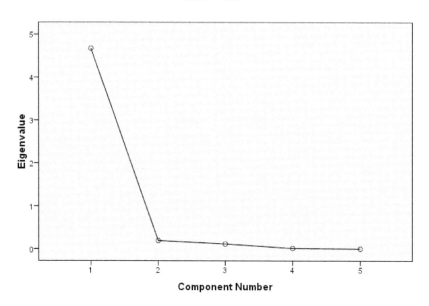

Scree Plot

Table A3.7   Component matrix[a] LSNS 2000–2006

	Component
	1
Number of shipping lines$_{IJt}$	.965
Number of vessels$_{IJt}$	.971
Number of services$_{IJt}$	.988
Average vessel size$_{IJt}$	.921
Capacity deployed TEU$_{IJt}$	.987

Notes: Extraction method: Principal component analysis. a. 1 components extracted

Appendix 4
Factor Analysis Liner Service Network Structure (LSNS), 2006

Table A4.1   Correlation matrix[a] LSNS 2006

	Number of ships deployed	TEU deployed	Number of carriers	Number of regular liner services	Max. ship size
Number of ships deployed$_{IJt}$	1.000	.985	.905	.987	.793
TEU deployed$_{IJt}$	.985	1.000	.838	.970	.772
Number of carriers$_{IJt}$	.905	.838	1.000	.885	.814
Number of regular liner services$_{IJt}$	.987	.970	.885	1.000	.756
Max. ship size$_{IJt}$	.793	.772	.814	.756	1.000

Note: a. Determinant = 1.90E–005

Table A4.2   Inverse of correlation matrix LSNS 2006

	Number of ships deployed	TEU deployed	Number of carriers	Number of regular liner services	Max. ship size
Number of ships deployed$_{IJt}$	182.367	−98.268	−36.600	−53.044	1.092
TEU deployed$_{IJt}$	−98.268	73.564	23.889	7.373	−3.869
Number of carriers$_{IJt}$	−36.600	23.889	14.187	2.583	−2.916
Number of regular liner services$_{IJt}$	−53.044	7.373	2.583	41.957	2.577
Max. ship size$_{IJt}$	1.092	−3.869	−2.916	2.577	3.548

Table A4.3   Anti-image matrices LSNS 2006

		Number of ships deployed	TEU deployed	Number of carriers	Number of regular liner services	Max. ship size
Anti-image Covariance	Number of ships deployed$_{IJt}$	.005	−.007	−.014	−.007	.002
	TEU deployed$_{IJt}$	−.007	.014	.023	.002	−.015
	Number of carriers$_{IJt}$	−.014	.023	.070	.004	−.058
	Number of regular liner services$_{IJt}$	−.007	.002	.004	.024	.017
	Max. ship size$_{IJt}$	.002	−.015	−.058	.017	.282
Anti-image Correlation	Number of ships deployed$_{IJt}$	.678[a]	−.848	−.720	−.606	.043
	TEU deployed$_{IJt}$	−.848	.705[a]	.739	.133	−.239
	Number of carriers$_{IJt}$	−.720	.739	.705[a]	.106	−.411
	Number of regular liner services$_{IJt}$	−.606	.133	.106	.881[a]	.211
	Max. ship size$_{IJt}$	.043	−.239	−.411	.211	.900[a]

Note: a. Measures of sampling adequacy (MSA)

Appendix 5
Ports List – Infrastructure Data

Table A5.1

Country	Port
Antigua and Barbuda	ST JOHNS
Argentina	BAHIA BLANCA, BUENOS AIRES, ROSARIO, USHUAIA, ZARATE
Aruba	ORANJESTAD
Bahamas, The	FREEPORT
Barbados	BRIDGETOWN
Belize	BELIZE CITY
Bermuda	ST GEORGE'S
Brazil	BELEM, IMBITUBA, ITAJAI, ITAQUI, MANAUS, PARANAGUA, PORT DE SALVADOR, PORT OF ILHEUS, PORTO DE SUAPE, PORTO DE SUAPE, RECIFE, RIO DE JANEIRO, RIO GRANDE, SANTAREM, SANTOS, SAO FRANCISCO, VILA DO CONDE, VITORIA
Cayman Islands	GEORGETOWN
Chile	ANTOFAGASTA, ARICA, BAHIA SAN VICENTE, CORONEL, IQUIQUE, LIRQUEN, PUERTO SAN ANTONIO, TALCAHUANO, VALPARAISO
Colombia	BARRANQUILLA, BUENAVENTURA, CARTAGENA, PUERTO BOLIVAR, SANTA MARTA
Costa Rica	PUERTO CALDERA, PUERTO LIMON
Dominica	ROSEAU
Dominican Republic	PUERTO DE HAINA
Ecuador	ESMERALDAS, GUAYAQUIL, MANTA, PUERTO BOLIVAR
El Salvador	ACAJUTLA
Grenada	ST GEORGE'S
Guadeloupe	POINTE A PITRE
Guatemala	PUERTO BARRIOS, PUERTO QUETZAL, SANTO THOMAS DE CASTILLA, SANTO THOMAS DE CASTILLA
Guyana	GEORGETOWN

Table A5.1   *Continued*

Country	Port
Haiti	PORT AU PRINCE
Honduras	LA CEIBA
Honduras	PUERTO CORTES
Jamaica	KINGSTON
Mexico	ALTAMIRA, ENSENADA, LAZARO CARDENAS, MANZANILLO, MAZATLAN, PROGRESO, SALINA CRUZ, TAMPICO, VERACRUZ
Montserrat	PLYMOUTH
Netherlands Antilles	WILLEMSTAD
Nicaragua	CORINTO
Panama	BALBOA, CHIRIQUI GRANDE, MANZANILLO, PUERTO CRISTOBAL
Paraguay	PUERTO DE ASUNCION
Peru	ILO, PAITA, PUERTO DEL CALLAO
Puerto Rico	SAN JUAN
Saint Kitts and Nevis	BASSETERRE
Saint Vincent and the Grenadines	KINGSTOWN
St. Lucia	CASTRIES, VIEUX FORT
Suriname	PARAMARIBO
Trinidad and Tobago	POINT LISAS PORT, PORT OF SPAIN
Uruguay	MONTEVIDEO
Venezuela	LA GUAIRA, MARACAIBO, PUERTO CABELLO
Virgin Islands	CHRISTIANSTED

Appendix 6
Port Infrastructure and Superstructure Variables

Table A6.1

Variable	Source
Terminals	Individual port websites and Containerization International
Berths	Individual port websites and Containerization International
Office hours	Individual port websites and Containerization International
Quayside hours	Individual port websites and Containerization International
Receive/Delivery hours	Individual port websites and Containerization International
Total area	Individual port websites and Containerization International
Storage capacity	Individual port websites and Containerization International
Electric reefer points	Individual port websites and Containerization International
Entrance restriction tide	National Geospatial-Intelligence Agency (NGA)
Entrance restriction swell	NGA
Entrance restriction ice	NGA
Entrance restriction other	NGA
Overhead limits	NGA
Turning area	NGA
Pilotage compulsory	NGA
Load offload wharves	NGA
Cranes fixed	NGA
Cranes mobile	NGA
Lifts 100 tons plus	NGA
Lifts 50 100 tons	NGA
Lifts 25 49 tons	NGA
Lifts 0 24 tons	NGA
Railway	NGA
Harbour Type	NGA
Maximum size vessel	NGA
Access depth	NGA
Pier depth	NGA
Anchorage depth	NGA

Appendix 7
Factor Analysis Port Variables (PCA1)

Table A7.1   Descriptive statistics

	Mean	Std. Deviation	Analysis N
Terminals	1.30	.684	71
Berths	4.03	4.246	71
Office hours	.07	.258	71
Quayside hours	.68	.471	71
Receive/Delivery hours	.34	1.121	71
Total area	253230.77	285284.650	71
Storage capacity	11553.07	41501.040	71
Electric reefer points	250.14	374.357	71

Table A7.2 Correlation matrix

	Terminals	Berths	Office hours	Quayside Hours	Receive/ Delivery Hours	Total Area	Storage Capacity	Electric Reefer Points
Terminals	1.000	.322	-.039	.213	.017	.281	.707	.614
Berths	.322	1.000	.142	.197	-.029	.230	.359	.154
Office hours	-.039	.142	1.000	.191	.065	.134	-.001	.178
Quayside hours	.213	.197	.191	1.000	.183	.277	.143	.330
Receive/Delivery hours	.017	-.029	.065	.183	1.000	.063	-.021	.063
Total Area	.281	.230	.134	.277	.063	1.000	.394	.388
Storage Capacity	.707	.359	-.001	.143	-.021	.394	1.000	.505
Electric Reefer Points	.614	.154	.178	.330	.063	.388	.505	1.000

Table A7.3 Inverse of correlation matrix

	Terminals	Berths	Office hours	Quayside Hours	Receive/ Delivery Hours	Total Area	Storage Capacity	Electric Reefer Points
Terminals	2.598	-.293	.309	-.093	-.033	.225	-1.300	-1.003
Berths	-.293	1.254	-.194	-.174	.070	-.122	-.309	.277
Office hours	.309	-.194	1.130	-.122	-.037	-.053	.054	-.326
Quayside hours	-.093	-.174	-.122	1.243	-.188	-.203	.180	-.304
Receive/Delivery hours	-.033	.070	-.037	-.188	1.044	-.039	.065	-.006
Total area	.225	-.122	-.053	-.203	-.039	1.335	-.443	-.335
Storage capacity	-1.300	-.309	.054	.180	.065	-.443	2.285	-.209
Electric reefer points	-1.003	.277	-.326	-.304	-.006	-.335	-.209	1.967

Table A7.4   KMO and Bartlett's test

Kaiser-Meyer-Olkin measure of sampling adequacy		.702
Bartlett's test of sphericity	Approx. Chi-Square	128.667
	df	28.000
	Sig.	.000

Table A7.5 Anti-image matrices

Anti-image Covariance	Terminals	Berths	Office hours	Quayside Hours	Receive/Delivery Hours	Total Area	Storage Capacity	Electric Reefer Points
Terminals	.385	-.090	.105	-.029	-.012	.065	-.219	-.196
Berths	-.090	.797	-.137	-.112	.053	-.073	-.108	.112
Office hours	.105	-.137	.885	-.087	-.031	-.035	.021	-.147
Quayside hours	-.029	-.112	-.087	.805	-.145	-.122	.063	-.124
Receive/Delivery hours	-.012	.053	-.031	-.145	.958	-.028	.027	-.003
Total area	.065	-.073	-.035	-.122	-.028	.749	-.145	-.128
Storage capacity	-.219	-.108	.021	.063	.027	-.145	.438	-.047
Electric reefer points	-.196	.112	-.147	-.124	-.003	-.128	-.047	.508
Terminals	.665[a]	-.162	.181	-.052	-.020	.121	-.534	-.444
Berths	-.162	.712[a]	-.163	-.140	.061	-.094	-.182	.176
Office hours	.181	-.163	.479[a]	-.103	-.034	-.043	.034	-.219
Quayside hours	-.052	-.140	-.103	.729[a]	-.165	-.158	.107	-.194
Receive/Delivery hours	-.020	.061	-.034	-.165	.573[a]	-.033	.042	-.004
Total area	.121	-.094	-.043	-.158	-.033	.772[a]	-.254	-.207
Storage capacity	-.534	-.182	.034	.107	.042	-.254	.723[a]	-.099
Electric reefer points	-.444	.176	-.219	-.194	-.004	-.207	-.099	.722[a]

Measures of sampling adequacy (MSA)

Table A7.6 Total variance explained

Component	Initial Eigenvalues			Extraction Sums of Squared Loadings			Rotation Sums of Squared Loadings		
	Total	% of Variance	Cumulative %	Total	% of Variance	Cumulative %	Total	% of Variance	Cumulative %
1	2.822	35.280	35.280	2.822	35.280	35.280	2.717	33.962	33.962
2	1.279	15.987	51.267	1.279	15.987	51.267	1.384	17.304	51.267
3	1.000	12.497	63.764						
4	.832	10.403	74.167						
5	.742	9.270	83.437						
6	.702	8.773	92.209						
7	.380	4.753	96.962						
8	.243	3.038	100.000						

Note: Extraction Method: Principal component analysis

Table A7.7   Communalities

	Initial	Extraction
Terminals	1.000	.766
Berths	1.000	.261
Office hours	1.000	.442
Quayside hours	1.000	.528
Receive/Delivery hours	1.000	.323
Total area	1.000	.410
Storage capacity	1.000	.764
Electric reefer points	1.000	.607

Extraction Method: Principal component analysis

Table A7.8   Scree plot

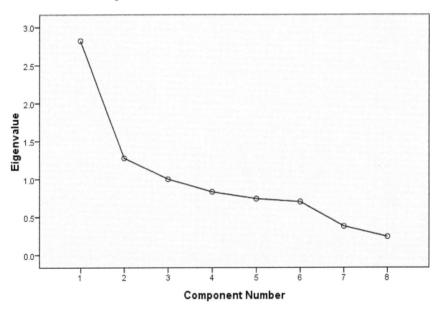

Table A7.9   Component matrix[a]

	Component	
	1	2
Terminals	.811	−.331
Storage Capacity	.800	−.352
Electric Reefer Points	.779	.029
Total Area	.618	.165
Berths	.510	−.029
Office hours	.197	.635
Receive/Delivery Hours	.094	.561
Quayside Hours	.478	.548

Extraction Method: Principal component analysis
a. 2 components extracted

Table A7.10   Rotated component matrix[a]

	Component	
	1	2
Terminals	.869	−.107
Storage capacity	.864	−.130
Electric reefer points	.744	.232
Total area	.554	.321
Berths	.500	.105
Office hours	.024	.664
Quayside hours	.318	.653
Receive/Delivery hours	−.056	.566

Extraction Method: Principal component analysis
Rotation Method: Varimax with Kaiser normalization
a. Rotation converged in 3 iterations

Table A7.11   Component transformation matrix

Component	1	2
1	.965	.261
2	−.261	.965

Extraction Method: Principal component analysis
Rotation Method: Varimax with Kaiser normalization

Table A7.12   Component plot in rotated space

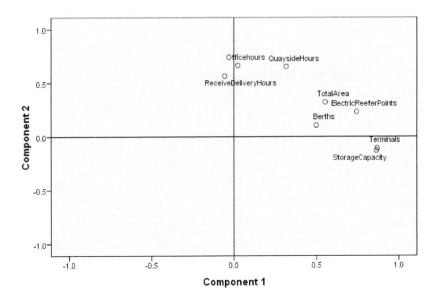

Table A7.13 Component score coefficient matrix

	Component	
	1	2
Terminals	.345	−.174
Berths	.180	.025
Office hours	−.062	.497
Quayside Hours	.052	.457
Receive/Delivery Hours	−.082	.432
Total Area	.178	.182
Storage Capacity	.346	−.191
Electric Reefer Points	.260	.094

Note: Extraction method: Principal component analysis
Rotation Method: Varimax with Kaiser normalization
Component scores

Table A7.14 Component score covariance matrix

Component	1	2
1	1.000	.000
2	.000	1.000

Note: Extraction method: Principal component analysis
Rotation method: Varimax with Kaiser normalization
Component scores

Appendix 8
Factor Analysis Port Variables (PCA 2)

Table A8.1 Descriptive statistics

	Mean	Std. Deviation	Analysis N
Berths	4.03	4.246	71
Terminals	1.30	.684	71
Total area	253230.77	285284.650	71
Storage capacity	11553.07	41501.040	71
Electric reefer points	250.14	374.357	71
Access depth	11.04	4.824	71
Pier depth	12.39	5.869	71
Anchorage depth	9.15	2.994	71
Berths	4.03	4.246	71
Terminals	1.30	.684	71

Table A8.2 Correlation matrix

	Berths	Terminals	Total Area	Storage Capacity	Electric Reefer Points	Access depth	Pier depth	Anchorage depth
Berths	1.000	.322	.230	.359	.154	.004	.018	.026
Terminals	.322	1.000	.281	.707	.614	-.022	-.052	.112
Total area	.230	.281	1.000	.394	.388	.045	-.234	-.033
Storage capacity	.359	.707	.394	1.000	.505	-.091	-.113	.046
Electric reefer points	.154	.614	.388	.505	1.000	.077	-.177	.017
Access depth	.004	-.022	.045	-.091	.077	1.000	.178	.072
Pier depth	.018	-.052	-.234	-.113	-.177	.178	1.000	.133
Anchorage depth	.026	.112	-.033	.046	.017	.072	.133	1.000

Table A8.3 Inverse of correlation matrix

	Berths	Terminals	Total Area	Storage Capacity	Electric Reefer Points	Access depth	Pier depth	Anchorage depth
Berths	1.195	-.241	-.174	-.284	.163	-.028	-.074	.013
Terminals	-.241	2.560	.192	-1.311	-.969	.040	-.121	-.184
Total area	-.174	.192	1.346	-.406	-.359	-.109	.234	.028
Storage capacity	-.284	-1.311	-.406	2.290	-.161	.203	.034	.019
Electric reefer points	.163	-.969	-.359	-.161	1.840	-.202	.200	.057
Access depth	-.028	.040	-.109	.203	-.202	1.084	-.221	-.062
Pier depth	-.074	-.121	.234	.034	.200	-.221	1.144	-.118
Anchorage depth	.013	-.184	.028	.019	.057	-.062	-.118	1.040

Table A8.4   KMO and Bartlett's test

Kaiser-Meyer-Olkin measure of sampling adequacy	.697
Bartlett's test of sphericity	118.943
	28.000
	.000

Table A8.5 Anti-image matrices

	Berths	Terminals	Total Area	Storage Capacity	Electric Reefer Points	Access depth	Pier depth	Anchorage depth
Berths	.837	-.079	-.108	-.104	.074	-.022	-.054	.010
Terminals	-.079	.391	.056	-.224	-.206	.015	-.041	-.069
Total area	-.108	.056	.743	-.132	-.145	-.075	.152	.020
Storage capacity	-.104	-.224	-.132	.437	-.038	.082	.013	.008
Electric reefer points	.074	-.206	-.145	-.038	.543	-.101	.095	.030
Access depth	-.022	.015	-.075	.082	-.101	.923	-.178	-.055
Pier depth	-.054	-.041	.152	.013	.095	-.178	.874	-.099
Anchorage depth	.010	-.069	.020	.008	.030	-.055	-.099	.962
Berths	.786[a]	-.138	-.137	-.171	.110	-.025	-.063	.011
Terminals	-.138	.665[a]	.103	-.541	-.446	.024	-.071	-.113
Total area	-.137	.103	.734[a]	-.231	-.228	-.090	.188	.024
Storage capacity	-.171	-.541	-.231	.727[a]	-.078	.129	.021	.013
Electric reefer points	.110	-.446	-.228	-.078	.731[a]	-.143	.138	.041
Access depth	-.025	.024	-.090	.129	-.143	.376[a]	-.198	-.058
Pier depth	-.063	-.071	.188	.021	.138	-.198	.568[a]	-.108
Anchorage depth	.011	-.113	.024	.013	.041	-.058	-.108	.565[a]

Table A8.6 Communalities

	Initial	Extraction
Berths	1.000	.332
Terminals	1.000	.759
Total area	1.000	.541
Storage capacity	1.000	.750
Electric reefer points	1.000	.643
Access depth	1.000	.909
Pier depth	1.000	.616
Anchorage depth	1.000	.436

Note: Extraction method: Principal component analysis

Table A8.7 Total variance explained

Component	Initial Eigenvalues			Extraction Sums of Squared Loadings			Rotation Sums of Squared Loadings		
	Total	% of Variance	Cumulative %	Total	% of Variance	Cumulative %	Total	% of Variance	Cumulative %
1	2.690	33.623	33.623	2.690	33.623	33.623	2.651	33.139	33.139
2	1.288	16.103	49.726	1.288	16.103	49.726	1.269	15.865	49.004
3	1.007	12.589	62.316	1.007	12.589	62.316	1.065	13.311	62.316
4	.919	11.483	73.799						
5	.811	10.136	83.935						
6	.615	7.683	91.618						
7	.423	5.294	96.912						
8	.247	3.088	100.000						

Note: Extraction method: principal component analysis

Table A8.8   Scree plot

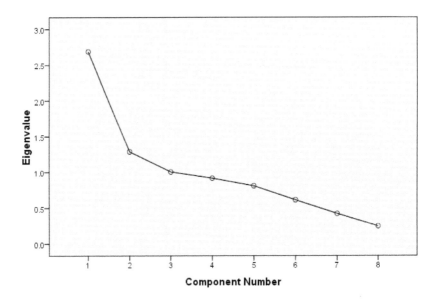

Table A8.9   Component matrix[a]

	Component		
	1	**2**	**3**
Storage capacity	.847	.037	−.177
Terminals	.840	.174	−.152
Electric reefer points	.768	.004	.230
Total area	.611	−.197	.359
Berths	.491	.191	−.233
Pier depth	−.240	.733	−.145
Anchorage depth	.062	.588	−.295
Access depth	−.027	.547	.780
Storage capacity	.847	.037	−.177
Terminals	.840	.174	−.152

Notes: Extraction method: principal component analysis
a. 3 components extracted

Table A8.10 Rotated component matrix[a]

	Component		
	1	2	3
Terminals	.866	.088	−.032
Storage capacity	.858	−.023	−.116
Electric reefer points	.736	−.218	.231
Total area	.544	−.427	.251
Berths	.532	.194	−.108
Pier depth	−.130	.750	.191
Anchorage depth	.165	.639	.001
Access depth	−.033	.147	.941
Terminals	.866	.088	−.032
Storage capacity	.858	−.023	−.116

Notes: Extraction method: principal component analysis
Rotation method: Varimax with Kaiser normalization
a. Rotation converged in 6 iterations

Table A8.11 Component transformation matrix

Component	1	2	3
1	.987	−.157	.030
2	.127	.885	.447
3	−.097	−.437	.894

Notes: Extraction method: principal component analysis
Rotation method: Varimax with Kaiser normalization
a. Rotation converged in 6 iterations

Table A8.12 Component plot in rotated space

Component Plot in Rotated Space

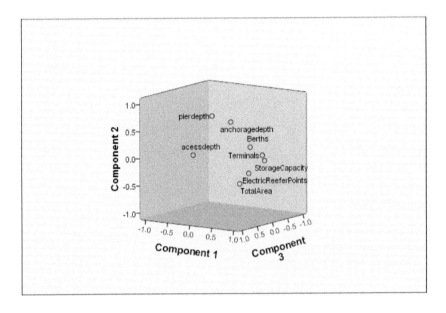

Table A8.13 Component score coefficient matrix

	Component		
	1	2	3
Berths	.222	.204	−.135
Terminals	.340	.137	−.065
Total area	.170	−.327	.257
Storage capacity	.331	.053	−.135
Electric reefer points	.260	−.142	.214
Access depth	−.031	.039	.882
Pier depth	−.002	.581	.123
Anchorage depth	.109	.528	−.057

Notes: Extraction method: Principal component analysis
Rotation Method: Varimax with Kaiser normalization
Component Scores

Table A8.14 Component score covariance matrix

Component	1	2	3
1	1.000	.000	.000
2	.000	1.000	.000
3	.000	.000	1.000

Notes: Extraction method: Principal component analysis
Rotation method: Varimax with Kaiser normalization
Component Scores

Table A8.15 Regression results: descriptive statistics – panel data regression, year 2000–2006

	Mean	Std. Deviation	N
Freight (US$/ton) ln	4.8117	.97247	608344
Unit value (US$/ton) ln	7.8520	1.28923	608344
Frequency of shipping services	1.1510	.07820	608344
Number of services	3.1478	.31789	608344
Reefer	.0084	.09142	608344
Open registry	.4553	.49799	608344
Volume of shipment – ln	1.0860	2.23628	608344
TEU deployed (region) – ln	10.5391	.68941	608344
Maritime trade imbalance (exporting country)	3.7823	10.85398	608344
Maritime trade imbalance (importing country)	1.2342	.81212	608344
Dummy year 2000	.1095	.31221	608344
Dummy year 2001	.1208	.32594	608344
Dummy year 2002	.1221	.32738	608344
Dummy year 2003	.1800	.38416	608344
Dummy year 2004	.1089	.31149	608344
Dummy year 2005	.1797	.38396	608344
Port infrastructure endowment (importing country)	3.3984	2.08725	608344
Port service level cluster variable (importing country)	2.0875	.65068	608344

Appendix 9
Correlations Regression Results

Table A9.1

		Freight (US$/ton) ln	LSNSij	Maritime distance (nm) ln
Pearson correlation	Freight (US$/ton) $\ln_{ijkt}$	1.000	−.272	.306
	LSNS_{IJ2006}	−.272	1.000	−.564
	Maritime distance (nm) $\ln_{IJ}$	.306	−.564	1.000
Sig. (1-tailed)	Freight (US$/ton) $\ln_{ijkt}$	.	.000	.000
	LSNS_{IJ2006}	.000	.	.000
	Maritime distance (nm) $\ln_{IJ}$	.000	.000	.
N	Freight (US$/ton) $\ln_{ijkt}$	115122	115122	115122
	LSNS_{IJ2006}	115122	115122	115122
	Maritime distance (nm) $\ln_{IJ}$	115122	115122	115122

Appendix 10
Descriptives Cross-sectional Regression Analysis, 2006

Table on following page.

Table A10.1

	N	Minimum	Maximum	Mean	Std. Deviation	Variance
LSNS$_{12006}$	134914	−3.37535	1.50518	.0000000	1.00000000	1.000
Maritime distance (nm) ln$_{ijkt}$	127379	4.89	8.74	7.2130	1.06084	1.125
Maritime trade imbalance (exporting country)$_{jt}$	148710	.04	842.40	3.1061	24.09727	580.678
Maritime trade imbalance (importing country)$_{It}$	150580	.25	1.74	.9234	.34221	.117
Unit value (US\$/ton) − ln$_{ijkt}$	150580	2.74	13.08	8.0874	1.31184	1.721
Volume of shipment − ln$_{ijkt}$	150580	−2.30	12.31	1.0746	2.26065	5.111
Reefer$_{ijkt}$	150580	.00	1.00	.0086	.09216	.008
Port infrastructure endowment (importing country)$_{jt}$	150580	1.36	8.74	3.0458	1.80467	3.257
Port service level (importing country)$_{jt}$	150580	.50	4.70	2.4506	1.03695	1.075
Port infrastructure endowment (exporting country)$_{jt}$	149913	1.27	10.00	3.1470	1.65388	2.735
Port service level (exporting country)$_{it}$	149913	.00	5.68	2.0929	.80746	.652
Port Quay accessibility PCA2 (exporting country)$_{it}$	149909	−2.63	2.86	.0090	.71071	.505
Port infrastructure endowment PCA2 (exporting country)$_{it}$	149909	−.81	6.68	1.1316	1.52798	2.335
Port Quay accessibility PCA2 (exporting country)$_{it}$	149909	−1.49	1.82	.0212	.84659	.717
Port accessibility PCA2 (importing country)$_{jt}$	150580	−1.08	1.00	−.1114	.52514	.276
Port infrastructure endowment PCA2 (importing country)$_{jt}$	150580	−.58	6.68	1.0366	1.78450	3.184
Port Quay accessibility PCA2 (importing country)$_{jt}$	150580	−.91	1.40	−.1570	.69743	.486
landlord ports$_{ijt}$	150580	.00	1.00	.6184	.48578	.236
service ports$_{ijt}$	150580	.00	1.00	.0835	.27664	.077
carrier number (ln)$_{It}$	139232	.00	3.30	2.3475	.75936	.577

Appendix 11

Descriptives Panel-data Regression Analysis, 2000–2006

Table A11.1

	Mean	Std. Deviation	N
Freight (USD/ton) $\ln_{ijkt}$	4.8715	.98178	608344
Unit value (USD/ton) $\ln_{ijkt}$	7.8923	1.28145	608344
Dummy year 2000	.1050	.30660	608344
Dummy year 2001	.1219	.32721	608344
Dummy year 2002	.1171	.32149	608344
Dummy year 2004	.1848	.38812	608344
Dummy year 2005	.1210	.32608	608344
Dummy year 2003	.1662	.37228	608344
TEU deployed (region) $\ln_{IJt}$	10.4753	.71289	608344
Number of services$_{IJt}$	3.1056	.31317	608344
Frequency of shipping services$_{IJt}$	1.1436	.07472	608344
Maritime trade imbalance (exporting country)$_{It}$	3.7212	11.03592	608344
Maritime trade imbalance (importing country)$_{Jt}$	1.2550	.78208	608344
Reefer$_{ijkt}$	.0085	.09165	608344
Open registry$_{ijkt}$	.3903	.48782	608344
Volume of shipment – $\ln_{ijkt}$	1.1042	2.25217	608344

Table A11.2

	Mean	Std. Deviation	N
Freight per ton – $\ln_{ijkt}$	4.9338	.99542	822100
Unit value – $\ln_{ijkt}$	7.9164	1.29402	822100
Open registry$_{ijkt}$	.40	.490	822100
Reefer$_{ijkt}$	.01	.091	822100
TEU deployed (region) – $\ln_{IJt}$	20.97	14.375	822100

Table A11.2 *Continued*

	Mean	Std. Deviation	N
Volume of shipment – $\ln_{ijkt}$	1.1760	2.27500	822100
Maritime corridor$_{IJ}$	.23	.418	822100
Corruption$_{ij}$	3.5909	1.19113	822100
Maritime trade imbalance (exporting country)$_{It}$	66.08	40.645	822100
Maritime trade imbalance (importing country)$_{Jt}$	1.2751	.79019	822100
Dummy year 2000	.10	.304	822100
Dummy year 2001	.12	.323	822100
Dummy year 2002	.12	.319	822100
Dummy year 2003	.17	.375	822100
Dummy year 2004	.19	.390	822100
Dummy year 2005	.12	.330	822100
Maritime Distance$_{IJ}$	42.99	42.326	822100

Table A11.3

	Mean	Std. Deviation	N
Freight per ton – $\ln_{ijkt}$	4.8651	1.03402	357706
Unit Value – $\ln_{ijkt}$	7.9579	1.22616	357706
Open registry$_{ijkt}$	.36	.479	357706
Reefer$_{ijkt}$	.01	.111	357706
TEU deployed (region) - $\ln_{IJt}$	23.37	17.880	357706
Volume of shipment - $\ln_{ijkt}$	1.8133	2.38720	357706
Maritime corridor$_{IJ}$	.42	.494	357706
Corruption$_{Jt}$	3.5706	1.23969	357706
Maritime trade imbalance (exporting country)$_{It}$	52.92	37.419	357706
Maritime trade imbalance (importing country)$_{Jtt}$	1.2781	.79639	357706
Dummy year 2000	.10	.304	357706
Dummy year 2001	.12	.323	357706
Dummy year 2002	.12	.326	357706
Dummy year 2003	.17	.371	357706
Dummy year 2004	.19	.393	357706
Dummy year 2005	.12	.330	357706
LSNS2000–2006$_{IJt}$	.0424	1.05142	357706
Landlord$_{ijt}$	.57	.496	357706

Appendix 12
Descriptives Panel-Data Regression Analysis by Country, 2000–2006

Table A12.1 Argentina

	Mean	Std. Deviation	N
Freight per ton – $\ln_{ijkt}$	4.3853	.94536	59473
Unit value – $\ln_{ijkt}$	8.2570	1.16248	59473
Open registry$_{ijkt}$	.46	.498	59473
Reefer$_{ijkt}$	.00	.038	59473
Volume of shipment – $\ln_{ijkt}$	1.6808	2.35895	59473
Maritime trade imbalance (exporting country)$_{It}$	51.85	25.301	59473
LSNS2000–2006$_{IJt}$	1.5071	.65831	59473
Dummy year 2000	.15	.357	59473
Dummy year 2001	.14	.350	59473
Dummy year 2002	.10	.293	59473
Dummy year 2003	.15	.355	59473
Dummy year 2004	.19	.389	59473
Dummy year 2005	.12	.321	59473

Table A12.2 Brazil

	Mean	Std. Deviation	N
Freight per ton – $\ln_{ijkt}$	4.6523	1.03534	36815
Unit Value – $\ln_{ijkt}$	7.8917	1.31257	36815
Open Registry$_{ijkt}$	.28	.447	36815
Reefer$_{ijkt}$	.04	.187	36815
Volume of Shipment – $\ln_{ijkt}$	2.4994	2.51877	36815
Maritime trade imbalance(exporting country)$_{It}$	54.55	44.949	36815
LSNS2000–2006$_{IJt}$	.3287	1.29723	36815

Table A12.2 *Continued*

	Mean	Std. Deviation	N
Dummy year 2000	.14	.344	36815
Dummy year 2001	.13	.335	36815
Dummy year 2002	.14	.343	36815
Dummy year 2003	.12	.328	36815
Dummy year 2004	.15	.355	36815
Dummy year 2005	.16	.370	36815

Table A12.3 **Chile**

	Mean	Std. Deviation	N
Freight per ton – $\ln_{ijkt}$	4.9448	1.09724	32827
Unit value – $\ln_{ijkt}$	8.0003	1.23353	32827
Open registry$_{ijkt}$	.01	.100	32827
Reefer$_{ijkt}$	.01	.100	32827
Volume of shipment – $\ln_{ijkt}$	1.7237	2.38854	32827
Maritime trade imbalance (exporting country)$_{It}$	65.15	34.269	32827
Maritime trade imbalance (importing country)$_{Jt}$	.7711	.47384	32827
Liner Shipping Network Structure (LSNS$_{IJt}$)	−.3561	.83919	32827
Dummy year 2000	.11	.313	32827
Dummy year 2001	.10	.304	32827
Dummy year 2002	.15	.354	32827
Dummy year 2003	.15	.353	32827
Dummy year 2004	.15	.354	32827
Dummy year 2005	.17	.377	32827

References

Abe, K. and Wilson, J. 2008. Trade, transparency, and welfare in the Asia Pacific. *Journal of International Economic Studies*, 12 (2), 33–77.

Amelung, T. 1990. Explaining Regionalization of Trade in Asia Pacific: A Transaction Cost Approach, *Kiel Working Paper* No. 423, Kiel: Institute of World Economics.

Amjadi A. and Winters L.A. 1997. Transport costs and 'natural' integration in Mercosur. *World Bank Policy Research Working Paper*, 1742; 1997. http://www.worldbank.org/research/trade/pdf/wp1742.pdf.

Amjadi A. and Yeats A.J. 1995. Have transport costs contributed to the relative decline of sub-Saharan African exports? Some preliminary empirical evidence. World Bank Policy Research Working Paper, 1559; 1995. http://www.econ.worldbank.org/files/391_wps1559.pdf.

Amjadi A., Reinke U. and Yeats A.J. 1996. Did external barriers cause the marginalization of sub-Saharan Africa in World Trade? *World Bank Policy Research Working Paper*, 1586; 1996. http://www.econ.worldbank.org/files/903_wps1586.pdf.

Anders, G. 1970. *Blick vom Mond*. Munich, Beck Verlag.

Anderson, J. and van Wincoop, E. 2003. Gravity with gravitas: a solution to the border puzzle. *American Economic Review*, 93, 170–92.

Anderson, J. and van Wincoop, E. 2004. Trade costs. *Journal of Economic Literature*, 42, 691–751.

Anderson, J.E. 2008. Economic integration and the civilizing commerce hypothesis. *The World Economy*, 31 (1), 141–57.

Anderson, J.E. and Marcouiller, D. 2002. Insecurity and the pattern of trade: an empirical investigation. *Review of Economics and Statistics*, 84 (2), 342–52.

Anderson, J.E. 2008. Economic Integration and the Civilising Commerce Hypothesis, The World Economy , 31 (1), 141–57.

Angeloudis, P., Bichou, K., Bell, M. and Fisk D. 2006. Security and reliability of the liner container shipping network: Analysis of robustness using a complex network framework, presented to IAME 2006 conference, Melbourne.

Australian Productivity Commission 1998. International Benchmarking of the Australian Waterfront, Canberra, Australia: Ausinfo.

Backhaus, K., Erichson, B., Plinke, W. and Weiber, R. 2006. Multivariate Analysemethoden. Springer, Berlin.

Baier, S.L. and Bergstrand, J.H. 2001. The growth of world trade: tariffs, transport costs and income similarity. *Journal of International Economics*, 53 (1), 1–27.

Barros, C.P. and Athanassiou, M. 2004. Efficiency in European Seaports with DEA: Evidence from Greece and Portugal, *Maritime Economics and Logistics*, 6, 122–40.

Behrens, K., Gaigné, C., Ottaviano, G.I.P. and Thisse J-F. 2006. How density economies in international transportation link the internal geography of trading partners. *Journal of Urban Economics*, 60, 148–263.

Bendall, H. and Stent, A. 1987. On measuring cargo handling productivity. *Maritime Policy and Management*, 14 (4), 337–43.

Bennathan, E. and Walters, A.A. 1969. The Economics of Ocean Freight Rates. NY: Praeger.

Beresford A.K.C. and Dubey, R.C. 1990. Handbook on the Management and Operation of Dry Ports. UNCTAD, Geneva.

Bergstrand, J.H. 1985. The gravity equation in international trade: Some microeconomic foundations and empirical evidence, *The Review of Economics and Statistics*, 67 (3), 474–81.

Bichou, K. and Gray, R. 2005. A critical review of conventional terminology for classifying seaports. *Transportation Research Part A*, 39 (1), 75–92.

Blainey, G. 1966. The Tyranny of Distance: How Distance Shaped Australia's History, *Sun*, Melbourne.

Blonigen, B.A. and Wilson, W.W. 2008. Port Efficiency and Trade Flows. *Review of International Economics*, 16, 21–36.

Boulho, H. and de Serres, A. 2008. Have Developed Countries Escaped the Curse of Distance? *OECD Economics Department Working Papers*, No. 610, OECD Publishing.

Boyer, K.D. 1998. *Principles of Transportation Economics*. Reading, MA: Addison-Wesley.

Branch, A.E. 2008. *Elements of Shipping*. Abingdon: Routledge.

Brooks, M., Wilmsmeier, G. and Sánchez, R.J. 2013. Developing Short Sea Shipping in South America – Looking beyond traditionalist perspectives. Ocean Yearbook, in press.

Bryan, I. 1974. Regression analysis of ocean liner freight rates on some Canadian export routes. *Journal of Transport Economics and Policy*, 8 (2), 161–71.

Carrere C. and Schiff, M. 2005. On the geography of trade: distance is alive and well, *Revue Economique* 56, 1249–74.

Chang Y.T. Lee, S-Y. Tongzon, J. Chou, C.C., Chu, C.W. and Liang, G.S. 2008, Port selection factors by shipping lines: Different perspectives between trunk liners and feeder service providers, *Marine Policy*, 32 (6), 877–85.

Chasomeris M.G. 2005. Assessing South Africa's Shipping Costs, *Journal of Development Perspectives*, September, 1 (1), 129–45.

Chou, C.C., Chu, C.W., Liang, G.S. 2003, Comparison of two models for port choice, *Journal of Maritime Quarterly*, 12, 45–61.

Chowdbury, A. and Erdenebileg, S. 2007. Geography Against Development – A Case for Landlocked Developing Countries, United Nations Publications.

Chowdhury, A.K. and Erdenebileg, E. 2006. Geography against Development: A Case for Landlocked Developing Countries. New York: United Nations.

Christaller, W. 1957. Zur Frage der Standort für Dienstleistungen, in Raumforschung und Raumordnung, 96–101.

Clark, X., Dollar, D. and Micco, A. 2004. Port efficiency, maritime transport costs, and bilateral trade. *Journal of Development Economics*, 75, 417–50.

Clyde, P.S. and Reitzes, J.D. 1995. The effectiveness of collusion under antitrust immunity. United States Federal Trade Commission, Bureau of Economics Staff Report, December.

Corbett, J.J., Winebrake, J. and Energy and Environmental Research Associates, 2008. The impacts of globalisation on international maritime transport activity. Past trends and future perspectives. *Global Forum on Transport and Environment in a Globalising World* 10–12 November 2008, Guadalajara, Mexico.

Coto Millán P., Baños, P. and Rodríguez Álvarez A. 1999. Allocative Efficiency and Over-Capitalization: an Application. *International Journal of Transport Economics*, Vol. XXVI, No 2, 181–200.

Coto Millán P., Baños, P. and Rodríguez Álvarez A. 2000. Economic efficiency in Spanish ports: Some empirical evidence, *Maritime Policy and Management* 27 (2), 169–74.

Cullinane, K.J.P. and Khanna, M. 2000. Economies of scale in large containership: optimal size and geographical implications, *Journal of Transport Geography*, Vol. 8, 181–95.

Cullinane, K.P.B. and Song, D-W. 2002. Port privatisation policy and practice. *Transport Reviews*, 22 (1), 55–75.

Cullinane, K.P.B., Khanna, M. and Song, D-W. 1999. How Big is Beautiful: Economies of Scale and the Optimal Size of Containership, *Proceedings of the International Association of Maritime Economists Annual Conference*, Dalhousie University, Halifax, 13–14 September.

Cullinane; K.P.B. and Khanna; M. 1999. Economies of Scale in Large Container Ships, *Journal of Transport Economics and Policy*, 33 (2), 185–208.

Davies, J.E. 1990. Destructive Competition and Market Sustainability in the Liner Shipping Industry. In: *International Journal of Transport Economics*, 27, 227–45.

de Langen, P. 2004. Governance in seaport clusters. *Maritime Economics and Logistics*, 6 (2), 141–56.

Deakin, B.M. and Seward, T. 1973. Shipping Conferences: A Study of Their Origins, Developments, and Economic Practices. Cambridge: Cambridge University Press.

Deardorff, A.V. 1995. Determinants of bilateral trade: Does gravity work in a Neo-classical world?, *NBER Working Paper* 5377.

Defilippi, E. 2004. Intra-Port Competition, Regulatory Challenges and the Concession of Callao Port, Maritime Economics and Logistics, Palgrave Macmillan, vol. 6 (4), pages 279–311, December.

Dicken, P. 1992. *Global shift: The internationalisation of economic activity.* Second edition. London: Paul Chapman Publishing Ltd.

World Bank 2013. Doing Business. www.doingbusiness.org.

Dollar, D., Micco, A. and Clark, X. 2002. Maritime transport costs and port efficiency. *World Bank Policy Research Working Paper* 2781. Washington, DC: World Bank.

Duranton, D. and Storper, M. 2008. Rising trade costs? Agglomeration and trade with endogenous transaction costs. *Canadian Journal of Economics*, 41 (1), 292–319.

Duranton, D. and Storper, M. 2008. Rising trade costs? Agglomeration and trade with endogenous transaction costs, *Canadian Journal of Economics*, 41 (1), 292–319.

Estache, A., Gonzalez, M. and Trujillo, L. 2001. Technical Efficiency Gains from Port Reform: The Potential for Yardstick Competition in Mexico. *World Bank Policy Research Working Paper* No. 2637, Washington, DC.

Exler, M. 1996. *Containerverkehr- Reichweiten und Sytemgrenzen in der Weltwirtschaft.* Dissertation. Erlangen Nürnberg: Friedrich-Alexander Universität.

Fagerholt, K. 2004. Designing optimal routes in a liner shipping problem, *Maritime Policy and Management*, 31 (4), 259–68.

Fasbender, K. and Wagner, W. 1973. Shipping conferences, rate policy and developing countries : the argument of rate discrimination, Verlag Weltarchiv, Hamburg.

Feenstra, R.C. 1996. U.S. Imports, 1972–1994: Data and Concordances. NBER Working Paper 5515s.

Feo, M., García, L., Martínez–Zarzoso, I. and Pérez, E. 2003. Determinants of modal choice for freight transport: consequences for the development of short sea shipping between Spain and Europe. In *Maritime Transport II. Second International Conference on Maritime Transport and Maritime History.* Volume I, 767–769. SCI UPC 2003, Barcelona, Spain.

Fink, C., Mattoo, A. and Neagu, I.C. 2002. Trade in international maritime services: How much does policy matter? *The World Bank Economic Review*, 16 (1), 81–108.

Fleming, D.K. and Hayuth, Y. 1994. Spatial Characteristics of Transportation Hubs: Centrality and Intermediacy, *Journal of Transport Geography*, 2 (1), 3–18.

Francois, J.F. and Wooton, I. 2001. Trade in International Transport Services: The Role of Competition, *Review of International Economics*, Blackwell Publishing, 9 (2), 249–61.

Frémont, A. and Soppé, M. 2007. Northern European range: shipping line concentration and port hierarchy, in: *Ports, cities, and global supply chains*, edited by Wang, J., Notteboom, T., Olivier, D. and Slack, B., Ashgate: Aldershot, 105–20.

Fuchsluger, J. 1999 (unpublished masters thesis). *Analysis of maritime transport costs in South America.* Karlsruhe: University of Karlsruhe.

Fuchsluger, J. 2000. An analysis of maritime transport and its costs for the Caribbean, ECLAC, LC/CAR/G.625, November 2000.

Geraci, V.J. and Prewo, W. 1977. Bilateral trade flows and transport costs. *Review of Economics and Statistics*, 59 (1), 67–74.

Ghosh, S. and Yamarik, S. 2004. Are regional trade agreements trade creating? An application of extreme bounds analysis. *Journal of International Economics*, 63 (2), 369–95.

Glaeser, E.L. and Kohlhase, J.E. 2003. Cities, regions and the Decline of transport Costs. Discussion Paper 2014, Harvard Institute of Economic Research.

Gonzalez, J.A., Guasch, J.L. and Serebrisky, T. 2008. Improving logistics costs for transportation and trade facilitation. Washington, DC: The World Bank Policy Research Working Paper No 4558.

Goss, R.O. 1990. Economic Policies and Seaports – Part 3: Are Port Authorities Necessary, *Maritime Policy and Management*, 17 (4), 257–71.

Gouvernal, E. and Slack, B. 2012. Container freight rates and economic distance: a new perspective on the world map. *Maritime Policy and Management*, 39 (2), 133–49.

Guy, E. 2003. Shipping lines networks and the integration of South America trades, *Maritime Policy and Management*, 30, 231–42.

Guy, E. and Urli, B. 2006. Port Selection and Multi-criteria Analysis: An Application to the Montreal–New York Alternative, *Maritime Economics and Logistics*, 8, 169–86.

Hanson, S. 1995. *Geography of Urban Transportation*. 2nd ed., New York. Guilford Press.

Haralambides, H.E. 2004. Determinants of Price and Price Stability in Line Shipping. Workshop on 'The Industrial Organization of Shipping and Ports': National University of Singapore.

Harding, A. and Hoffmann, J. 2003. Trade between Caribbean Community (CARICOM) and Central American Common Market (CACM) countries: the role to play for ports and shipping services, Serie de la CEPAL 52, Santiago de Chile, May.

Head, K. and Mayer, T. 2001. Illusory Border Effects: Distance mis-measurement inflates estimates of home bias in trade. CEPII, mimeo.

Heaver, T.D. 1973. The structure of liner conference rates. *Journal of Industrial Economics*, 21 (3), 257–65.

Heaver, T.D. 1995. The Implications of Increased Competition among Ports for Port Policy and Management, *Maritime Policy and Management*, 22 (2), 125–33.

Heaver, T.D. 2006. The Evolution and Challenges of Port Economics. *Research in Transportation Economics*, 16, 11–41, Elsevier.

Hesse M. and Rodrigue J-P. 2004 The transport geography of logistics and freight distribution, *Journal of Transport Geography* 12 (3), 171–84.

Hilling, D. 1996. *Transport and developing countries*. London: Routledge.

Hoffmann, J. 2001. Latin American ports: results and determinants of private sector participation. *International Journal of Maritime Economics*, 3 (2), 221–41.

Hoffmann, J. 2002. El costo del transporte internacional, y la integración y competitividad de América Latina y el Caribe. *Boletín Fal No. 191,* July 2002. United Nations ECLAC, Santiago.

Hoffmann, J., Sánchez, R.J. and Talley, W. 2005. Determinants of vessel flag. In: K. Cullinane, ed. 2005. *Research in Transportation Economics Volume 12: Shipping Economics.* Amsterdam: Elsevier.

Hoffmann, J., Pérez, G., Wilmsmeier, G. 2002. International Trade and Transport Profiles of Latin American Countries, year 2000. Serie Manuales No. 19. United Nations ECLAC, Santiago.

Hoyle B.S. and Knowles, R.D. 1998. *Modern Transport Geography* (second ed.), Wiley, Chichester and New York.

Hummels, D. 1999a. *Have International Transport Costs Declined?* Department of Economics Working Paper, Purdue University.

Hummels, D. 1999b. *Toward a Geography of Trade Costs,* University of Chicago, Chicago, United States. Mimeo.

Hummels, D. 2000. Time as a Trade Barrier. Purdue University, October, http://www.mgmt.purdue.edu/faculty/hummelsd/research/time3b.pdf, 2001.

Hummels, D. 2001. Have International Transport Costs declined? *Journal of International Economics,* 54 (1): 75–96.

Hummels, D. and Lugovskyy, V. 2006. Are Matched Partner Trade Statistics a Usable Measure of Transportation Costs?, *Review of International Economics,* 14 (1), 69–86.

Hummels, D. and Skibba, A. 2002. A Virtuous Circle? Regional Tariff Liberalization and Scale Economies in Transport. Purdue University. Working Paper.

Hummels, D., Lugovskyy, V. and Skibba, A. 2009. The trade reducing effects of market power in international shipping. *Journal of Development Economics,* 89 (1), 84–97.

Huybrechts, M., Meersman, H., Van De Voorde, E., Van Hooydonk, E., Verbeke, A. and Winkelmans, W. 2002. *Port Competitiveness: an Economic and Legal Analysis of the Factors Determining the Competitiveness of Seaports,* Editions De Boeck, Antwerp.

Janelle, D.G and Beuthe, M. 1997. Globalization and Research Issues in Transportation, *Journal of Transport Geography* 5, 199–206.

Janelle, D.G. 1991. Global Interdependence and Its Consequences, in Leinbach, T. and Brunn, S.D., eds, *Collapsing Space and Time* (Unwin-Hyman, 1991) 49–81.

Jansson, J.O. 2001. Optimal transport pricing. *Journal of Transport Economics and Policy,* 35 (3), 353–62.

Jansson, J.O. and Shneerson, D. 1982. The optimal ship size. *Journal of Transport Economics and Policy,* 16 (3), 217–38.

Jansson, J.O. and Shneerson, D. 1987. *Liner Shipping Economics.* London: Chapman and Hall.

Jonkeren, O., Demirel, E., van Ommeren, J. and Rietveld, P. 2008. Endogenous Transport Prices and Trade Imbalances. *Tinbergen Institute Discussion Paper,* TI 2008-088/3.

Journal of Maritime Economics and Logistics, 6, 279–311.

Kachigan S.K. 1986: Statistical Analysis: An Interdisciplinary Introduction to Univariate and Multivariate Methods. New York: Radius Press.

Kent P. and Fox A.K. 2005. Is Puerto Limón a Real Lemon? Port Inefficiency and its Impact, Nathans for USAID.

Kindleberger, C.P. 1962. *Foreign Trade and the National Economy*. New Haven: Yale University Press.

Kindleberger, C.P. 1973. *The World in Depression: 1929–1939*. University of California Press.

Knowles, R., Shaw J. and Docherty, I. (eds), 2008. *Transport Geographies: Mobilities, Flows and Spaces*. Oxford. Blackwell-Wiley.

Koopmans, T. 1939, Tanker Freight Rates and Tankship Building, An Analysis of Cyclical Fluctuations. *Netherlands Economic Institute report* no. 27. Haarlem: De Erven F. Bohn N.V.

Krugman, P. 1991. Increasing returns and economic geography. *The Journal of Political Economy*, 99 (3), 483–99.

Krugman, P. 1996. *Internationalism*, Cambridge, Mass: MIT Press.

Kumar, S. and Hoffmann, J. 2002. Globalization, the maritime nexus, in *Handbook of Maritime Economics and Business*, edited by Grammenos, C., London: LLP, 35–62.

Kuwamori H. 2006. The Role of Distance in Determining International Transport Costs: Evidence from Philippine Import Data, *IDE Discussion Paper Series*, No. 60.

Laing, E.T. 1977. Shipping freight rates for developing countries. Who ultimately pays? *Journal of Transport Economics and Policy*, 11 (3), 262–76.

Läpple, D. 1995. Hafenwirtschaft, in Treuner, P. ed., *Handwörterbuch der Raumordnung*, 2nd edition. Braunschweig, 462–7.

Lim, S.M. 1998. Economies of scale in container shipping. *Maritime Policy and Management*, 25 (4), 361–73.

Limão, N. and Venables A.J. 2001. Infrastructure, geographical disadvantage, transport costs, and trade. *The World Bank Economic Review*, 15 (3), 451–79.

Limão, N. and Venables A.J. 2000. Infrastructure, geographical disadvantage, transport costs. London, London School of Economics, mimeo.

Linnemann, H. 1966. *An Econometric Study of International Trade Flows*, North Holland Publishing Company, Amsterdam.

Lirn, T.C., Thanopoulou, H.A., Beynon, M.J. and Beresford, A.K.C. 2004. An application of AHP on transhipment port selection: a global perspective, *Maritime Economics and Logistics*, 6, 70–91.

Liu, Z. 1995. The comparative performance of public and private enterprises: The case of British ports, *Journal of Transport Economics and Policy*, 29 (3), 263–74.

Lloyd's Register Technical Association, 2002. Ultra-Large Container Ships (ULCS): Designing to the limit of current and projected terminal infrastructure capabilities. Lloyd's Register.

McCalla, R, Slack, B. and Comtois, P. 2005. The Caribbean basin: adjusting to global trends in containerization, in *Maritime Policy and Management*, 32: 245–61.

McConville, J. 1999. International Trade and Transport Costs, in *Economics of Maritime Transport: Theory and Practice*, 1st edition, the Institute of Chartered Shipbrokers: London.

Magala, M. and Sammons, A. 2008. A New Approach to Port Choice Modelling, *Maritime Economics and Logistics*, 10 (1–2), 9–34.

Malchow, M. and Kanafani, A. 2001, A disaggregate analysis of factors influencing port selection, *Maritime Policy and Management*, 28, 265–77.

Márquez-Ramos, L., Martínez-Zarzoso, I., Pérez-García, E. and Wilmsmeier, G. 2007. Transporte Marítimo: Costes de Transporte y Conectividad en el Comercio Exterior español. In Lecciones de Economía Marítima. La Coruña. Spain. ISBN: 978-84-9745-052-3.

Márquez-Ramos, L., Martínez-Zarzoso, I., Pérez-García, E. and Wilmsmeier, G. 2011. Maritime Networks, Services Structure and Maritime Trade. In Special Issue on Latin-American Research, *Networks and Spatial Economics* 11 (3), 555–76.

Martínez-Budria, E., Diaz-Armas, R., Navarro-Ibafiez, M. and Ravelo-Mesa, T. 1999. A Study of the Efficiency of Spanish Port Authorities Using Data Envelopment Analysis. *International Journal of Transport Economics* 2: 237–53.

Martínez-Zarzoso, I. and Nowak-Lehmann F. 2007. Is distance a good proxy for transport costs? The case of competing transport modes, *Journal of International Trade and Economic Development*, 16(3), 411–34.

Martínez-Zarzoso, I. and Suárez-Burguet C. 2008, Do transport costs have a differential effect on trade at the sectoral level?, *Applied Economics*, 40, 3145–57.

Martínez-Zarzoso, I., Pérez-García E. and Suárez-Burguet C. 2005, Transport costs and trade: empirical evidence for Latin American imports from the European Union, *Journal of International Trade and Economic Development*, 14, 353–71.

Martínez-Zarzoso, I. and Nowak-Lehmann F.D. 2007. Is Distance a Good Proxy for Transport Costs?: The Case of Competing Transport Modes, *The Journal of International Trade and Economic Development* 16 (3), 411–34.

Martínez-Zarzoso, I. and Wilmsmeier, G. 2008. Determinants of Maritime Transport Costs. A Panel Data Analysis for Latin American Trade, Ibero America Institute for Econ. Research (IAI) Discussion Papers 172, Ibero-America Institute for Economic Research.

Martínez-Zarzoso, I. García-Menendez, L. and Suárez-Burguet, C. 2003. The impact of transport cost on international trade: the case of Spanish ceramic exports. *Maritime Economics and Logistics*, 5 (2), 179–98.

Martínez-Zarzoso, I., Suarez-Burguet, C. and Garcia-Menendez, L. 2002. Transport Costs and Infrastructures: Do They Influence Exports? *Papers de*

Discussión (Pd-Eco 2002–2003), Facultat de Ciencias Juridicas y Economicas, Universitat Jaume I. Castellón, Spain.

Mesquita-Moreira, M., Volpe, C. and J.S. Blyde, 2008. *Unclogging the Arteries: The Impact of Transport Costs on Latin American and Caribbean* Trade Inter-American Development Bank/DRCLAS, Harvard University.

Micco, A. and Pérez, N. 2001. *Maritime transport costs and port efficiency.* Inter-American Development Bank, Research Working Paper.

Morales-Sarriera, J., Araya, G., Serebrisky, T., Briceño-Garmendía, C. and Schwartz, J. 2013. Benchmarking Container Port Technical Efficiency in Latin America and the Caribbean – A Stochastic Frontier Analysis. The World Bank. Policy Research Working Paper 6680, October 2013.

Murphy, P. and Daley, J. 1994. A comparative analysis of port selection factors, *Transportation Journal*, 3, 15–21.

Murphy, P., Daley, J. and Dalenberg, D. 1992. Port selection criteria: an application of a transportation research framework, *Logistics and Transportation Review*, 28, 237–55.

Naudé, W. 1999. The Impact of International Transport Costs on the Exports of a Developing Country: The Case Study of South Africa. Presented at the TIPS Annual Forum at Glenburn Lodge, Muldersdrift, 19–22 September.

Neary, J.T. 2001. Of Hype and Hyperbolas: Introducing the New Economic Geography, *Journal of Economic Literature*, 39, 2: 536–61.

Ng, A.K.Y. and Wilmsmeier G. 2012. The geography of maritime transportation: space as a perspective in maritime transport research. *Maritime Policy and Management*, 39(2), 127–32.

Nir An-Shuen, Lin Kuang, Liang Gin-Shun, 2003. Port Choice Behaviour – from the Perspective of the Shipper, *Maritime Policy and Management*, 30, 165–73.

Njinkeu, D., Wilson, J. and Powo Fosso, B. 2008. *Intra Africa trade constraints: the impact of trade facilitation.* Mimeo. Washington, DC: World Bank.

Notteboom, T. 2002. Consolidation and contestability in the European container handling industry, *Maritime Policy and Management*, 29, 257–69.

Notteboom, T. 2004. A carrier's perspective on container network configuration at sea and on land, *Journal of International Logistics and Trade*, 1 (2), 65–87.

Notteboom, T. 2006a. The Time Factor in Liner Shipping Services, in *Maritime Economics and Logistics*, 8, 19–39.

Notteboom, T. 2006b. Traffic inequality in seaport systems revisited, in *Journal of transport geography*, 14:2 (2006): 95–108.

Notteboom, T. 2009. Complementarity and substitutability among adjacent gateway ports, *Environment and Planning A*, 41, 743–62.

Notteboom, T. and Rodrigue, J.-P. 2005. Port regionalization: towards a new phase in port development, *Maritime Policy and Management*, 32, 297–313.

Nuhn, H. and Hesse, M. 2006. *Verkehrsgeographie.* Paderborn: Schöningh.

Ogueldo, V.I. and Macphee, C.R. 1994. Gravity models: a reformulation and an application to discriminatory trade arrangements. *Applied Economics*, 26, 107–20.

Ottaviano G.I.P. and Puga, D. 1998. Agglomeration in the global economy: a survey of the 'new economic geography'. *World Economy* 21, 707–31.

Palander, T. 1935. *Beiträge zur Standorttheorie*. Uppsala.

Pedersen, P.O. 2001. Freight transport under globalisation and its impact on Africa. *Journal of Transport Geography*, 9 (2), 85–99.

Peters, H.J.F. 2001. Developments in Global Seatrade and Container Shipping Markets: Their Effects on the Port Industry and Private Sector Involvement organic growth container. *International Journal of Maritime Economics*, 3 (1), 3–26.

Portugal-Perez, A. and Wilson, J.S. 2009. Why trade facilitation matters to Africa. *World Trade Review*, 8 (3), 379–416.

Pöyhönen, P. 1963. A tentative model for the volume of trade between countries, *Weltwirtschaftliches Archiv*, 90, 93–9.

Predöhl, A. 1958. *Verkehrspolitik*, Göttingen: Vandenhoeck and Ruprecht.

Raballand, G. and Macchi, P. 2008. Transport Prices and Costs: The Need to Revisit Donors' Policies in Transport in Africa, *BREAD Working Paper* No. 190, October 2008.

Radelet, S. and Sachs, J. 1998. Shipping Costs, Manufactured Exports, and Economic Growth. Paper presented at the American Economic Association Meetings, Harvard University. Mimeo.

Rankin, K.S. 2002. *Thomas' Stowage*, Glasgow: Brown, Son and Ferguson.

Rodrigue, J., Comtois, C. and Slack, B. 1997. Transportation and spatial cycles: evidence from maritime systems, *Journal of Transport Geography* 5 (2), 87–98.

Rodrigue, J., Comtois, C. and Slack, B. 2006. *The geography of transport systems*. London Routledge.

Rodrigue, J.P. 2009. *The Geography of Transport Systems*. http://www.people. hofstra.edu/geotrans/eng/ch7en/conc7en/table_conditionstransport.html (visited June, 2009).

Rodrigue, J.P. and Browne, M. 2008. International Maritime Freight Movements and Logistics. In Knowles, R.D., Shaw, J. and Docherty, I. eds., *Transport Geographies: Mobilities, Flows and Spaces*, London: Blackwell, 156–78.

Roll, Y. and Hayuth, Y. 1993. Port performance comparison applying data envelopment analysis (DEA). *Maritime Policy and Management: an International Journal of Shipping and Port Research*, 20 (2), 153–61.

Saggar, R.K. 1970. Turnaround and Costs of Conventional Cargo Liners: U.K.–India Route, *Journal of Transport Economics and Policy*, 4 (1), 53–65.

Sampson, G.P. and Yeats, A.J. 1977. The Incidence of Transport Costs and Tariffs on the United Kingdom's Exports, *Journal of Transport Economics and Policy*, 10.

Sánchez, R.J., Hoffmann, J., Micco, A., Pizzolitto, G., Sgut, M. and Wilmsmeier, G. 2003. Port Efficiency and International Trade: Port Efficiency as a Determinant of Maritime Transport Cost; *Maritime Economics and Logistics*, 5, 199–218.

Sánchez, R.J., Wilmsmeier, G. and Doerr, O. 2008. Interport Competition in a Single Market: Lessons from the Central Chilean Port Range. Proceedings of 2008 International Conference on Shipping, Port and Logistic Management. Kainan University, Taiwan, March 28–29, 2008.

Sánchez, R.J., Wilmsmeier, G., Pérez, G. and Hesse, M. 2008. Latin America – Modal Split in International Transport, year 2006. CEPAL – http://www.cepal.org/cgi–bin/getProd.asp?xml=/Transporte/noticias/noticias/4/34754/P34754.xml&xsl=/Transporte/tpl/p1f.xsl&base=/transporte/tpl/top–bottom.xslt.

Sanchez, R.J. and Perrotti, D. 2012. Looking into the future: big full containerships and their arrival to South American ports. Maritime policy and Management, 39 (6), 571–88.

Schätzl, L. 1998. *Wirtschaftsgeographie 1. Theorie.* 6. edition, Paderborn: UTB.

Schmitz, H. 1990. Small firms and flexible specialization in developing countries, *Labour and Society*, 15 (3).

Shneerson, D. 1976. The structure of liner freight rates. A comparative route study. *Journal of Transport Economics and Policy*, 10 (1), 52–67.

Simon, D. 1996. Transport and development in the third world. London: Routledge.

Sjostrom, W. 1988. Monopoly exclusion of lower cost entry: loyalty contracts in ocean shipping conferences. *Journal of Transport Economics and Policy*, 22 (3), 339–44.

Sjostrom, W. 1992. Price discrimination by shipping conferences. *Logistics and Transportation Review* 28, 207–16.

Skjølsvik, K.O., Andersen, A.B., Corbett, J.J. and Skjelvik, J.M. 2000. *Study of Greenhouse Gas Emissions from Ships* (MEPC 45/8 Report to International Maritime Organization on the outcome of the IMO Study on Greenhouse Gas Emissions from Ships), MARINTEK Sintef Group, Carnegie Mellon University, Center for Economic Analysis, and Det Norske Veritas, Trondheim, Norway.

Song, D.W. and Yeo, K.T. 2004. A Competitive Analysis of Chinese Container Ports Using the Analytic Hierarchy Process, *Maritime Economics and Logistics*, 6, 34–52.

Song, D.W., Cullinane, K. and Roe, M. 2001. The productive efficiency of container terminals. An application to Korea and the UK. Ashgate Publishing Company, England.

Stopford, M. 1997. *Maritime Economics.* 2nd Revised Edition. Abingdon, UK: Routledge.

Stopford, M. 2009. *Maritime Economics.* 3rd Edition. Abingdon, UK: Routledge.

Storper, M. and Walker, R. 1989. The capitalist imperative: Territory, technology and economic growth. Oxford: Blackwell.

Sturmey, S.G. 1967. Economics and international liner services. *Journal of Transport Economics and Policy*, 1 (2), 190–203.

Taaffe, E.J. and Gauthier, H.L. 1973. *Geography of Transportation*, Prentice Hall, Englewood Cliffs, USA.

Taaffe, E.J. and Gauthier, H.L. 1994. Transportation geography and geographic thought in the United States: an overview, *Journal of Transport Geography* 2 (3), 155–68.

Talley, W.K. 1990. Optimal Containership Size, *Maritime Policy and Management*, 17 (3), 165–75.

Talley, W.K. and Pope, J.A. 1985. Determinants of Liner Conference Rates under Containerization. *International Journal of Transport Economics* 12, 145–55.

Thoman, P.B. and Corbin, R.S. 1974. The Geography of Economic Activity, New York: McGraw-Hill.

Thomas, O.O. 2002. Thomas Stowage, Fourth Edition, Brown, Son and Ferguson, Ltd.

Thrift, N. 2004. Intensities of Feeling: Towards a Spatial Politics of Affect. *Geografiska Annaler B*, 86, 57–78.

Thünen, J.H. von 1875. Der isolierte Staat in Beziehung auf Landwirtschaft und Nationalökonomie, 3rd edition, Wiegardt, Hempel & Parey, Berlin.

Tinbergen, J. 1959. Tonnage and freight. In *Jan Tinbergen Selected Papers*, L.H. Klassen.

Tinbergen, J. 1962. Shaping the world economy. Suggestions for an international economic policy, New York.

Tiwari, P. Itoh, H., and Doi, M. 2003. Shipper's containerized cargo transportation behaviour in China: a discrete choice analysis. *Journal of Transportation Economics and Statistics* , vol. 6, no. 1, pp. 71–87.

Tolofari S.R. 1989. Open Registry Shipping – a comparative study of costs and freight rates, Gordon and Breach Science Publishers.

Tongzon, J. 2001. Efficiency measurement of selected Australian and other international ports using data envelopment analysis, *Transportation Research Part A: Policy and Practice* 35 (2), 113–28.

Tovar, B., Jara-Díaz, S. and Trujillo, L 2003. *Production and cost functions and their application to the port sector, a literature survey.* World Bank Policy Research Working Paper 3123. Washington, DC: World Bank.

Tozer, D.R. and Penfold, A. 2000. Container Ships: Design Aspects of Larger Vessels, *Lloyd's Register and Ocean Shipping Consultants Ltd.*, RINA/IMarE Presentation, London, UK.

UNCTAD, 1992. Port marketing and the challenge of the third generation port. Geneva: UNCTAD. 2005 review of Maritime Transport.

UNCTAD, 2008a. Transport Newsletter, fourth quarter and earlier. Geneva: UNCTAD.

UNCTAD, 2008b. Review of Maritime Transport, 2008 and earlier. New York/ Geneva.

United Nations 1974. United Nations Conference of Plenipotentiaries on a Code of Conduct for Liner Conferences, April 6, I974, U.N. Doc. TD/CODE/Ii/Rev. r and Corr. 1 (1974)

UNCTAD, 2013. Review of Maritime Transport, 2013. New York/Geneva.

UN-ECLAC 2002. El Costo del Transporte Internacional, y la Integración y Competitividad de América Latina y el Caribe. Boletin Fal. Edición No. 191, June 2002, Santiago, Chile.

UNOHRLLS 2013. Landlockedness: Understanding the development costs of being landlocked, New York

USAID, 2007. Calculating Tariff Equivalents for Time in Trade. Nathan Associates.

Vagle, Ruth. 2012. 'Maritime Reefer Trade in West Coast South America: The case of fruits', Boletín Marítimo, N° 50, October, [on-line] http://www.cepal. org/id.asp?id=48153.

Vagle, Ruth. 2013. 'Maritime Reefer Trade in East Coast of South America', Boletín Marítimo, N° 52, February, [on-line] http://www.cepal.org/id.asp?id=49297.

van Houtum, H. 2000. Borders, distances and spaces, *Journal of Borderlands Studies*/2000.

Veenstra, A.W. and Bergantino A.S. 2002. Networks in Liner Shipping – interconnection and coordination. *International Journal of Maritime Economics* 4 (3), 210–29.

Voigt, F. 1973. Verkehr. Volumen 1 – Theorie der Verkehrswirtschaft, Berlin: Duncker and Humblot.

Wang, T., Cullinane, K. and Song, D. 2005. *Container Port Production and Economic efficiency*. London: Palgrave.

Weber, A. 1909. *Theorie des Standortes*, Tübingen.

Weigmann, H. 1933. Standortheorie und Raumwirtschaft, Rostock.

Wiegmans, B., Van Der Hoest, A. and Notteboom, T. 2008. Port and terminal selection by deep-sea container operators, *Maritime Policy and Management*, 35 (6), 517–34.

Wilmsmeier, G., Tovar, B. and Sanchez, R.J. 2013. The evolution of container terminal productivity and efficiency under changing economic environments, Research in Transportation Business & Management, Volume 8, October 2013, Pages 50–66, ISSN 2210-5395, http://dx.doi.org/10.1016/j.rtbm.2013.07.003.

Wilmsmeier, G. 2013. Liner Shipping Markets, Networks and Strategies. The implications for port development on the West Coast of South America. The case of Chile, ITF Discussion Paper No 2013–22, November 2013.

Wilmsmeier, G. 2003. Modal Choice in South American Freight Transport: Analysis of Constraint Variables and a Perspective for Diversified Modal Participation in South America. Unpublished master's thesis, Technische Universität Dresden.

Wilmsmeier, G. 2009. The Role of Transport and Logistics Costs on Food Imports. Policy Guidance Note – Working Paper, The World Bank, Washington.

Wilmsmeier, G. and Hoffmann, J. 2008. Liner shipping connectivity and port infrastructure as determinants of freight rates in the Caribbean. *Maritime Economics and Logistics*, 10 (1), 130–51.

Wilmsmeier, G. and Martínez-Zarzoso, I. 2010. Determinants of maritime transport costs – a panel data analysis, *Transportation Planning and Technology* 33 (1), 117–36.

Wilmsmeier, G. and Notteboom, T. 2011. Determinants of Liner Shipping Network Configuration – A Two Region Comparison. *GeoJournal*, 76 (3), pp. 213–28. ISSN 0343-2521.

Wilmsmeier, G. and Pérez, G. 2005. Maritime Transport Costs and Connectivity on Maritime routes to South America. *13th Annual Congress of the International Association of Maritime Economists (IAME)*, Cyprus.

Wilmsmeier, G. and Sánchez, R.J. 2008. Shipping Networks in International Containerized Trade – Market Evolution on the West Coast of South America. In *Handbook of Container Shipping* Vol. 2 ISL, ISSN 0174-5728, Bremen, Germany.

Wilmsmeier, G. and Sánchez, R.J. 2009. The relevance of international transport costs on food prices: Endogenous and exogenous effects. *Research in Transportation Economics*. 25, 1, 56–66.

Wilmsmeier, G. and Sánchez, R.J. 2011. Liner shipping networks and market concentration. In *International Handbook of Maritime Economics*. K.P.B. Cullinane (ed.), Edward Elgar, Cheltenham.

Wilmsmeier, G., Hoffmann, J. and Sánchez, R.J. 2006. The impact of port characteristics on international maritime transport costs. In *Research in Transportation Economics Volume 16: Port Economics*. edited by K. Cullinane and W. Talley, Amsterdam: Elsevier, 117–42.

Wilmsmeier, G., Tovar, B., Sanchez, R.J. 2013. The evolution of container terminal productivity and efficiency under changing economic environments, *Research in Transportation Business and Management*, Volume 8, October 2013, pp. 50–66, ISSN 2210-5395, http://dx.doi.org/10.1016/j.rtbm.2013.07.003.

Wilson, J.S., Mann, C.L. and Otsuki, T. 2003. Trade facilitation and economic development: a new approach to measuring the impact. *World Bank Economic Review*, 17 (3), 367–89.

World Bank 2001. Global Economic Prospects and the Developing Countries 2002: Making Trade Work for the Poor, Washington DC. World Bank.

Woudsma, C. and Andrey, J. 2004. Introductory remarks: special papers in transport geography. *Canadian Geographer*, 48 (4), 446–7.

Yeats A.J. 1986. Do International Transport Costs Increase with Fabrication? Some empirical evidence. *Oxford Economics Papers*, 29, 3, 458–71.

Yeats, A.J. 1986. The Incidence of Transport Costs on Indonesia's Exports to the United States, *Bulletin of Indonesian Development Studies*, 14.

Index

For Product Safety Concerns and Information please contact our EU
representative GPSR@taylorandfrancis.com
Taylor & Francis Verlag GmbH, Kaufingerstraße 24, 80331 München, Germany

www.ingramcontent.com/pod-product-compliance
Ingram Content Group UK Ltd.
Pitfield, Milton Keynes, MK11 3LW, UK
UKHW021612240425
457818UK00018B/527